BLOOM'S

HOW TO WRITE ABOUT

Ralph Waldo Emerson

FABIAN IRONSIDE

BLOOM'S
LITERARY CRITICISM
An imprint of Infobase Publishing

Bloom's How to Write about Ralph Waldo Emerson

Copyright © 2009 by Fabian Ironside

Bloom's Literary Criticism
An imprint of Infobase Publishing
132 West 31st Street
New York NY 10001

Library of Congress Cataloging-in-Publication Data

Ironside, Fabian.
  Bloom's how to write about Ralph Waldo Emerson / Fabian Ironside ; introduction by Harold Bloom.
       p. cm.— (Bloom's how to write about literature)
  Includes bibliographical references and index.
    ISBN 978-0-7910-9833-2 (acid-free paper) 1. Emerson, Ralph Waldo, 1803–1882—Criticism and interpretation. 2. Criticism—Authorship. 3. Report writing. I. Bloom, Harold. II. Title. III. Title: How to write about Ralph Waldo Emerson. IV. Title: Ralph Waldo Emerson. V. Series.
  PS1638.I76 2009
  814'.3—dc22   2008005710

Bloom's Literary Criticism books are available at special discounts when purchased in bulk quantities for businesses, associations, institutions, or sales promotions. Please call our Special Sales Department in New York at (212) 967-8800 or (800) 322-8755.

You can find Bloom's Literary Criticism on the World Wide Web at
http://www.chelseahouse.com

Text design by Annie O'Donnell
Cover design by Ben Peterson

Printed in the United States of America

Bang MSRF 10 9 8 7 6 5 4 3 2 1

This book is printed on acid-free paper.

CONTENTS

SERIES
INTRODUCTION

BLOOM's How to Write about Literature series is designed to inspire students to write fine essays on great writers and their works. Each volumes in the series begins with an introduction by Harold Bloom, meditating on the challenges and rewards of writing about the volume's subject author. The first chapter then provides detailed instructions on how to write a good essay, including how to find a thesis; how to develop an outline; how to write a good introduction, body text, and conclusions; how to cite sources; and more. The second chapter provides a brief overview of the issues involved in writing about the subject author and then a number of suggestions for paper topics, with accompanying strategies for addressing each topic. Succeeding chapters cover the author's major works.

The paper topics suggested within this book are open ended, and the brief strategies provided are designed to give students a push forward on the writing process rather than a road map to success. The aim of the book is to pose questions, not answer them. Many different kinds of papers could result from each topic. As always, the success of each paper will depend completely on the writer's skill and imagination.

HOW TO WRITE ABOUT EMERSON: INTRODUCTION

by Harold Bloom

M Y FIRST essay on Emerson was written in 1964, 44 years ago. There are sections on him in every book I have written since then, and he pervades my huge work-in-progress, *Living Labyrinth: Literature and Influence*. Frequently I am asked why I have not devoted an entire book to him and do not know the answer. For me, he is more than a writer: He is *the* American sage, my Gentile rabbi. The question of how to write about Emerson is therefore a daily reality in my life.

There is an immense body of work by Emerson. I have read all of it so many times that much of his prose is embedded in me, and I possess him by memory. The first observation I offer as advice is a universal aid in writing about any great spirit, but is particularly essential for Emerson: Read him and reread him, for everything is in him. John Jay Chapman, in an otherwise admiring response, said that you could learn more about life by going to the Italian opera than attending to Emerson, for at least the opera would teach you that there are two sexes. But that was a poor summary of Emerson: consult his essay, "Love."

Emerson the essayist, at his strongest, was the American Montaigne, a judgment that would have delighted him. Though Emerson remains the strongest American essayist, his authentic greatness is in his vast journals, from which his essays and lectures were quarried. Read often from the journals, and gradually you will realize that Emerson's mind became and amazingly still is the mind of America. The Sage of Concord founded our current politics, in his distinction between the Party of Hope (the Democrats) and the Party of Memory (the Republicans). He revised our imaginative literature into our Native Strain, breaking with English models, and helped transform his disciples, Walt Whitman and Thoreau. Most profoundly and subtly, he became the theologian of self-reliance, which resulted in the ongoing American Religion.

As our national sage, now appropriated both by the Right and the Left, he himself would advise you to write about your own authentic innermost self in relation to your reading of him. Like Walt Whitman, Emerson still stops somewhere waiting for you.

HOW TO WRITE
A GOOD ESSAY

W HILE THERE are many ways to write about literature, most assignments for high school and college English classes call for analytical papers. In these assignments, you are presenting your interpretation of a text to your reader. Your objective is to interpret the text's meaning in order to enhance your reader's understanding and enjoyment of the work. Without exception, strong papers about the meaning of a literary work are built upon a careful, close reading of the text or texts. Careful, analytical reading should always be the first step in your writing process. This volume provides models of such close, analytical reading, and these should help you develop your own skills as a reader and as a writer.

As the examples throughout this book demonstrate, attentive reading entails thinking about and evaluating the formal (textual) aspects of the author's works: theme, character, form, and language. In addition, when writing about a work, many readers choose to move beyond the text itself to consider the work's cultural context. In these instances, writers might explore the historical circumstances of the period in which the work was written. Alternatively, they might examine the philosophies and ideas that a work addresses. Even in cases where writers explore a work's cultural context, though, papers must still address the more formal aspects of the work itself. A good interpretative essay that evaluates Charles Dickens's use of the philosophy of utilitarianism in his novel *Hard Times*, for example, cannot adequately address the author's treatment of the philosophy without firmly grounding this discussion in the book itself. In other words, any analytical paper about a text, even one that seeks to evaluate the work's cultural context, must also have a

1

firm handle on the work's themes, characters, and language. You must look for and evaluate these aspects of a work, then, as you read a text and as you prepare to write about it.

WRITING ABOUT THEMES

Literary themes are more than just topics or subjects treated in a work; they are attitudes or points about these topics that often structure other elements in a work. Writing about theme therefore requires that you not just identify a topic that a literary work addresses but also discuss what that work says about that topic. For example, if you were writing about the culture of the American South in William Faulkner's famous story "A Rose for Emily," you would need to discuss what Faulkner says, argues, or implies about that culture and its passing.

When you prepare to write about thematic concerns in a work of literature, you will probably discover that, as most works of literature do, your text touches upon other themes in addition to its central theme. These secondary themes also provide rich ground for paper topics. A thematic paper on "A Rose for Emily" might consider gender or race in the story. While neither of these could be said to be the central theme of the story, both are clearly related to the passing of the "old South" and could provide plenty of good material for papers.

As you prepare to write about themes in literature, you might find a number of strategies helpful. After you identify a theme or themes in the story, you should begin by evaluating how other elements of the story—such as character, point of view, imagery, and symbolism—help develop the theme. You might ask yourself what your own responses are to the author's treatment of the subject matter. Do not neglect the obvious, either: What expectations does the title set up? How does the title help develop thematic concerns? Clearly, the title "A Rose for Emily" says something about the narrator's attitude toward the title character, Emily Grierson, and all she represents.

WRITING ABOUT CHARACTER

Generally, characters are essential components of fiction and drama. (This is not always the case, though; Ray Bradbury's "August 2026:

There Will Come Soft Rains" is technically a story without characters, at least any human characters.) Often, you can discuss character in poetry, as in T. S. Eliot's "The Love Song of J. Alfred Prufrock" or Robert Browning's "My Last Duchess." Many writers find that analyzing character is one of the most interesting and engaging ways to work with a piece of literature and to shape a paper. After all, characters generally are human, and we all know something about being human and living in the world. While it is always important to remember that these figures are not real people but creations of the writer's imagination, it can be fruitful to begin evaluating them as you might evaluate a real person. Often you can start with your own response to a character. Did you like or dislike the character? Did you sympathize with the character? Why or why not?

Keep in mind, though, that emotional responses like these are just starting places. Truly to explore and evaluate literary characters, you need to return to the formal aspects of the text and evaluate how the author has drawn these characters. The 20th-century writer E. M. Forster coined the terms *flat* characters and *round* characters. Flat characters are static, one-dimensional characters who frequently represent a particular concept or idea. In contrast, round characters are fully drawn and much more realistic characters who frequently change and develop over the course of a work. Are the characters you are studying flat or round? What elements of the characters lead you to this conclusion? Why might the author have drawn characters like this? How does their development affect the meaning of the work? Similarly, you should explore the techniques the author uses to develop characters. Do we hear a character's own words, or do we hear only other characters' assessments of him or her? Or, does the author use an omniscient or limited omniscient narrator to allow us access to the workings of the characters' minds? If so, how does that help develop the characterization? Often you can even evaluate the narrator as a character. How trustworthy are the opinions and assessments of the narrator? You should also think about characters' names. Do they mean anything? If you encounter a hero named Sophia or Sophie, you should probably think about her wisdom (or lack thereof), since *Sophia* means "wisdom" in Greek. Similarly, since the name *Sylvia* is derived from the word *sylvan,* meaning "of the wood," you might want to evaluate that character's relationship with nature. Once again, you might look to the title of the work. Does Herman Melville's "Bartleby, the Scrivener" signal anything about Bartleby himself? Is Bartleby adequately defined by his job as scrivener? Is this part of Melville's point? Pursuing questions like these can help you develop thorough papers about characters from psychological, sociological, or more formalistic perspectives.

WRITING ABOUT FORM AND GENRE

Genre, a word derived from French, means "type" or "class." Literary genres are distinctive classes or categories of literary composition. On the most general level, literary works can be divided into the genres of drama, poetry, fiction, and essays, yet within those genres there are classifications that are also referred to as genres. Tragedy and comedy, for example, are genres of drama. Epic, lyric, and pastoral are genres of poetry. *Form,* on the other hand, generally refers to the shape or structure of a work. There are many clearly defined forms of poetry that follow specific patterns of meter, rhyme, and stanza. Sonnets, for example, are poems that follow a fixed form of 14 lines. Sonnets generally follow one of two basic sonnet forms, each with its own distinct rhyme scheme. Haiku is another example of poetic form, traditionally consisting of three unrhymed lines of five, seven, and five syllables.

While you might think that writing about form or genre might leave little room for argument, many of these forms and genres are very fluid. Remember that literature is evolving and ever changing, and so are its forms. As you study poetry, you may find that poets, especially more modern poets, play with traditional poetic forms, bringing about new effects. Similarly, dramatic tragedy was once quite narrowly defined, but over the centuries playwrights have broadened and challenged traditional definitions, changing the shape of tragedy. When Arthur Miller wrote *Death of a Salesman*, many critics challenged the idea that tragic drama could encompass a common man like Willy Loman.

Evaluating how a work of literature fits into or challenges the boundaries of its form or genre can provide you with fruitful avenues of investigation. You might find it helpful to ask why the work does or does not fit into traditional categories. Why might Miller have thought it fitting to write a tragedy of the common man? Similarly, you might compare the content or theme of a work with its form. How well do they work together? Many of Emily Dickinson's poems, for instance, follow the meter of traditional hymns. While some of her poems seem to express traditional religious doctrines, many seem to challenge or strain against traditional conceptions of God and theology. What is the effect, then, of her use of traditional hymn meter?

WRITING ABOUT LANGUAGE, SYMBOLS, AND IMAGERY

No matter what the genre, writers use words as their most basic tool. Language is the most fundamental building block of literature. It is essential that you pay careful attention to the author's language and word choice as you read, reread, and analyze a text. Imagery is language that appeals to the senses. Most commonly, imagery appeals to our sense of vision, creating a mental picture, but authors also use language that appeals to our other senses. Images can be literal or figurative. Literal images use sensory language to describe an actual thing. In the broadest terms, figurative language uses one thing to speak about something else. For example, if I call my boss a snake, I am not saying that he is literally a reptile. Instead, I am using figurative language to communicate my opinions about him. Since we think of snakes as sneaky, slimy, and sinister, I am using the concrete image of a snake to communicate these abstract opinions and impressions.

The two most common figures of speech are similes and metaphors. Both are comparisons between two apparently dissimilar things. Similes are explicit comparisons using the word *like* or *as*; metaphors are implicit comparisons. To return to the previous example, if I say, "My boss, Bob, was waiting for me when I showed up to work five minutes late today—the snake!" I have constructed a metaphor. Writing about his experiences fighting in World War I, Wilfred Owen begins his poem "Dulce et decorum est" with a string of similes: "Bent double, like old beggars under sacks, / Knock-kneed, coughing like hags, we cursed through sludge." Owen's goal was to undercut clichéd notions that war and dying in battle were glorious. Certainly, comparing soldiers to coughing hags and to beggars underscores his point.

"Fog," a short poem by Carl Sandburg, provides a clear example of a metaphor. Sandburg's poem reads:

> The fog comes
> on little cat feet.
>
> It sits looking
> over harbor and city
> on silent haunches
> and then moves on.

Notice how effectively Sandburg conveys surprising impressions of the fog by comparing two seemingly disparate things—the fog and a cat.

Symbols, by contrast, are things that stand for, or represent, other things. Often they represent something intangible, such as concepts or ideas. In everyday life we use and understand symbols easily. Babies at christenings and brides at weddings wear white to represent purity. Think, too, of a dollar bill. The paper itself has no value in and of itself. Instead, that paper bill is a symbol of something else, the precious metal in a nation's coffers. Symbols in literature work similarly. Authors use symbols to evoke more than a simple, straightforward, literal meaning. Characters, objects, and places can all function as symbols. Famous literary examples of symbols include Moby Dick, the white whale of Herman Melville's novel, and the scarlet *A* of Nathaniel Hawthorne's *The Scarlet Letter.* As both of these symbols suggest, a literary symbol cannot be adequately defined or explained by any one meaning. Hester Prynne's Puritan community clearly intends her scarlet *A* as a symbol of her adultery, but as the novel progresses, even her own community reads the letter as representing not just *adultery,* but *able, angel,* and a host of other meanings.

Writing about imagery and symbols requires close attention to the author's language. To prepare a paper on symbolism or imagery in a work, identify and trace the images and symbols and then try to draw some conclusions about how they function. Ask yourself how any symbols or images help contribute to the themes or meanings of the work. What connotations do they carry? How do they affect your reception of the work? Do they shed light on characters or settings? A strong paper on imagery or symbolism will thoroughly consider the use of figures in the text and will try to reach some conclusions about how or why the author uses them.

WRITING ABOUT HISTORY AND CONTEXT

As noted earlier, it is possible to write an analytical paper that also considers the work's context. After all, the text was not created in a vacuum. The author lived and wrote in a specific period and in a specific cultural context and, as all of us are, was shaped by that environment. Learning more about the historical and cultural circumstances that surround the author and the work can help illuminate a text and provide you with productive material for a paper. Remember, though, that when you write analytical papers, you should use the context to illuminate the text. Do not lose sight of your goal—to interpret the meaning of the literary work. Use historical or philosophical research as a tool to develop your textual evaluation.

Thoughtful readers often consider how history and culture affected the author's choice and treatment of his or her subject matter. Investigations into the history and context of a work could examine the work's relation to specific historical events, such as the Salem witch trials in 17th-century Massachusetts or the restoration of Charles to the British throne in 1660. Bear in mind that historical context is not limited to politics and world events. While knowing about the Vietnam War is certainly helpful in interpreting much of Tim O'Brien's fiction, and some knowledge of the French Revolution clearly illuminates the dynamics of Charles Dickens's *A Tale of Two Cities,* historical context also entails the fabric of daily life. Examining a text in light of gender roles, race relations, class boundaries, or working conditions can give rise to thoughtful and compelling papers. Exploring the conditions of the working class in 19th-century England, for example, can provide a particularly effective avenue for writing about Dickens's *Hard Times.*

You can begin thinking about these issues by asking broad questions at first. What do you know about the period and about the author? What does the editorial apparatus in your text tell you? These might be starting places. Similarly, when specific historical events or dynamics are particularly important to understanding a work but might be somewhat obscure to modern readers, textbooks usually provide notes to explain historical background. These are a good place to start. With this information, ask yourself how these historical facts and circumstances might have affected the author, the presentation of theme, and the presentation of character. How does knowing more about the work's specific historical context illuminate the work? To take a well-known example, understanding the complex attitudes toward slavery during the time Mark Twain wrote *Adventures of Huckleberry Finn* should help you begin to examine issues of race in the text. Additionally, you might compare these attitudes to those of the time in which the novel was set. How might this comparison affect your interpretation of a work written after the abolition of slavery but set before the Civil War?

WRITING ABOUT PHILOSOPHY AND IDEAS

Philosophical concerns are closely related to both historical context and thematic issues. As historical investigation does, philosophical research can provide a useful tool as you analyze a text. For example, an investigation into the working class in Dickens's England might lead you to a topic on the philosophical doctrine of utilitarianism in *Hard Times.* Many other works explore philosophies and ideas quite explicitly. Mary Shelley's famous novel *Frankenstein,* for example, explores John Locke's tabula rasa theory of human knowledge as she portrays the intellectual and emotional development of Victor Frankenstein's creature. As this example indicates, philosophical issues are somewhat more abstract than investigations of theme or historical context. Some other examples of philosophical issues include human free will, the formation of human identity, the nature of sin, or questions of ethics.

Writing about philosophy and ideas might require some outside research, but usually the notes or other material in your text will provide you with basic information and often footnotes and bibliographies suggest places you can go to read further about the subject. If you have identified a philosophical theme that runs through a text, you might ask yourself how the author develops this theme. Look at character development and the interactions of characters, for example. Similarly, you might examine whether the narrative voice in a work of fiction addresses the philosophical concerns of the text.

WRITING COMPARISON AND CONTRAST ESSAYS

Finally, you might find that comparing and contrasting the works or techniques of an author provides a useful tool for literary analysis. A comparison and contrast essay might compare two characters or themes in a single work, or it might compare the author's treatment of a theme in two works. It might also contrast methods of character development or analyze an author's differing treatment of a philosophical concern in two works. Writing comparison and contrast essays, though, requires some special consideration. While they generally provide you with plenty of material to use, they also come with a built-in trap: the laundry list. These papers often become mere lists of connections between the works. As this chapter will discuss, a strong thesis must make an assertion that you want to prove or validate. A strong comparison/contrast thesis, then, needs to comment on the significance of the similarities and differences you observe. It is not enough merely to assert that the works contain similarities and differences. You might, for example, assert why the similarities and differences are important and explain how they illuminate the works' treatment of theme. Remember, too, that a thesis should not be a statement of the obvious. A comparison/contrast paper that focuses only on very obvious similarities or differences does little to illuminate the connections between the works. Often, an effective method of shaping a strong thesis and argument is to begin your paper by noting the similarities between the works but then to develop a thesis that asserts how these apparently similar elements are different. If, for example, you observe that Emily Dickinson wrote a number of poems about spiders, you might analyze how she uses spider imagery differently in two poems. Similarly, many scholars have noted that Hawthorne created many "mad scientist" characters, men who are so devoted to their science or their art that they lose perspective on all else. A good thesis comparing two of these characters—Aylmer of "The Birth-mark" and Dr. Rappaccini of "Rappaccini's Daughter," for example—might initially identify both characters as examples of Hawthorne's mad scientist type but then argue that their motivations for scientific experimentation differ. If you strive to analyze the similarities or differences, discuss significances, and move beyond the obvious, your paper should bypass the laundry list trap.

PREPARING TO WRITE

Armed with a clear sense of your task—illuminating the text—and with an understanding of theme, character, language, history, and philosophy, you are ready to approach the writing process. Remember that good writing is grounded in good reading and that close reading takes time, attention, and more than one reading of your text. Read for comprehension first. As you go back and review the work, mark the text to chart the details of the work as well as your reactions. Highlight important passages, repeated words, and image patterns. "Converse" with the text through marginal notes. Mark turns in the plot, ask questions, and make observations about characters, themes, and language. If you are reading from a book that does not belong to you, keep a record of your reactions in a journal or notebook. If you have read a work of literature carefully, paying attention to both the text and the context of the work, you have a leg up on the writing process. Admittedly, at this point, your ideas are probably very broad and undefined, but you have taken an important first step toward writing a strong paper.

Your next step is to focus, to take a broad, perhaps fuzzy, topic and define it more clearly. Even a topic provided by your instructor will need to be focused appropriately. Remember that good writers make the topic their own. There are a number of strategies—often called "invention"—that you can use to develop your own focus. In one such strategy, called *freewriting*, you spend 10 minutes or so just writing about your topic without referring to the text or your notes. Write whatever comes to mind; the important thing is that you just keep writing. Often this process allows you to develop fresh ideas or approaches to your subject matter. You could also try *brainstorming*: Write down your topic and then list all the related points or ideas you can think of. Include questions, comments, words, important passages or events, and anything else that comes to mind. Let one idea lead to another. In the related technique of *clustering*, or *mapping*, write your topic on a sheet of paper and write related ideas around it. Then list related sub-points under each of these main ideas. Many people then draw arrows to show connections between points. This technique helps you narrow your topic and can also help you organize your ideas. Similarly, asking journalistic questions—Who? What? Where? When? Why? and How?—can develop ideas for topic development.

Thesis Statements

Once you have developed a focused topic, you can begin to think about your thesis statement, the main point or purpose of your paper. It is imperative that you craft a strong thesis; otherwise, your paper will probably be little more than random, disorganized observations about the text. Think of your thesis statement as a kind of road map for your paper. It tells your reader where you are going and how you are going to get there.

To craft a good thesis, you must keep a number of points in mind. First, as the title of this subsection indicates, your paper's thesis should be a statement, an assertion about the text that you want to prove or validate. Beginning writers often formulate a question that they attempt to use as a thesis. For example, a writer exploring the theme of society in Emerson's essay "Self-Reliance" might ask, Why does Emerson present such a negative image of society in "Self-Reliance"? While a question like this is a good strategy to use in the invention process to help narrow your topic and find your thesis, it cannot serve as the thesis statement because it does not tell your reader what you want to assert about society. You might shape this question into a thesis by instead proposing an answer to that question: In "Self-Reliance," Emerson gives us a predominantly negative image of society, suggesting that all social institutions are corrupt because they demand conformity and consistency. The essay ultimately argues that self-reliance necessarily involves the rejection of society and institutions as they are and calls for a revolution based on self-trust. Notice that this thesis provides an initial plan or structure for the rest of the paper, and notice, too, that the thesis statement does not necessarily have to fit into one sentence. After discussing Emerson's attitude to society, you could examine the ways in which society is represented in this essay, and then theorize about what Emerson is saying about society more generally; perhaps you could discuss how notions of society were being readdressed with advances in industry and the growth of urban centers.

Second, remember that a good thesis makes an assertion that you need to support. In other words, a good thesis does not state the obvious. If you tried to formulate a thesis about society by simply saying, Society is important in "Self-Reliance," you have done nothing but rephrase the obvious. Since Emerson's essay is centered on the self's relationship to the "NOT ME," or the outside world, there would be no point in spending three to five pages supporting that assertion. You might try to develop a thesis from that point by asking yourself some further questions: What does it mean to keep "with perfect sweetness the independence of solitude"? Does the essay seem to indicate that all institutions are corrupting, or are there some redeeming exceptions? Does it present withdrawal as the only solution, and, if so, is this a defeatist's manifesto? Such a line of questioning might lead you to a more viable thesis, like the one in the preceding paragraph.

As the comparison with the road map also suggests, your thesis should appear near the beginning of the paper. In relatively short papers (three to six pages) the thesis almost always appears in the first paragraph. Some writers fall into the trap of saving their thesis for the end, trying to provide a surprise or a big moment of revelation, as if to say, "TA-DA! I've just proved that in 'Fate' Emerson does not portray hope through imagery of children and youths, but uses them to symbolize defeat." Placing a thesis at the end of an essay can seriously mar the essay's effectiveness. If you fail to define your essay's point and purpose clearly at the beginning, your reader will find it difficult to assess the clarity of your argument and understand the points you are making. When your argument comes as a surprise at the end, you force your reader to reread your essay in order to assess its logic and effectiveness.

Finally, you should avoid using the first person ("I") as you present your thesis. Though it is not strictly wrong to write in the first person, it is difficult to do so gracefully. While writing in the first person, beginning writers often fall into the trap of writing self-reflexive prose (writing *about* their paper *in* their paper). Often this leads to the most dreaded of opening lines: "In this paper I am going to discuss. . . ." Not only does this self-reflexive voice make for very awkward prose, it frequently allows writers to announce a topic boldly while completely avoiding a thesis statement. An example might be a paper that begins as follows: "Fate," one of Emerson's later essays, contains reflections on fate with a number of examples and images drawn from Emerson's life and travels. In this paper I am going to discuss the images Emerson uses of infancy and childhood. The author of this paper has done little more than announce a general topic for the paper (imagery of birth and infancy used in the essay). While the last sentence might be a thesis, the writer fails to present an opinion about the significance of the imagery. To improve this "thesis," the writer would need to back up a couple of steps. First, the announced topic of the paper is too broad; it vaguely summarizes the scope of the essay, without saying anything about the ideas in the essay. The writer should highlight what she considers the purpose of the essay: What does Emerson conclude? The writer might suggest that Emerson's depiction of children is a gauge of his optimism. From here, the author could select the means by which Emerson communicates these ideas and then begin to craft a specific thesis. A writer who chooses to explore Emerson's use of images of children might, for example, craft a thesis that reads, "Fate" is an essay that explores the extent to which individuals are in control of their lives and to what degree the individual is powerless and led, inevitably, by irresistible forces. Images of childhood and infancy are used to illustrate Emerson's point.

Outlines

While developing a strong, thoughtful thesis early in your writing process should help focus your paper, outlining provides an essential tool for logically shaping that paper. A good outline helps you see—and develop—the relationships among the points in your argument and assures you that your paper flows logically and coherently. Outlining not only helps place your points in a logical order but also helps you subordinate supporting points, weed out any irrelevant points, and decide whether there are any necessary points that are missing from your argument. Most of us are familiar with formal outlines that use numerical and letter designations for each point. However, there are different types of outlines; you may find that an informal outline is a more useful tool for you. What is important, though, is that you spend the time to develop some sort of outline—formal or informal.

Remember that an outline is a tool to help you shape and write a strong paper. If you do not spend sufficient time planning your supporting points and shaping the arrangement of those points, you will probably construct a vague, unfocused outline that provides little, if any, help with the writing of the paper. Consider the following example.

Thesis: "Fate" is an essay that explores the extent to which individuals are in control of their lives and to what degree the individual is powerless and led, inevitably, by irresistible forces. Images of childhood and infancy are used to illustrate Emerson's point.

I. Introduction and thesis

II. Infancy and childhood
   A. Generation
   B. Sons and mothers
   C. Childhood in *The American Scholar* and "Experience"
   D. Fate

III. Nature

IV. Biology
   A. Evolution

V. Conclusion
   A. Emerson believes Fate is unavoidable and we see this in his portrayal of generation and childhood

This outline has a number of flaws. First, the major topics labeled with the roman numerals are not arranged in a logical order. If the paper's aim is to show how fate is portrayed through images of infancy, the writer should establish the particulars of Emerson's account of fate before showing how he shows this through images of childhood and the earliest infancy. Similarly, the thesis makes no reference to nature or to biology, but the writer includes both of them as major sections of this outline. As a central theme in much of his best-known writing, nature might well have a place in this paper, but the writer fails to provide details about its place in the argument. Biology, too, though it might be relevant to considerations of childhood and generation, does not logically merit a major section. The writer could, however, discuss biology in another section of the essay. Third, the writer includes the idea of fate as one of the lettered items in section II. Letters *A*, *B*, and *C* all refer to specific instances where representations of childhood and infancy will be discussed; fate as an idea does not belong in this list. The writer could argue that fate is the idea that is illustrated by these scenes of birth and infancy (therefore, it is the idea that encompasses all these scenes), but it itself is not an image of childhood or infancy. A fourth problem is the inclusion of a section A in sections IV and V. An outline should not include an A without a B, a 1 without a 2, and so forth. The final problem with this outline is the overall lack of detail. None of the sections provide much information about the content of the argument, and it seems likely that the writer has not given sufficient thought to the content of the paper.

A better start to this outline might be the following:

Thesis: "Fate" is an essay that explores the extent to which individuals are in control of their lives and to what degree the individual is powerless and led, inevitably, by irresistible forces. Images of childhood and infancy are used to illustrate Emerson's point.

   I. Introduction and thesis

  II. "Fate in matter" and its illustrating examples

        1. In "generation"—before birth
        2. Cellular development—"vesicles"
        3. In childhood

    III. Earlier   images   of   children   in   Emerson's
         writing
        1. In *Nature*
        2. In *The American Scholar*
        3. In "Experience"

    IV. Emerson's change of philosophy
        1. "Fall of man" and original sin
        2. Adulthood as corruption
        3. Solution: "Beautiful Necessity"

    V. Conclusion

This new outline would prove much more helpful when it came time to write the paper.

An outline like this could be shaped into an even more useful tool if the writer fleshed out the argument by providing specific examples from the text to support each point. Once you have listed your main point and your supporting ideas, develop this raw material by listing related supporting ideas and material under each of those main headings. From there, arrange the material in subsections and order the material logically.

For example, you might begin with one of the theses cited previously: In "Self-Reliance," Emerson gives us a predominantly negative image of society, suggesting that all social institutions are corrupt because they demand conformity and consistency. The essay ultimately argues that self-reliance necessarily involves the rejection of society and institutions as they are and calls for a revolution based on self-trust. As noted, this thesis already gives you the beginning of an organization: Start by supporting the notion that Emerson presents society and institutions as corrupt. You might begin your outline, then, with four topic headings: (1) examples of society and its institutions as corrupting, (2), expectations and influences of society, (3) the essay's context in Emerson's personal history and in national history, and (4) Emerson's solution. Under each of those headings you could list ideas that support the particular point. Be sure to include references to parts of the text that help build your case.

An informal outline might look like this:

In "Self-Reliance," Emerson gives us a predominantly negative image of society, suggesting that all social institutions are corrupt because they demand conformity and consistency. The essay ultimately argues that self-reliance necessarily involves the rejection of society and institutions as they are and calls for a revolution based on self-trust.

1. Examples of society and its institutions as corrupting
   - Images of jail and prison
   - The joint stock company
   - The public street
   - Church
     - "Dead church," "dead Bible-society" (181)
     - "Society is a wave" (201)
     - "Society everywhere is in conspiracy against the manhood of every one of its members" (178; also 192)

2. Expectations and influences of society are at fault
   - Conformity
     - "Whoso would be a man must be a nonconformist" (178)
     - Soul versus NOT-ME; reason and understanding
   - Consistency
     - "The hobgoblin of little minds" (183)
     - "this corpse of your memory" (183)

- Imitation and deference
  - "The world has been instructed by its kings" (186)
  - "Imitation is suicide" (176)
- Ignorance
  - "Ignorance of self" (Pattee, 631)
  - "False estimates of men" (Pattee, 631)

3. Context of Emerson's philosophy in his personal and national history
   - First note that Emerson wrote "Self-Reliance" over two years shortly after the Divinity School Address and its attendant controversy, and his attitude was hardened to the church
     - Andrews Norton
     - Emerson's last sermon (January 20, 1839) (Rusk, 273)
   - Emerson barred from speaking at Harvard after the Divinity School Address (Rusk, 435)
   - Images of the crowd and the street; Jacksonian democracy
     - "when the unintelligent brute force that lie at the bottom of society is made to growl and mow" (182)
     - "sour faces of the multitude" (182)
     - "The thousand-eyed present" (183)
     - Edgar Allan Poe, "The Man of the Crowd"
     - Factory towns of Massachusetts (Lynn, Lawrence, Lowell)
   - Slavery and abolitionism

4. Emerson's solution
   - Withdrawal
     - "This pleasing, contrite wood-life which God allows me" (183)

      ○ Thoreau's retreat at Walden
      ○ The community at Brook Farm
- Whim
      ○ "I would write on the lintels of the door-post, *Whim*." (179)
      ○ Nonchalant boys (177)
      ○ Pit in the playhouse (178)
      ○ "I am the Devil's child." (179)
- Self-trust
      ○ Independent and revolutionary (reflects nationalism)
      ○ Originality
      ○ "An institution is the lengthened shadow of one man." (185)
      ○ "Trust thyself; every heart vibrates to that iron string." (177)
      ○ "The relations of the soul to the divine spirit" (188)
      ○ Solipsism?
      ○ "Self-reliance is its aversion." (178)

Conclusion
- Opposite poles of self and society
- No room for reconciliation
- Emerson's reconciliation later, in "The Transcendentalist" and "Fate": "Double consciousness"

You would set about writing a formal outline with a similar process, though in the final stages you would label the headings differently. A formal outline for a paper that argues the thesis about "Fate" cited earlier—that the protagonist's frustration and isolation are communicated by her actions, thoughts, and clothing—might look like this:

Thesis: "Fate" is an essay that explores the extent to which individuals are in control of their lives and to what degree the individual is powerless and led, inevitably, by irresistible forces. Images of childhood and infancy are used to illustrate Emerson's point.

I. Introduction and thesis—"Thus we trace Fate in matter, mind and morals" (373)

II. "Fate in matter" and its illustrating examples
   A. In "generation"—i.e., before birth
      1. Brutal attitude, anticipates eugenics: "The more of these drones perish, the better for the hive" (367)
      2. "We must begin our reform earlier still,—at generation" (362)
   B. Cellular development
      1. We are fated at a microscopic level, from the smallest "vesicles"—"All we know of the egg, from each successive victory, is, *another vesicle*." (368)
      2. "vesicles, vesicles"—a negative echo of "Patience,—patience" in *The American Scholar* (104), or "Simplify, simplify" from Thoreau's *Walden*
   C. In childhood
      1. Parenting
         a. Closeness of mothers: "Men are what their mothers made them." Why mothers, and not fathers?
         b. Emerson's own background: Father died when Emerson was seven. "William's premature death created a great deficit among the boys, and in some ways Ralph probably never fully recovered from it" (Barish, 52; also Cole, 102)
         c. Emerson in flight from his past: "How shall a man escape from his ancestors . . . ?"

      d. Emerson's flight from history. *Nature:* "Our age is retrospective" (35)

   2. Image of the father as fate: "We stand against Fate, as children stand up against the wall in their father's house and notch their height from year to year" (378–379)

   3. In childhood, still the belief that fate can be resisted or diverted

      a. Imagery of the childish fantasy: "Every brave youth is in training to ride and rule this dragon" (379)

      b. Childish contest reimagined by the adult Emerson: nature and thought (or, fate and power) imagined as "two boys pushing each other on the curbstone of a pavement" (386)

III. Earlier images of children in Emerson's writing: By his changing representations of children, show the evolution of Emerson's philosophy

  A. *Nature*

    1. Children as at one with nature

    2. "I have no hostility to nature, but a child's love for it." (70)

    3. See also "The Sphinx," in which children are identified as favored by nature: "The sun is its toy." (44)

  B. "Self-Reliance"

    1. Youth is self-reliant and nonchalant: "independent, irresponsible, looking out from his own corner." (177, 178)

        2. "Young America" movement and American nationalism

   C. "Experience"

       1. After the death of Waldo, aged five

       2. Childhood as sacred but perhaps doomed

       3. "Threnody"

       4. Is this where Emerson's hope for youth as a symbol fades?

IV. Emerson's change of philosophy

   A. Stephen Whicher's thesis (freedom and fate) that Emerson's philosophy became progressively darker after the death of Waldo

   B. "Fall of Man" and original sin

       1. "When each comes forth from his mother's womb, the gate of gifts closes behind him." (366)

       2. Yearning for life in the womb

   C. Adulthood as corruption

       1. "In youth we clothe ourselves with rainbows and go as brave as the zodiac. In age we put out another sort of perspiration,—gout, fever, rheumatism, caprice, doubt, fretting and avarice." (385)

       2. A sense of a grim, or cursed, wish fulfillment: "And the moral is that what we seek we shall find; what we flee from flees from us; as Goethe said, 'what we wish for in youth, comes in heaps on us in old age.'" (389)

       3. Adulthood still viewed through childish images:

      a. "The world of men show like a comedy without laughter: populations, interests, government, history; 'tis all toy figures in a toy house." (376)

      b. "As once he found himself among toys, so now he plays a part in colossal systems, and his growth is declared in his ambition, his companions and his performance." (386)

      c. "Man is the arch machine of which all these shifts drawn from himself are toy models." (370)

D. Emerson's "solution"

  1. "Double consciousness"

      a. "A man must ride alternately on the horses of his private and public nature." (389)

      b. "Double consciousness" in "The Transcendentalist"

      c. Ages in "The Transcendentalist"—"grave seniors" (256) and transcendentalists

      d. Transcendentalists like children: "not good citizens, not good members of society" (251)—recalls the boys in the pit in "Self-Reliance"

  2. "Beautiful Necessity"

      a. "If we thought men were free . . . it were all one as if a child's hand could pull down the sun." (390)

      b. Same image as used in "The Sphinx"

V. Conclusion
    A. How "Fate" addresses the inevitability of
       forces and the extents of our resistance
    B. How Emerson uses images of childhood
       to represent freedom and adulthood to
       represent fate
    C. Even childhood is—finally—corrupted

As in the previous example outline, the thesis provided the seeds of a structure, and the writer was careful to arrange the supporting points in a logical manner, showing the relationships among the ideas in the paper.

Body Paragraphs

Once your outline is complete, you can begin drafting your paper. Paragraphs, units of related sentences, are the building blocks of a good paper, and as you draft you should keep in mind both the function and the qualities of good paragraphs. Paragraphs help you chart and control the shape and content of your essay, and they help the reader see your organization and your logic. You should begin a new paragraph whenever you move from one major point to another. In longer, more complex essays you might use a group of related paragraphs to support major points. Remember that in addition to being adequately developed, a good paragraph is both unified and coherent.

Unified Paragraphs

Each paragraph must be centered around one idea or point, and a unified paragraph carefully focuses on and develops this central idea without including extraneous ideas or tangents. For beginning writers, the best way to ensure that you are constructing unified paragraphs is to include a topic sentence in each paragraph. This topic sentence should convey the main point of the paragraph, and every sentence in the paragraph should relate to that topic sentence. Any sentence that strays from the central topic does not belong in the paragraph and needs to be revised or deleted. Consider the following paragraph about the expectations and influences of society in "Self-Reliance." Notice how the paragraph veers away from the main point that consistency and conformity are the chief enemies of self-reliance:

Emerson rails against conformity. "Whoso would be a man, must be a nonconformist," he writes (178). The examples given of conformity are drawn from the central institutions in Emerson's New England. There is the church; Emerson recalls an exchange with a "valued adviser" who pestered him with "the dear old doctrines of the church" and "the sacredness of traditions" (179). Emerson recoils from the idea of tradition and institution, taking rather the name of the devil: "if I am the Devil's child, I will live then from the Devil" (179). Emerson's hostility to the church was hardly surprising, since he had been publicly challenged and criticized for his address, which he delivered at Harvard's Divinity School in 1838. Emerson was still embittered about his reception by the members of the Unitarian church orthodoxy when he was writing "Self-Reliance." Unitarianism was, ironically, a liberal branch of Christianity, while Emerson at times sounds more like a 17th-century Puritan, both in his rhetoric and in his language. He rails furiously, calling Unitarianism a "game" of "blind-man's-buff" (181), recalling Emerson's recurring theme of eyes and perception, established in *Nature* with the famous image of the "transparent eyeball." In that essay, Emerson says that he can bear any calamity, "leaving me my eyes" (39). This statement inevitably causes us to consider the loss of the eyes, which is a castration symbol. Perhaps the classic literary scene of blinding representing castration occurs in Sophocles' *Oedipus Rex*, where Oedipus blinds himself after he finds out that he has killed his father and married his mother. Emerson uses Sophocles' figure of the sphinx as an enigmatic riddler in his poem "The Sphinx" but also as a symbol of nature in the essay of that name.

Although the paragraph begins solidly, and the second sentence provides the central idea of the paragraph, the author soon goes on a tangent. If the purpose of the paragraph is to demonstrate that society and its institutions necessitate conformity and consistency, the sentences about the Divinity School Address and Unitarianism, *Nature,* and Oedipus are all tangential here. Some may find a place later in the paper, but they should be deleted from this paragraph.

Coherent Paragraphs

In addition to shaping unified paragraphs, you must also craft coherent paragraphs, paragraphs that develop their points logically with sentences that flow smoothly into one another. Coherence depends on the order of your sentences, but it is not strictly the order of the sentences that is important to paragraph coherence. You also need to craft your prose to help the reader see the relationship among the sentences.

Consider the following paragraph about Emerson's criticism of the expectations of society in "Self-Reliance." Notice how the writer uses the same ideas as the previous paragraph yet fails to help the reader see the relationships among the points.

One target of Emerson's critique is conformity. "Whoso would be a man, must be a conformist," Emerson writes (178). His division between self and society is like that of the polar opposites of *Nature,* the Soul and the NOT-ME (36), or between "Reason" and "Understanding." Conformity is, to Emerson, a sin against God since by following society one ignores "the divine idea which each of us represents" (176). Emerson rails against consistency, which he says is the "hobgoblin of little minds" (183). People are afraid to act out of character. Emerson calls the memory of one's own events and behavior a "corpse" and argues that it is all right to contradict oneself and to be misunderstood. Emerson rejects all deference, including that paid to kings. "The world has been instructed by its kings, who have so magnetized the eyes of nations" (186). A king is a "symbol" and a "hieroglyphic," and men take joy in suffering loyalty to a king, or a noble, or a great proprietor because that king's arbitrary power represents "the right of every man" (186-187). Emerson argues that "imitation is suicide" and "envy is ignorance." Only by recognizing one's own self can one be "relieved and gay" (176). Society likes to keep its people in ignorance of themselves and others, so that they peep, steal, and skulk up and down (186).

This paragraph demonstrates that unity alone does not guarantee paragraph effectiveness. The argument is hard to follow because the author fails both to show connections between the sentences and to indicate how they work to support the overall point.

A number of techniques are available to aid paragraph coherence. Careful use of transitional words and phrases is essential. You can use transitional flags to introduce an example or an illustration (*for example, for instance*), to amplify a point or add another phase of the same idea (*additionally, furthermore, next, similarly, finally, then*), to indicate a conclusion or result (*therefore, as a result, thus, in other words*), to signal a contrast or a qualification (*on the other hand, nevertheless, despite this, on the contrary, still, however, conversely*), to signal a comparison (*likewise, in comparison, similarly*), and to indicate a movement in time (*afterward, earlier, eventually, finally, later, subsequently, until*).

In addition to transitional flags, careful use of pronouns aids coherence and flow. If you were writing about *The Wizard of Oz,* you would not want to keep repeating the phrase *the witch* or the name *Dorothy.* Careful substitution of the pronoun *she* in these instances can aid coherence. A word of warning, though: When you substitute pronouns for proper names, always be sure that your pronoun reference is clear. In a paragraph that discusses both Dorothy and the witch, substituting *she* could lead to confusion. Make sure that it is clear to whom the pronoun refers. Generally, the pronoun refers to the last proper noun you have used.

While repeating the same name over and over again can lead to awkward, boring prose, it is possible to use repetition to help your paragraph's coherence. Careful repetition of important words or phrases can lend coherence to your paragraph by reminding readers of your key points.

Admittedly, it takes some practice to use this technique effectively. You may find that reading your prose aloud can help you develop an ear for effective use of repetition.

To see how helpful transitional aids are, compare the paragraph that follows to the preceding paragraph about the capitulations demanded by society in "Self-Reliance." Notice how the author works with the same ideas and quotations but shapes them into a much more coherent paragraph whose point is clearer and easier to follow.

One target of Emerson's critique is conformity. "Whoso would be a man, must be a conformist," he writes (178). His stark differentiation between self and society recalls the division between those polar opposites of *Nature*, the Soul and the NOT-ME (36), or in the same essay between "Reason" and "Understanding." Indeed, the identification of soul with self and, conversely, society with NOT-ME is apt, since by following society one ignores "the divine idea which each of us represents" (176). Conforming, then, is to turn away from God, even if that conformity is to the church. Emerson next rails against consistency, which he says is the "hobgoblin of little minds" (183). People are afraid to act out of character, in case they are caught in a public self-contradiction. Emerson compares the memory of one's own events and behavior to a "corpse" and praises self-contradiction and misunderstanding. Constancy, dependability, loyalty—Emerson challenges the fundamental roots of polite society. He continues by rejecting all deference, including (indeed, particularly) that paid to kings. "The world has been instructed by its kings, who have so magnetized the eyes of nations," he writes (186). But a king is merely a "symbol," a "hieroglyphic," and men in fact take joy in suffering loyalty to kings and nobility, because their arbitrary power supposedly represents "the right of every man" (186–187). Emerson argues that, with regard to such people, "imitation is suicide" and "envy is ignorance." Society likes to keep its people in this ignorance of themselves and others, so that they remain peeping and stealing and skulking up and down (186). Only by recognizing one's own self and shrugging away the tyranny of society can one be "relieved and gay" (176).

Similarly, the following paragraph from a paper on "Fate in matter" and its illustrating examples in "Fate" demonstrates both unity and coherence. In it, the author argues that while Emerson has moved beyond his earlier optimism in regard to children, he still uses images orginating in the playroom or schoolyard.

By "Fate in matter," Emerson means, for the better part, the expression of Fate in the human body and its development. His emphasis on the body is unusual for Emerson—an often squeamish and ethereal writer who elsewhere defined his own body as "NOT-ME"—and itself suggests a change in his thinking since 1836. Reform cannot be achieved in the classroom, Emerson remarks regretfully; "We must begin our reform earlier still,— at generation: that is to say, there is Fate, or laws of the world" (362). When children provided hope for a younger Emerson, now he finds them corrupted—that is, fated—at birth; so he decides to go further back, before fate enters, his faith in childhood turned into a science-fiction nightmare of excess. We are fated by our breeding (or "generation"), so breeding must be controlled. Later, Emerson will remark like a sinister scientist, "The more of these drones perish, the better for the hive" (367). However far he takes his reader, Emerson finds Fate. Even at the microscopic level, he finds Fate in the smallest "vesicles." Where earlier (in *The American Scholar*) he reassured his readers with hope—"Patience,—patience"—now he can only bark its negative echo: "vesicles, vesicles" (104; 368). Since reform (that is, resistance against Fate) is doomed even in childhood, Emerson's view of parenting is similarly gloomy. Predating Freud's discoveries by half a century, Emerson writes that "men are what their mothers made them" (366). Why mothers, we might ask, and not fathers? Emerson's own father died when he was seven; this death "created a great deficit among the boys, and in some ways Ralph probably never fully recovered from it," writes Evelyn Barish (52). When Emerson's father does appear in the essay, it is as Fate personified: "We stand against Fate, as children stand up against the wall in their father's house and notch their height from year to year" (378–379). Perhaps Emerson's own issues with his father—about whom he conspicuously wrote nothing of consequence—influenced his perception of fate. Yet Emerson still conceives fate in childish images—as a father or a dragon—while the epic contest between nature and thought (or, fate and power) he imagines as "two boys pushing each other on the curbstone of a pavement" (386). Even while Emerson's argument abandons the hope of classroom reform, his choice of images maintains the children's crusade.

Introductions

Introductions present particular challenges for writers. Generally, your introduction should do two things: capture your reader's attention and explain the main point of your essay. In other words, while your introduction should contain your thesis, it needs to do a bit more work than that. You are likely to find that starting that first paragraph is one of the most difficult parts of the paper. It is hard to face that blank page or screen, and, as a result, many beginning writers, in desperation to start somewhere, start with overly broad, general statements. While it is often a good strategy to start with more general subject matter and narrow your focus, do not begin with broad sweeping statements such as Everyone likes to be creative and feel understood. Such sentences are nothing but empty filler. They begin to fill the blank page, but they do nothing to advance your argument. Instead, you should try to gain your readers' interest. Some writers like to begin with a pertinent quotation or with a relevant question. Or, you might begin with an introduction of the topic you will discuss. If you are writing about Emerson's depiction of infancy and childhood in "Fate," for instance, you might begin by talking about how children have been represented historically in 19th-century literature. Another common trap to avoid is depending on your title to introduce the author and the text you are writing about. Always include the work's author and title in your opening paragraph.

Compare the effectiveness of the following introductions.

1) Throughout history, people have wondered about fate and destiny. Think about how you feel about destiny. Is it a good thing or is it a bad thing? It depends on what you are destined for. In this essay, Emerson shows how fate works through images of childhood and infancy.

2) Nineteenth-century American literary representations of childhood have traditionally emphasized values of innocence and purity, hope, and potential in children (at least, until *The Adventures of Tom Sawyer*, 1876). Children could be used to signify the young republic, for instance, which entailed showing how children have a potential for greatness like the United States, especially as it continued a national policy of aggressive expansion. In his essay "Fate" (186), Ralph Waldo Emerson's representations of childhood and infancy challenge these notions of innocence and hope, suggesting that corruption has already occurred by the time children have entered school. By employing negative images of children and even embryos, Emerson reflects on how the individual's destiny—and perhaps America's also—is a dark one.

The first introduction begins with a vague, overly broad sentence; cites unclear, undeveloped examples; and then moves abruptly to the thesis. Notice, too, how a reader deprived of the paper's title does not know the title of the essay that the paper will analyze. The second introduction works with the same material and thesis but provides more detail and is consequently much more interesting. It begins by discussing the traditional representations of children in American culture, tying them to ideas of the national destiny. The paragraph ends with the thesis, which includes both the author and the title of the work to be discussed.

The next paragraph provides another example of an opening strategy. It begins by introducing the author and the text it will analyze, and then it moves on to briefly introducing relevant details of the story in order to set up its thesis.

> Ralph Waldo Emerson's essay "Self-Reliance" examines the division and conflict felt by the author between the individual self and his or her surrounding society. This division has provided the substance for countless works of modern literature. However, Raymond Williams finds that Emerson's particular use of the word, in which an abstract society is opposed to the individual, first came into use in the 19th century (246), so Emerson's reaction against society was at the time still fairly novel. The concept of the individual, as we now use it, was likewise used first in the same period (Williams, 136). Emerson was born in 1803, and "Self-Reliance" was published in 1841, when the terminology was coming into use. Also in this time—that period between 1800 and 1840—the number of urban territories in America rose from 322 to 1,845 (United States, 12). As cities amassed residents and population increased, city dwellers and visitors to cities felt menaced by the sheer numbers of people and the anonymity of the crowds around them. In "Self-Reliance," Emerson gives us a predominantly negative image of society, suggesting that all social institutions are corrupt because they demand conformity and consistency. The essay ultimately argues that self-reliance necessarily involves the rejection of society and institutions as they are and calls for a revolution based on self-trust.

Conclusions

Conclusions present another series of challenges for writers. No doubt you have heard the old adage about writing papers "Tell us what you are going to say, say it, and then tell us what you've said." While this formula does not necessarily result in bad papers, it does not often result in good ones, either. It will almost certainly result in boring papers (especially boring conclusions). If you have done a good job establishing your points in the body of the paper, the reader already knows and understands your argument. There is no need merely to reiterate. Do not just summarize your main points in your conclusion. Such a boring and mechanical conclusion does nothing to advance your argument or interest your reader. Consider the following conclusion to the paper about negative images of childhood in "Fate."

> In conclusion, Emerson presents the individual, even in childhood, as doomed and corrupted. Reform cannot be achieved in the classroom; nor can it be managed at "generation." The only solution lies in accepting your lot gracefully. I guess that is true for all of us.

Besides starting with a mechanical transitional device, this conclusion does little more than summarize the main points of the outline (and it does not even touch on all of them). It is incomplete and uninteresting (and a little too depressing).

Instead, your conclusion should add something to your paper. A good tactic is to build upon the points you have been arguing. Asking "why?" often helps you draw further conclusions. For example, in the paper on "Self-Reliance," you might speculate or explain how Emerson's sense of Fate was revised or resolved in later works, and in his own life. Some scholars consider "Fate" to be Emerson's final relevant expression, discounting his subsequent career, and your conclusion might challenge this by considering his subsequent writings. Another method for successfully concluding a paper is to speculate on other directions in which to take your topic by tying it into larger issues. You might do this by envisioning your paper as just one section of a larger paper. Having established your points in this paper, how would you build upon this argument? Where would you go next? In the following conclusion to the paper on "Fate," the author reiterates some of the main points of the paper but does so in order to amplify the discussion of the essay's central polarity and to connect it to other texts by Emerson:

> In the end, Emerson's solution to the problem of submitting to fate is in a compromise that also involves a periodical resistance: "double consciousness" (389). If Emerson's solution rings hollow (take solace that "universal benefit" results from your pain and suffering), his imagery remains on the axis between the polar opposites, infancy and old age. The image he chooses to represent double consciousness, the "equestrians in the circus" who "throw themselves nimbly from horse to horse," is conspicuously childish and recalls the earlier image of the "brave youth" who rides his fate like a dragon, to "make weapons and wings of these passions and retarding forces" (379). Childhood, or youth, remains a symbol of hope, if a compromised hope. Old age, conversely, is the negative side of the compromise—sciatica in the loins, cramp in the mind, a club-footed "daemon" (389). Even in his mature "acquiescence," Emerson still venerates youth as an ideal. As he wrote four years later in his journal, "Within I do not find wrinkles and used heart, but unspent youth" (Whicher, 169).

Similarly, in the following conclusion to a paper on society and institutions in "Self-Reliance," the author draws a conclusion about what the essay is saying about the individual-society conflict in Emerson's writing more broadly.

> Ultimately, "Self-Reliance" epitomizes Emerson's early philosophy of vigorous resistance, following from *Nature* and the Divinity School Address, in which he aggressively challenges the society he lives in. As with many of his essays, Emerson structures his

prose around polar opposites, here the self against society (or, the self against the NOT-ME). Rather than seeking reconciliation of these opposites, he seeks "a revolution in all the offices and relations of men" (195). Emerson's earlier essays and addresses were resolved with uplifting exhortations with apocalyptic undertones, such as the one in *Nature:* "Build therefore your own world. . . . A correspondent revolution in things will attend the influx of the spirit" (81). *The American Scholar* and the Divinity School Address similarly call for or predict spiritual revolutions, with no room for compromise. In later works, however, Emerson ends his essays in more somber tones, signaling a rapprochement with forces such as history and society. In "Circles," then, he concludes: "True conquest is the causing the calamity to fade and disappear" (238). In "Experience," he rallies the reader (or himself): "Never mind the ridicule, never mind the defeat; up again, old heart!" (311). Finally, in "Fate" (1860), Emerson seems to have made his necessary peace with fate (or history, or society), concluding, "Let us build altars to the Beautiful Necessity" (390). Ultimately, Emerson's career, viewed over the decades and the spread of his works, marks the evolution of the self and society from a state of war to one of acquiescence. However, it is not that Emerson's perceptions of society improve, but that his faith in the fight fails.

Citations and Formatting

Using Primary Sources

As the examples included in this chapter indicate, strong papers on literary texts incorporate quotations from the text in order to support their points. It is not enough for you to assert your interpretation without providing support or evidence from the text. Without well-chosen quotations to support your argument you are, in effect, saying to the reader, "Take my word for it." It is important to use quotations thoughtfully and selectively. Remember that the paper presents *your* argument, so choose quotations that support *your* assertions. Do not let the author's voice overwhelm your own. With that caution in mind, there are some guidelines you should follow to ensure that you use quotations clearly and effectively.

Integrate Quotations:

Quotations should always be integrated into your own prose. Do not just drop them into your paper without introduction or comment. Otherwise, it is unlikely that your reader will see their function. You can integrate textual support easily and clearly with identifying tags, short phrases that identify the speaker. For example:

```
Emerson describes fate as "a limp band softer than
silk" (372).
```

While this tag appears before the quotation, you can also use tags after or in the middle of the quoted text, as the following examples demonstrate:

```
"The book of Nature is the book of Fate," Emerson
claims.
```

```
"You may as well ask a loom which weaves huckabuck why
it does not make cashmere," Emerson remarks, "as expect
poetry from this engineer."
```

You can also use a colon to introduce a quotation formally:

```
In "Fate" Emerson is reconciled to the pseudo-
sciences: "the cab-man is phrenologist so far,
he looks in your face to see if his shilling is
sure."
```

When you quote brief sections of poems (three lines or fewer), use slash marks to indicate the line breaks in the poem:

As the poem ends, Emerson confounds Christian ideas of the afterlife: "But thou, meek lover of the good! / Find me, and turn thy back on heaven."

Longer quotations (more than four lines of prose or three lines of poetry) should be set off from the rest of your paper in a block quotation. Double-space before you begin the passage, indent it 10 spaces from your left-hand margin, and double-space the passage itself. Because the indentation signals the inclusion of a quotation, do not use quotation marks around the cited passage. Use a colon to introduce the passage:

The larger narrative of fate is described, repeatedly, in terms that recall the child's playpen:

> And of all the drums and rattles by which men are made willing to have their heads broke, and are led out every solemn morning to parade,—the most admirable is this by which we are brought to believe that events are arbitrary and independent of actions. At the conjuror's, we detect the hair by which he moves his puppet, but we have not eyes sharp enough to descry the thread that ties cause and effect.

Images of drums, rattles, and puppets suggest that childhood penetrates all stages and stations of life.

The whole of Emerson's poem recalls the Brook Farm experiment:

> For joy & beauty planted it
> With faerie lustres cheered,
> And boding Fancy haunted it,
> With men & women weird.

The description somewhat resembles a little Hawthorne's portrait of the community in *The Blithedale Romance.*

It is also important to interpret quotations after you introduce them and explain how they help advance your point. You cannot assume that your reader will interpret the quotations the same way that you do.

Quote Accurately

Always quote accurately. Anything within quotations marks must be the author's exact words. There are, however, some rules to follow if you need to modify the quotation to fit into your prose.

1. Use brackets to indicate any material that might have been added to the author's exact wording. For example, if you need to add any words to the quotation or alter it grammatically to allow it to fit into your prose, indicate your changes in brackets:

   > Emerson favors the "Eastern" reconciliation
   > with fate: "It [is] a poetic attempt to lift the
   > mountain of Fate, to reconcile this despotism
   > of race with liberty, which [leads] the Hindoos
   > to say, 'Fate is nothing but the deeds committed
   > in a prior state of existence.'"

2. Conversely, if you choose to omit any words from the quotation, use ellipses (three spaced periods) to indicate missing words or phrases:

   > Like everybody else (except Walt Whitman),
   > Emerson was spellbound by the "Swedish
   > Nightingale": "It would not be safe to say when
   > . . . a singer like Jenny Lind . . . would be
   > born in Boston."

3. If you delete a sentence or more, use the ellipses after a period:

   > Emerson recalls the death of Margaret Fuller in
   > surprisingly cold terms: "I seemed in the height
   > of a tempest to see men overboard struggling in

quotation marks when you use language from your source, even if you use just one or two words. For example, if you wrote, to a certain extent, Emerson felt that his faith *was* skepticism, you would be guilty of plagiarism, since you used Stephen Whicher's distinct language without acknowledging him as the source. Instead, you should write: Emerson was aware that, to some degree, "his faith *was* skepticism" (Whicher, 113). In this case, you have properly credited Whicher.

Similarly, neither summarizing the ideas of an author nor changing or omitting just a few words means that you can omit a citation. Robert D. Richardson's intellectual biography of Emerson contains the following passage about the essay "Fate":

> "Fate" is Emerson's long deferred, full-dress confrontation with the dark side of life, with evil, with indifference, with violence and savagery, with entropy and cold obstruction and rot. But even though he spends half the essay on the subject of evil, giving it full weight and expression, he does not accept it as the last word. Earlier essays such as "The Poet" might begin with a sentence or two deprecating false views. Now his method is different. Now he lets half the essay go by before turning the tables.

The following are two examples of plagiarized passages:

> In "Fate" Emerson wrote what he had long put off: to unflinchingly address the problem of evil. However, while half the dissertation is taken up with exploring the darkest sides of his thought, he does not leave it at that. In his earlier essays he might have spent the first few sentences voicing negative views before changing tack; here he takes half the essay to turn his argument on itself.

> "Fate" sees Emerson confronting the dark side of life. While he spends half the essay considering this dark

> side, he does not accept it as the final word. Earlier
> essays (like "The Poet") might start out with a sentence
> or two of negative, bleak accounts of their subject. In
> "Fate" he continues for half the essay before turning
> the tables (Richardson, 501–502).

While the first passage does not use Richardson's exact language, it does list the same ideas he proposes as the critical themes behind two stories without citing his work. Since this interpretation is Richardson's distinct idea, this constitutes plagiarism. The second passage has shortened his passage, changed some wording, and included a citation, but some of the phrasing is Richardson's. The first passage could be fixed with a parenthetical citation. Because some of the wording in the second remains the same, though, it would require the use of quotation marks, in addition to a parenthetical citation. The passage that follows represents an honestly and adequately documented use of the original passage:

> Robert D. Richardson argues that "Fate" is Emerson's
> "long-deferred, full-dress confrontation with the dark
> side of life" (501). While earlier essays (Richardson
> suggests "The Poet") opened with negative and "false
> views," these views Emerson speedily challenged and
> righted thereafter. However, in "Fate," Richardson claims,
> Emerson continues in this negative vein for a whole half
> of the essay before "turning the tables" (502).

This passage acknowledges that the interpretation is derived from Richardson while appropriately using quotations to indicate his precise language.

While it is not necessary to document well-known facts, often referred to as "common knowledge," any ideas or language that you take from someone else must be properly documented. Common knowledge generally includes the birth and death dates of authors or other well-documented facts of their lives. An often-cited guideline is that if you can find the information in three sources, it is common knowledge. Despite this guideline, it is, admittedly, often difficult to know whether the facts you uncover are common knowledge or not. When in doubt, document your source.

Sample Essay

Elias Nebula
Professor Lanidrac
English II
October 20, 2008

NEGATIVE IMAGES OF SOCIETY IN "SELF-RELIANCE"

Ralph Waldo Emerson's essay "Self-Reliance" examines the division and conflict felt by the author between the individual self and the surrounding society. This division has provided the substance for countless works of modern literature. However, Raymond Williams finds Emerson's particular meaning associated with the word, in which an abstract society is opposed with the individual, first came into use in the 19th century (246), so Emerson's reaction against society was at the time still fairly novel. The concept of the beleaguered (and capitalized) "Individual," as we now use it, was likewise forming in the same period (Williams, 136). Emerson was born in 1803, and "Self-Reliance" was published in 1841, when these connotations and representations were coming into use. Also, and not coincidentally, in this time (that period between 1800 and 1840) the number of urban territories in America rose from 322 to 1,845 (United States 12). As cities amassed residents and population increased, city dwellers and visitors to cities felt menaced by the sheer numbers of people and the anonymity of the crowds around them. In "Self-Reliance," Emerson gives us a predominantly negative image of society, suggesting that all social institutions are corrupt because they demand conformity and consistency. The essay ultimately argues that self-reliance necessarily involves the rejection of society and institutions as they are and calls for a revolution based on self-trust.

In "Self-Reliance" Emerson chooses certain institutions as representative of society at its most oppressive. For example, Emerson says that "society is a joint-stock company, in which the members agree, for the better securing of his bread to each shareholder, to surrender the liberty and culture of the eater" (178). Such an image possibly reflects Emerson's anxiety about the increasing emphasis on industry and finances in New England. In several instances, additionally, Emerson invokes imagery of jail: "the man is as it were clapped into jail by his consciousness" (178) while "nature is not slow to equip us in the prison-uniform of the party to which we adhere" (182). The "public street" reflects another phobia for Emerson (who idealized its logical antithesis, the untouched countryside). Emerson recoils from "the crowd" (181), "mobs" (202), "by-standers . . . in the public street" (182), "the ignorant and the poor" (182), and "the unintelligent brute force that lies at the bottom of society" (182). Edgar Allan Poe, Emerson's contemporary, gave a similar portrait in his story "The Man of the Crowd" (first published, interestingly, in the period when Emerson was writing "Self-Reliance"). In Poe's story, set in a London street, the narrator follows "the man of the crowd" for twenty-four hours, concluding finally that he is "the type and the genius of deep crime" (396). Emerson, though not (supposedly) a writer of eerie or sensational fiction, uses the same images and tone as Poe, arriving at a similar conclusion—that the crowd is criminal.

Perhaps the most stinging attack in "Self-Reliance" is reserved, however, for the "dead church" (181). Much of Emerson's attack recalls his address given at the Divinity School at Harvard University in July 1838. Indeed, "Self-Reliance" can be seen as that address revisited, with its target expanded. The church, for a

Massachusetts son of a preacher (which Emerson was), was the ultimate and representative institution. It is to a "valued adviser" who would pester Emerson with "the dear old doctrines of the church" that Emerson makes perhaps his most audacious (and, perhaps, petulant) claim: "What have I to do with the sacredness of traditions, if I live from within? . . . if I am the Devil's child, I will live then from the Devil" (179). Emerson is no satanist—indeed, the essay only affirms God and (as Harold Bloom calls it) "God-Reliance" (Newfield, 25)—but the devil is also the opposite of the church, so at this present time Emerson finds such an identification useful (if not theologically correct). Emerson overwhelms his reader with images from one institution or another until, as he no doubt intends, the institutions blur into one, and the joint-stock company is the church, which is also the prison. Such a blurring makes Emerson's point, that society is a many-headed hydra; a Proteus, changing form; a sinister "conspiracy against the manhood of everyone of its members" (178). Making society one amorphous monolith also makes it more susceptible, rhetorically speaking, to toppling.

One of society's manifestations is in conformity. "Whoso would be a man, must be a conformist," he writes (178). His stark differentiation between self and society recalls the division between those polar opposites of nature, the soul and the NOT-ME (36), or in the same essay between "Reason" and "Understanding." Indeed, the identification of soul with self and, conversely, society with NOT-ME is apt, since by following society one ignores "the divine idea which each of us represents" (176). Conforming, then, is to turn away from God, even if that conformity is to the church. Emerson next rails against consistency, which he says is the "hobgoblin of little minds" (183). People are afraid to act out of character, in case they are caught in a public self-contradiction. Emerson compares the memory of one's own events and behavior to a "corpse" and praises self-contradiction and misunderstanding. Constancy, dependability, loyalty— Emerson challenges the fundamental roots of polite society. He continues by rejecting all deference, including (indeed, particularly) that paid to kings. "The world has been instructed by its kings, who have so magnetized the eyes of nations," he writes (186). But a king is merely a "symbol," a "hieroglyphic," and men in fact take joy in suffering loyalty to kings and nobility, because their arbitrary power supposedly represents "the right of every man" (186–187). Emerson argues that, with regard to such people, "imitation is suicide" and "envy is ignorance." Society likes to keep its people in this ignorance of themselves and others, so that they remain peeping and stealing and skulking up and down (186). Only by recognizing one's own self and shrugging away the tyranny of society can one be "relieved and gay" (176).

What is the source of Emerson's animus against these "institutions"? While he endeavors to keep his account fairly abstract, historical precedents can be identified both from Emerson's personal history and from the national history of the 1830s. "Self-Reliance" was written in the protracted fallout from his controversial reading of the Divinity School Address. That he saw church and state, company, college, and mob all blurring into one large conspiracy is hardly surprising, considering that the rejection of Emerson after the address continued beyond the walls of the Divinity School. He was barred from reading at Harvard for the next 30 years (Rusk 435)—was this, perchance, the "college of fools" (180)? Emerson was shunned socially across the board, indeed; by the old and the young, the high-up and the common (Rusk 271–273). Genteel Boston families were urged to "abhor & abominate R. W. Emerson as a sort of mad dog" (Rusk 272). Were these the "sour-faces of the multitude" (182)? Emerson had given up even the occasional supply preaching he had been maintaining in January 1839 and was completely free of church ties (Rusk 273). "Self-Reliance" might be read as an explosion, then; a protracted "good riddance to that." Also discernible is Emerson's response to the Jacksonian democracy, which celebrated the common man. "Self-Reliance" was written and published under the administration of President Martin Van Buren, Andrew Jackson's former vice president and a maintainer of Jacksonian values. Emerson—sometimes haughty, with patrician tastes—recoiled from such a culture.

Emerson's solution to both his real-life excommunication and his abstract in-the-text battle against an abstract society in the essay is found in self-trust: "Trust thyself: every heart vibrates to that iron string" (177). Emerson's original controversy at the Divinity School had been the same doctrine—that "If . . . a man claims to know and speak of God and carries you backward to the phraseology of some old mouldered nation in another country . . . believe him not" (188). Instead, disregard time and space (or the past, and the allure of foreign countries) and look within: "Bid the invaders take the shoes from off their feet, for God is here within" (191). That was the theology, but socially, his model was equally controversial. A doctrine of "self-existence" (190, 191) emphasized whim, spontaneity, and withdrawal, all three of which flout society. Emerson's defense of "*Whim*" and self-contradiction unnerves readers to this day, who do not know when (or whether) to believe Emerson in his texts. Emerson identifies with children, who in Victorian America were essentially outside "society"—the nonchalant boys in the parlor and the playhouse pit (177, 178), the Devil's *child* (179; italics mine). He withdrew from society also spatially, by shunning the city and staying in the country—"This pleasing, contrite wood-life which God allows me" (183)—a position already fully established in the earlier, more sedate book *Nature* (1836). Emerson's vilification after the Divinity School Address, combined with his already stated tendency to withdraw from social hubs, made his solutions genuinely realizable for him, if not for the rest of society. This—the singular unattractiveness and unfashionableness of his solution—may explain why Emerson's exhortations fell on deaf ears outside his immediate circle, the "Transcendental Club." More than any person (including Emerson), Henry David Thoreau, who lived at the shack at Walden for "two years and two months" (1), followed the ideal of "Self-Reliance." But he was hardly typical. While "Self-Reliance" survives as a great essay and a noble ideal, it failed to produce the sought-after revolution.

Ultimately, "Self-Reliance" epitomizes Emerson's early philosophy of vigorous resistance, following from the Divinity School Address, in which he aggressively challenges the society he lives in. As in many of his essays, Emerson structures his essay around polar opposites; here the self against society (or, the self against the NOT-ME). Rather than seeking reconciliation of these opposites, he seeks "a revolution in all the offices and relations of men" (195). Emerson's earlier essays and addresses were resolved with uplifting exhortations with apocalyptic undertones, such as the one in *Nature*: "Build therefore your own world. . . . A correspondent revolution in things will attend the influx of the spirit" (81). *The American Scholar* and the Divinity School Address similarly call for or predict spiritual revolutions, with no room for compromise. In later works, however, Emerson ends his essays in more somber tones, signaling a rapprochement with forces such as history and society. In "Circles," then, he concludes: "True conquest is the causing the calamity to fade and disappear" (238). In "Experience," he rallies the reader (or himself): "Never mind the ridicule, never mind the defeat; up again, old heart!" (311). Finally, in "Fate" (1860), Emerson seems to have made his necessary peace with fate (or history, or society), concluding, "Let us build altars to the Beautiful Necessity" (390).

Ultimately, Emerson's career, viewed over the decades and the spread of his works, marks the evolution of the self and society from a state of war to one of acquiescence. However, it is not that Emerson's perceptions of society improve, but that his faith in the fight fails.

WORKS CITED

Barish, Evelyn. *Emerson: The Roots of Prophesy.* Princeton, NJ: Princeton University Press, 1989.

Cole, Phyllis. "Emerson Father and Son. A Precedent for 'The American Scholar'" New England Quarterly, 78:1 (March 2005): 101–24.

Emerson, Ralph Waldo. *Nature and Selected Essays.* 1836. New York: Penguin, 1985.

——. "Self-Reliance." Emerson 175–203.

——. *Nature.* Emerson 35–82.

——. "Circles." Emerson 225–238.

——. "Fate." Emerson 361–391.

Poe, Edgar Allan. "The Man of the Crowd." *Poetry and Tales.* New York: Library of America, 1984. 388–396.

Newfield, Christopher. *The Emerson Effect: Individualism and Submission in America.* Chicago: U of Chicago P, 1996.

Richardson, Robert D. *Emerson: The Mind of Fire.* Berkeley: U of California P, 1995.

Rusk, Ralph. *The Life of Ralph Waldo Emerson.* New York: Charles Scribner's Sons, 1949.

Thoreau, Henry David. *Walden and Civil Disobedience.* New York: W. W. Norton, 1966.

United States. Department of Commerce. Bureau of the Census. *Historical Statistics of the United States.* Bicentennial Edition. 2 vols. Washington, DC: GPO, 1975.

Whicher, Stephen E. *Freedom and Fate: An Inner Life of Ralph Waldo Emerson.* Philadelphia: U of Pennsylvania P, 1953.

Williams, Raymond. *Keywords: A Vocabulary of Culture and Society.* Glasgow: Fontana, 1976.

HOW TO WRITE ABOUT RALPH WALDO EMERSON

AN OVERVIEW

THE WORKS of Ralph Waldo Emerson are, and always have been, acknowledged for their complexity. Emerson gained a reputation for his brilliance and his poetry, but also for the obscurity and mysticism of his words. In his essay "Experience," he seems to tease the reader even, crowing paradoxically that "I am explained without explaining." As a touring lecturer, he gave addresses to audiences throughout the United States, many of whom exited the Lyceum no wiser than when they went in; yet often they felt they had got their money's worth. Readers of his essays and poems were equally stumped, but entranced. Emerson knew this, accepted it, and could even laugh at it. "A little guessing does [the reader] no harm, so I would assist him with no connections," he wrote in his journal.

To be aware of Emerson's national legend, however, does not mean we should conspire in it. Emerson exhibited a distinct style, adopting a sometimes antiquated tone. This should not be mistaken for the "typical" language of its day—we assume wrongly if we believe that Emerson's language has somehow become archaic and strange over the last 150 years; it was so in its own day. One critic calls it "scripturese" (Buell 2003, 118), while Emerson's friend James Russell Lowell wrote that "a diction at once so rich and so homely as his we know not where to match in these days of writing by the page; it is like homespun cloth-of-gold."

Many of the greatest and most esteemed critics to this day have freely conceded that Emerson is puzzling to them. This puzzlement makes his works especially amenable to criticism—the circuit is not resolved, the questions not answered. Numerous essays on Emerson— essays by established, experienced, and adroit critics—begin with the caveat that he is difficult to understand; such a preface becomes almost a convention. Emerson, indeed, occasionally found himself frowning over his own sentences, unable to decipher what he had meant by them. This biographical addendum does not suggest, however, that any Emerson essay is nonsensical, nor that it can be read to mean whatever the reader wishes it to mean.

A greater understanding of Emerson's work can be gleaned from exploring his process as a writer. Emerson scholars have collated his journals and "Miscellaneous Notebooks" as well as his correspondence, and so it has become easier to identify sources for his enigmatic sentences in the context in which those ideas first came to Emerson. Clues to meaning can be found in tracing the process of composition. Where does one sentence originate? By scanning the journals, you might find the situation from which an apparently cryptic remark originated organically. Emerson called his journals his "savings bank." A remark may have trickled from his journal to a comment in a letter, then into a lecture, and finally into the printed essay.

Each reader has his own Emerson. Every person's reading of Emerson will reflect his or her own bent, his or her own interests. Emerson has his famous lines, but the student should not feel compelled only to take note of these enduring quotes. Look for those phrases and thoughts that seem the most provocative and pertinent to your study. Familiarize yourself with the full variety of the texts—their sheer amount. We come to Emerson, often, through anthologies or selections, and editors and anthologists share a tendency to return to the same essays and poems repeatedly. While it is of course important to be aware of those texts that are deemed by consensus canonical, core pieces, even a canon is not universally agreed on. Reading Emerson's lesser-known works can prove just as advantageous and rewarding. Among the essays that might have been included in this study are "The Method of Nature," "Man the Reformer," "History," "Compensation," "The Poet," "Plato," "Montaigne," "Power," "Worship," and "Illusions." Emerson's study of *English*

Traits contains valuable thoughts, particularly regarding his developing view on "Fate." Among the poetry, "The Rhodora," "The Humble-Bee," "Threnody," "Uriel," "Merlin," "Hamatreya," "Ode to W. H. Channing," and the long poem "The Adirondacs" might also have been included and are deemed significant by critics of Emerson's verse. Emerson was prolific—he plundered his journals and letters extensively, and his output can be overwhelming. When you read criticism, you will find that there are some critics you agree with and prefer to others. Those critics you like may refer to less "core" Emerson texts and suggest a direction of original reading you can follow. Similarly, be aware of and then ready to challenge clichés. Even that term most frequently applied to Emerson, *transcendentalist,* was one that Emerson resisted. More recently, a trend emerged among critics in the 1980s to "de-transcendentalize" Emerson.

Emerson criticism is by now what can be termed an "industry." Only specialists can hope to keep up with all the new currents and writings on Emerson. Again, you should not be daunted by this. The bibliography of any good study of Emerson will direct you to the fundamental works of scholarship. When studying Emerson, the use of such sources is essential. Direction is needed, if only to understand the specific ways in which Emerson uses terms (for instance, his confusing but central interpretation of the words *reason* and *understanding*). Scholarship can also provide you with interpretations to challenge in your own reading of Emerson. An argument is, of course, vital to a good essay—and it is the scholars you can argue your position with.

For all of Emerson's essays, it is useful to know where they came from: their contexts in time and space. Then, cross-references can be made to Emerson's journals, his correspondence, and his biographies. What was occurring "behind the scenes" of these texts? There is a school of thought that maintains that that which occurs to the author outside the text is of no possible relevance to the text itself; this is, however, only a matter of opinion. Emerson, as a writer, had an unusually prominent place in history and society. His renown, or notoriety, resulted from his writings and his lecture tours. He could be seen giving readings by anybody who could pay the price for a Lyceum show. Additionally, he was arguably connected to more of the important thinkers and writers American and English than anybody of his age. Emerson was the intimate of Henry Thoreau, Bronson Alcott, Margaret Fuller, and

Jones Very; he was friends with Walt Whitman, James Russell Lowell, Nathaniel Hawthorne, John Greenleaf Whittier, and Thomas Carlyle and met with Charles Dickens, William Makepeace Thackeray, William Wordsworth, Arthur Hugh Clough, Robert Browning, Lord Tennyson, and John Ruskin, among others. He knew the central figures in American politics, including Horace Greeley, Charles Sumner, and Abraham Lincoln, who visited him after a lecture. He knew the abolitionists William Lloyd Garrison, and John Brown. Despite his doctrine of self-reliance and solitude, he was visible to all—not a recluse like Nathaniel Hawthorne or Emily Dickinson—and received pilgrims with patience, if he abandoned them in time. Although his image might be of the haughty sage in Massachusetts, he was, like Whitman, democratic, at least in the span of his contacts. He traveled across America, and he met its people, even on the frontier. You can read, for instance, the account of Emerson giving a lecture above a stable in Rock Island, Illinois (Scott, 84).

Questions calling for the comparison and contrast of one text with another, or one writer with another, are intended to serve a useful purpose, rather than being a mere exercise in showing similarities and differences. When done well, identifying these similarities and differences illuminates the respective texts involved in a new way, a way that an isolated reading of the texts separately would have missed. Importantly, the student should comment on the significance of these similarities or differences; simply noting them is not sufficient.

As a writer who was extremely public and well known and thus extremely influential, plenty of comparisons are suggested. It was difficult for a thinking person of Emerson's time to avoid Emerson. He was a figure to be measured against, or to challenge. One finds such challenges in the works of Nathaniel Hawthorne, Herman Melville, and Edgar Allan Poe. One finds resonances of and recognition of Emerson in the works of Henry David Thoreau, Walt Whitman, and William James. Most of the major writers of the time orbited at some point around Emerson, from William Dean Howells to Samuel Clemens to Henry James. Emerson sat in or convened salons and clubs, where he entered into conversation with many writers. Comparison can bring to light the effect Emerson had on them, personally, intellectually, and as writers. This is done, not only by textual comparison, but by research (through correspondence, journals, and biographies) into their relationships. Even when Emerson did not know a specific writer personally—even after his death—his influence endures through his writing, so that writers today (John Updike and William Gass, for example) continue to write toward, about, after, and against Emerson.

TOPICS AND STRATEGIES

The following section suggests several possible topics for essays on Ralph Waldo Emerson. They can and should be used as starting points for your own, independent exploration of the essay.

Themes

Certain themes recur in Emerson's writing, although their treatment might be different each time. "By harping, or, if you will, pounding on each string, we learn at last its power," Emerson writes in "Fate." The critic O. W. Firkins remarked that "Emerson's wish to get his whole philosophy into each essay tended toward sameness and promiscuity at once; it made the *essays similar* and the *paragraphs diverse*" (quoted in Packer, 155). Sensitivity to these recurrences can aid you in tracing Emerson's developing ideas. Emerson is, effectively, in dialogue with himself: revising, modifying, and correcting earlier statements. "Emerson speaks back to his former selves as Krishna did to Arjuna," writes Laurence Buell, recalling the exchanges that take place in the Bhagavad Gita, an important influence on Emerson (175). There is an advantage, then, in viewing the course of Emerson's career to find how pet subjects fluctuate in Emerson's thought. Such fluctuations of development, or pulses, are essential to Emerson's theory in "Circles." When you find a motif or image or subject that rings familiar, circle it and cross-reference it.

The most significant recurring subject for Emerson is probably nature. Emerson founded his entire doctrine on his study *Nature* (1836), the work that spawned his reputation, the formation of a transcendentalist movement and circle, and, ultimately, a tradition in American literature. Polarities—grouping of opposites—also recur in Emerson's work. One opposition that absorbed Emerson was between society and solitude. Enduring through Emerson's work and his life is a dialogue between withdrawal—whether it is political or simply social—and participation. This can at times be a manifestation of another ongoing inquiry into the duality of idealism and its opposite, materialism. Equally, this concern might express a historical ambivalence Emerson had toward the rise of the city against an idyllic conception of the country. Which does Emerson choose, ultimately?

Sample Topics:

1. **Nature:** How does Emerson's portrayal of nature change over his writing career?

   Emerson's writing about nature (or Nature) covers his career as a writer. This question asks you to decide which essays you consider to be most representative of an evolving attitude and to analyze them alongside each other, emphasising their differences and their similarities. Compare *Nature* (1836) with "Experience" (1844), for instance. In the earlier essay, Emerson famously imagines himself as a "transparent eyeball" when in nature. In the later essay, he snaps that "nature does not like to be observed, and likes that we should be her fools and playmates." Does Emerson recast nature here? How is nature dramatized? As resentful? If so, of what? Of Emerson's earlier prying, in 1836? Emerson repeats the charge: "Nature hates peeping." Is nature vengeful? Is Emerson now abandoning his earlier, central premise? What does the negation of such a central totem suggest? Is Emerson's portrayal of nature from text to text an index to his own philosophy, and does a negative portrayal of nature reflect a general skepticism on Emerson's part? In the later essay, Emerson writes, "I am not the novice I was fourteen, nor yet seven years ago."

   In a still later essay, "Fate" (1860), Emerson writes that "the book of Nature is the book of Fate." Nature "is no sentimentalist." You might look at the poetry too. For example, in *Nature* Emerson characterizes nature as "the Sphinx at the roadside." In the poem "The Sphinx," then, does the Sphinx represent nature? This question requires that, beyond identifying differences and similarities between the essay and poem, you interpret them. Is nature truly the best gauge of Emerson's developing philosophy, for instance, or is this a scholarly commonplace, inadequately challenged? Does his perception of nature really become increasingly negative? Or is nature redeemed in the end? The question is not only about Emerson's view of nature, but what he perceived through nature—how he used nature to manifest his own thoughts.

2. **Society and solitude:** Does Emerson choose society or solitude?

Emerson's last book completed without assistance was titled *Society and Solitude* (1870). What is the significance of this polarity to Emerson? It can be traced from chapter 1 of *Nature* (1836), when Emerson declares, "To go into solitude, a man needs to retire as much from his chamber as from society." Alone in nature, Emerson becomes the transparent eyeball. Is solitude the requisite state for such a revelation, then? Look at other essays that treat ideas of "society" (such as "Friendship," "Love," or "The Over-Soul,") in which revelation is achieved through conversation, when a "third party"—God—becomes present. Emerson's remarks about friendship reveal in turn his feelings about society and solitude. These fluctuate from essay to essay. Find examples from a number of texts and compare Emerson's conclusions.

Look also at Emerson's own life. In practice, did he embrace society or solitude? You might compare his life's philosophy with Henry David Thoreau's. Emerson was a family man, a member of the community who spoke at bicentennials and graduations; one who edited journals and led salons. He was a minister and a lecturer. How does his biography accord (or jar) with his writing? (For instance, how does the "Concord Hymn" stand alongside "Self-Reliance"?) Is the reconciliation to society necessarily a rejection of solitude? How does this duality reflect other recurring dualities in Emerson's thought, such as materialism and idealism, me and NOT-ME, reading and acting, or the city and the country? "I affirm melioration

. . . I affirm also the self-quality of nature," Emerson wrote in his journal; "but I cannot reconcile these two statements. I affirm the sacredness of the individual . . . I see also the benefits of cities . . . But I cannot reconcile these oppositions." Does Emerson ever reconcile these oppositions? What are his solutions, drawn from life? For instance, could Concord, Massachusetts, be called a middle ground between country and city, society and solitude?

3. **Idealism and materialism:** How does Emerson's notion of "idealism" develop in his writing?

"There are degrees in idealism," Emerson writes in "Circles." "We learn first to play with it academically, as the magnet was once a toy." How does Emerson define idealism in *Nature* (1836), the discussion of which makes up a full chapter of the whole? Perhaps of all Emerson's persisting beliefs, idealism is the most unnerving. Does Emerson believe that the visible, palpable world is unreal? Is he a solipsist, believing nobody is real except him? Where do his friendships and correspondences (not to mention his marriages and family) stand in such a view? And does this view of idealism change in later works, such as "Circles," "The Transcendentalist," or "Experience"? Is it an academic concept or an enduring belief for Emerson?

Conversely, how does materialism find form in Emerson's essays? Is it only the rejected opposite pole to idealism, or does Emerson ever embrace materialism? Think, for instance, of "Experience," when Emerson pronounces, "We live amid surfaces, and the true art of life is to skate well on them." He goes on, "Let us treat the men and women well; treat them as if they were real; perhaps they are." Is this view finally defeated? What does Emerson conclude in "Experience" and in later works?

History and Context

Emerson's writing career covers a period in which the United States went though some of its most considerable changes. Emerson was born in 1803, when the American Revolution was still a relatively fresh memory. Survivors of the battles were still alive, and Emerson interviewed some who fought at the Battle of Concord when he wrote his *Historical Discourse* address for the bicentennial celebrations in Concord in 1835. Emerson saw the rise of the "common man" under Andrew Jackson's presidency and the attendant emergence of a celebrated democracy. He was witness to the rise of an industrial, urban North and to the stubborn stasis of a South that persisted in a livelihood based on slavery. Although it is facile, strictly, to define the decades before the Civil War solely in terms of the war they led to, those decades were dominated by presentiments of disaster, held together by a series of "compromises" (often brokered by Henry Clay) that only held off, but never prevented, the Civil War. In his earliest writings, Emerson upset the orthodoxy with his radical views. Banished from Harvard, vilified by the Unitarian church leaders, Emerson forged his identity and his canon in the thick of these changing days—and emerged, into the era of Reconstruction, an old and respected man. Many of the companions of his radical times were gone. Many friends had not survived the Civil War. It killed off (it is argued) Nathaniel Hawthorne. Margaret Fuller died in 1850, Henry David Thoreau in 1862. John Brown was hanged and Abraham Lincoln assassinated. How are these volatile times reflected in Emerson's writing?

Does Emerson's writing reflect the history of the nation in his time, or is it turned predominantly inward, to the interior, to Emerson's mind or the Concord countryside? Is Emerson's history only of Concord and its haughty salons, or does he trace the divided, conflicted, whimsical, paradoxical course of the country as a whole?

Sample Topics:

1. **Concord, Massachusetts:** To what extent was Emerson's thought a product of his situation in Concord, Massachusetts?

   Emerson and Concord are indivisible in the popular mythology of literary history. Emerson has been dubbed "the Sage of Concord," and he was always identified with the ancestral home. Emerson was born in Boston, moving to Concord at the age of

11. How has that community infiltrated his writing? Was Concord a rarefied, artificial atmosphere, untypical of the United States? Or was it, as the site of "the shot heard round the world" ("Concord Hymn"), a seat for revolutionary thought and deed? This question requires a consideration of the site of Emerson's writing and how it might have influenced his philosophy. Various histories have been written of Concord, including Emerson's own *Historical Discourse, Delivered before the Citizens of Concord, 12th September 1835* (published in the *Complete Works* in volume 11, *Miscellanies*). From such research, you can deduce a sociological and historical portrait of Concord. How are these aspects related to qualities found in Emerson's writings? Would Emerson have emphasized nature in his philosophy, for instance, had he remained in Boston—or had he moved to New York? Was Concord's rural setting, replete with its proximity to Boston, a source of Emerson's ambivalence to cities? And was Concord an inward-looking community? How would this be relevant to Emerson's philosophy?

Look at the history of the town as well. How does its placement at the heart of fighting in the American Revolution emerge in Emerson's work? Is this expressed in Emerson's emphasis on independence ("Self-Reliance") and his rejection of European influence (*The American Scholar*)? Or was Concord a predominantly intellectual community, tending toward bookishness and even a preference for European culture? How was Concord transformed, finally, in Emerson's lifetime? Did Emerson's notoriety turn it into a writers' community, a mecca for transcendentalist pilgrims?

2. **American society:** How did the United States change over the course of Emerson's lifetime, and how is this reflected in his writings?

Emerson's writings roughly coincide with a period that begins with the aftermath of revolution (and is still apparently reeling from Puritanism) and runs to the industrial age, the Civil War, and beyond. How is this change reflected in the writing of Emerson? To answer this question, you might identify key moments, ruptures, or advances in the development of the United States. For instance, find the dates of prominent political events—the presidential campaigns and elections; various periods of warfare; sundry financial panics; the setbacks, twists, and triumphs of the abolitionist struggle; short-lived experiments in utopian reform (such as the community called Brook Farm) as well as singular events such as the beating of Senator Charles Sumner on the floor of the Senate and John Brown's execution. Align these events with Emerson's personal and literary chronology. What was he writing when each event occurred? How is this reflected in his journal, his correspondence, his verse, and his essays?

With these data recorded, interpret them. Was Emerson outward looking in his work? Were his seemingly abstract meditations actually precipitated by events that marked the nation's history? What might this mean, if his writings do reflect the nation's development? Does it make Emerson a more successful writer? Or a more "American" writer? Or does it mark a failure by Emerson, whose avowed aim was—at least at one stage—to ignore time and space?

Philosophy and Ideas

Emerson surprises many readers when he announces, in "Circles," this apparently minor caveat:

> But lest I should mislead any when I have my own head and obey my whims, let me remind the reader that I am only an experimenter. Do not set the least value on what I do, or the least discredit on what I do not, as if I pretended to settle any thing as true or false. I unsettle all things. No facts are to me sacred; none are profane; I simply experiment, an endless seeker with no Past at my back.

What does an announcement like this imply for the reader of Emerson's works? Does this revise and recast everything that preceded it as unreliable? In that case, how are we to read any of Emerson's statements? And when Emerson claims in "Experience" that "I have set my heart on honesty in this chapter," are we to believe a word of it? What is an essay that lies—and how is it different from fiction?

With the creeping introduction of doubt to his readers, Emerson also presents—or makes more visible—his use of multiple voices and multiple views in his essays. This is perhaps best demonstrated in "Experience," when Emerson goes through seven different voices (or "lenses") without declaring definitively which is the "honest" one. Again, the reader might wonder whether Emerson's work has always been concerned with dialogues—or dialectics—between polar opposites, without actually identifying and clearly defining these positions.

Another factor influencing the analysis of Emerson's writing is the critical tradition that views Emerson's work as a decline (or "declension") from a position of optimism and self-trust in the early work, gradually descending into a position of skepticism and doubt. This decline was punctuated by the death in 1842 of Emerson's firstborn son, Waldo. This thesis was made popular by the scholar Stephen Whicher in his study *Freedom and Fate* (Philadelphia, 1953). It has been the prevalent view (if not among specialists) ever since. Is the Whicherian thesis, this narrative of decline, correct?

Sample Topics:

1. **Narration:** Is Emerson a reliable narrator?

Unreliable narrator is a literary term to describe (as it suggests) a narrator who cannot be relied on or trusted. You might explore this topic by investigating examples of this literary conceit, usually used in fiction. How is such a state signaled to the reader by the author? If the narrator is unreliable, how are we to understand the author behind the narrator? And how do we separate author from narrator?

Certain of Emerson's texts more than others conspicuously use the unreliable narrator. Perhaps the best-known examples are in "Circles" and "Experience," where the unreliability of the narrative is actually admitted—even boasted. How does this awareness make us reassess Emerson's other narratives? You might reread certain essays, looking now for narrative ambiguities. You will find, for instance, that even as early as *Nature*, Emerson shifts tone when he speaks as the "Orphic Poet." Who, then, is the speaker for the rest of the essay? If the speaker shifts, whom are we to trust? Which other essays (or indeed addresses and lectures) of Emerson's are fragmented? Analyze the tone and form of deliberately unsettling essays such as "Circles" and "Experience" (or indeed some of the poems written in the voice of personae, for instance, "The Sphinx" or "Brahma") and compare them with those ostensibly "honest" essays in which the speaker is not attempting to distort or misrepresent. (Which essays, after all, do we read as "honest," and why?) Who is the whimsical author of "Self-Reliance," for instance, who preaches a "doctrine of hatred" and asks, "Are they *my* poor?" Who, indeed, is the firebrand speaker of the Divinity School Address? Is he really the same as the modest and polite former student of divinity? Can we divorce Emerson from the speaker's role and see his essays as a form of fiction or dramatic monologue?

2. **Polarity:** How does Emerson use polarity in his writing?

In a number of essays, Emerson draws particular attention to the idea of polarity. First, you should identify instances of opposing elements being discussed in Emerson's works. An obvious example is in "The Transcendentalist," in which he somewhat painstakingly relates the opposition between idealism and materialism. How does he resolve this polarity in "The Transcendentalist"? Identify other examples of polarities and how they are used by Emerson. How does he resolve them? Next, what does this resolution show or prove?

Think also of historical reasons for why Emerson—and other Americans—were thinking so much about polar opposites and their possible reconciliation. Slavery was perhaps a defining obsession in the United States in the 19th century, dividing black and white, North and South, proslavery and abolitionist. Is Emerson's method of reasoning a reflection of his nation's history? Or is he purposely applying the "dialectic" technique familiar to readers of Plato's Socratic dialogues? What other reasons can you find for Emerson's use of this technique? Isolate cases and analyze them.

3. **Whicher's thesis—freedom and fate:** Does Emerson's writing follow a course from optimism to skepticism? If not, is there any pattern to his developing thought?

Stephen Whicher's thesis was that all Emerson's best work was done in his early career, up to the death of his son Waldo (1842). Whicher coolly calls the years 1841 to 1882 (when Emerson died) the "period of acquiescence." Do you agree? This question asks you to pay special attention, inevitably, to those works written after 1841. This gives you a large palette to work from, the "second series" of *Essays* and everything published after it. Choose several essays and investigate them. Do you find them to be statements of "acquiescence" (submission)? Look at "Experience," for instance, in which—after numerous statements of "acquiescence" but also of resilience—Emerson concludes:

> Never mind the ridicule, never mind the defeat; up again, old heart! . . . there is victory yet for all justice; and the true romance which the world exists to realize will be the transformation of genius into practical power.

Can you identify expressions of either acquiescence or resilience here or elsewhere? Equally, can you find instances of acquiescence in pre-1842 writings?

The question also asks whether, if you disagree with Whicher's thesis, you can find an alternative pattern. Try to recognize consistent elements to Emerson's narrative, particularly anything that recurs from 1836 through Emerson's last works.

Form and Genre

Emerson's friend the poet and critic James Russell Lowell wrote that

> the bother with Mr. Emerson is, that, though he writes in prose, he is essentially a poet. If you undertake to paraphrase what he says, and to reduce it to words of one syllable for infant minds, you will make [a] sad . . . work of it.

This quotation squarely identifies one of the perennial arguments among readers of Emerson. Was he, first, a poet or an essayist? To the philosopher William James he was an "artist." William's brother, the novelist Henry James, meanwhile carped that it was "hardly too much, or too little, to say of Emerson's writings in general that they were not composed at all." This in turn alerts us to the third argument, that an Emerson text was an unstructured hodgepodge, composed of fragments, joined arbitrarily.

Sample Topics:

1. **The essay:** Was Emerson an essayist?

   While this question seems to seek a somewhat obvious answer, it clearly requires a more thorough and sophisticated consideration. Emerson wrote essays, but were they typical of the essay form? What resemblance do they bear to earlier essays and those by contemporaries? You should fully equip yourself (and so your reader) with a definition and history of the essay form. You should also make a study of several examples of the essay. The word was coined by the French writer Michel de Montaigne to describe his first book, *Essais* (1580). Emerson particularly admired Montaigne, including an essay about him in his book *Representative Men* (1850). Reading that work could provide a useful starting point for exploring this topic. What does Emerson say about Montaigne, and what does he value most in his work? Survey other masters of the essay form such as the English contemporary of Shakespeare Francis Bacon or the English humorists Joseph Addison and Richard Steele, beloved of Benjamin Franklin, among others.

Other names mentioned in Emerson's essay as authorities on Montaigne are Leigh Hunt and William Hazlitt, British essayists who wrote mostly in the first half of the 19th century. You might look also at their works. What similarities are there between these British essays and Emerson's work? Is there a classic essay form, and, if so, does Emerson follow it? After identifying similarities and differences, it is important to ask what reconsidering these works within the context of their genre adds to our appreciation of Emerson.

2. **The poem:** Was Emerson a poet?

Again, this question might seem to invite a one-word response, but a more complex nuanced answer requires engaging the debate that involves, on one side, the contention that Emerson was foremost a writer of prose (or a philosopher) and, on the other, that he was a poet. Many critics have faulted Emerson for his inexact meter or for his failure to engage in radical poetic structures (as, say, Walt Whitman did) such as free verse. Do you agree? Find examples of different critical views and challenge (or confirm) their findings with your own readings from a selection of Emerson's verses. The comparison with Walt Whitman can be fruitful, since the two were acquaintances (if not exactly friends) and readers of each others' poetry. Does Emerson influence Whitman as a poet or as a prose stylist? Is Emerson's style really conventional and prone to hiccup, or is it—as some scholars attest—a deliberate confounding of exact meter? How would such a purposeful subversion of expectation accord with other aspects of Emerson's work?

Language, Symbols, and Imagery

In Emerson's essays, certain stylistic features recur. Readers cannot help noticing the fragmentary nature of some of Emerson's paragraphs; there is no set length to paragraphs (some paragraphs run to pages, some to a few lines) and no clear thread that runs throughout any essay. Emerson himself remarked ruefully, "I have often found cause to complain that my thoughts have an ebb & flow. . . . The worst is, that the ebb is certain, long, & frequent, while the flow comes transiently & seldom." The essay "Experience," which follows a tortuous form through seven different tones, is almost the paradigm of the Emerson essay, emphasizing as it does its variety and adaptability as a form. Is this fragmentary, dislocated structure a deliberate innovation or a mark of error on Emerson's part?

Another stylistic signature of Emerson's essays is the inclusion of a verse motto at the beginning. What is the purpose of these poems? Do they encapsulate the essay to follow, or do they provide a key to its understanding, or are they simply red herrings, planted by a saboteur to comprehension, who seeks only to "unsettle"?

Sample Topics:

1. **"Fragment aesthetics":** Are Emerson's essays fragmentary, or do they have a definitive structure?

> One of the chief charges against Emerson is that his writing is fragmentary. Do you agree? One way to ascertain the extent of Emerson's structuring is to research the progress certain ideas or sentences make from the journals to a final printed form. How does Emerson arrange and craft the text from his journals? With the availability of Emerson's *Journals and Miscellaneous Notebooks* in a multivolume set, it is possible to trace the way Emerson plundered his journals for sentences and transposed them into essay form. Does this reveal a sophisticated, even tedious deliberation, or a pattern, or does it betray a slapdash and random cut-and-paste methodology? Look also at Emerson's own philosophy: How might his method of structuring precisely reflect his own ideas and thoughts? How does the form of the text reflect the content?
>
> Consider the work "Experience," for instance, with its multiplicity of narrative voices and philosophies. How does the seemingly jumbled structure of the essay, which begins, after all, "In a series of which we do not know the extremes," reflect its disorienting intention? Can you assign a purpose to Emer-

son's seeming lack of structure or system by locating the ways Emerson's content is reflected in his chosen form?

2. **Mottoes:** What is the significance of the mottoes that head many of Emerson's essays? Do they serve as prefatory summaries to the essays they precede? Or are they red herrings, intended to violate the reader's expectations?

This topic requires you to assemble several of the mottoes that precede essays by Emerson. There are mottoes for many of the *Essays* in the first and second series. Is it preferable to be well versed in the motto before you read the essay or to read it afterward? How do you think Emerson intended the mottoes to be read? Survey several mottoes and the several essays that contain them as well. You need a good knowledge of the essays to compare their content to that of the mottoes. Do all mottoes serve a similar purpose?

Look at the motto for "Experience," for instance. It introduces the notion of "the lords of life, the lords of life," but their identity and relevance to the essay are lost to us until we have read the entirety of the essay, when (three paragraphs from the end) their meaning is revealed. How does the motto function in this case? Does it confirm and explain aspects of the poem, or does it further complicate our understanding of the essay? Once you have established a purpose for these mottoes, what does this then reveal about Emerson's tone in the essays? Does it reveal Emerson to be deliberately cryptic—even playful with the reader? Or does it show Emerson trying to assist the reader with clues to understanding? Or, finally, does it reveal Emerson as an unsettler, deliberately preventing us from formulating a secure understanding of his work?

Bibliography and Online Resources

Allen, Gay Wilson. *American Prosody.* New York: American Book Company, 1935.

Buell, Lawrence. "Reading Emerson for the Structures: The Coherence of the Essays." *Critical Essays on Ralph Waldo Emerson.* Ed. Robert E. Burkholder and Joel Myerson. Boston: G. K. Hall, 1983. 399–413.

———. *Emerson.* Cambridge, MA: Harvard UP, 2003.

Packer, Barbara. *Emerson's Fall: A New Interpretation of the Major Essays.* New York: Continuum, 1982.

Scott, Eleanor Bryce. "Emerson Wins the Nine Hundred Dollars." *American Literature* 17 (1945): 78–85.

Whicher, Stephen. *Freedom and Fate: An Inner Life of Ralph Waldo Emerson.* Philadelphia: U of Pennsylvania P, 1953.

NATURE

READING TO WRITE

*N*ATURE WAS Emerson's first published essay (1836), establishing many images, themes, and ideas that would recur and endure, not only in Emerson's own writing but also in a vigorous tradition in American literature that extends to this day. *Nature* has been described as the inspiration for a larger American body of meditative writing "that centers on a perceiver trying to make sense of his or her physical surroundings."

One critical position maintains that *Nature* is more tidily structured than Emerson's subsequent essays. While it is a long essay, it is conveniently divided into constituent subchapters. Still, given the size of the essay, its complexity, and its tendency to interweave certain ideas and terms, it is helpful to note in summary the arguments of each chapter. What structure do you notice? *Nature* has been found to have a clear shape and to follow an internal logic, traits arguably harder to locate in many of Emerson's later studies. There have been many critical attempts to interpret this internal logic, well worth perusing.

For hints regarding how to read the essay for the purpose of writing, the first authority to be considered should be Emerson himself. The student should note any time the author comments on the act of writing. Such pronouncements provide signposts and assurances, perhaps otherwise lacking, on how to read Emerson's work. For instance, Emerson implicitly acknowledges that his own "theory" is imperfect and anticipates the many critics who remark (both favorably and not) on his propensity for clumping fragmentary sentences:

We learn to prefer imperfect theories, and sentences which contain glimpses of truth, to digested systems which have no one valuable suggestion.

Emerson acknowledges that his study is a "general" one, and that accuracy is of little consequence:

In inquiries so general as our present one, the inaccuracy is not material.

The author anticipates the criticism that his ideas may seem implausible:

That which seems faintly possible . . . is often faint and dim because it is deepest seated among the eternal verities.

Finally, he concedes that the theories he is propounding and assimilating in his own theory can be difficult to follow:

The doctrine is abstruse.

In each case Emerson seems to be reassuring readers who may be cowed or flagging or confused as they try to trace a strict system to his narrative. To prevent obscurity, at other times Emerson makes his aims explicit:

"Every scripture is to be interpreted by the same spirit which gave it forth,"—is the fundamental law of criticism.

The true philosopher and the true poet are one, and a beauty, which is truth, and a truth, which is beauty, is the aim of both.

A wise writer will feel that the ends of study and composition are best answered by announcing undiscovered regions of thought, and so communicating, through hope, new activity to the torpid spirit.

Does Emerson meet his own standards? Does he follow his own advice? Keep such questions in mind as you read *Nature* and Emerson's other essays.

Emerson is committed to writing about large, abstract concepts, and sometimes his use of words denoting cosmic, metaphysical abstractions may seem frustratingly vague or loaded in some unobvious way. Emerson complained that in group discussions his questioners "drive me into a corner—I must not suggest, I must define." In lieu of definition, you must take the time to clarify what you understand Emerson to be "suggesting" by certain words and keep these definitions at hand for times when the word recurs. Sometimes Emerson uses a word in a highly particular way, as it is used in philosophical discourse rather than the more familiar colloquial usage. The reader needs, therefore, to ascertain how Emerson means these words to be understood. *Type* is a good example of this, derived specifically from Emerson's reading of the English poet Samuel Taylor Coleridge. Two other central concepts for navigating Emerson's theory are "reason" and "understanding"; yet, as one critic has noted, Emerson's use of the word *reason* (again, drawn from Coleridge) was modified to mean "not methodological ratiocination but its conventional opposite, intuitive grasp of Truth." In this instance a word is used to mean its conventional opposite, so let the reader beware and mark Emerson's interpretations of words. Follow his hints at sources, and if you would understand *Nature,* read Coleridge.

The following passage is from the first subchapter, "Nature":

> Nature is a setting that fits equally well a comic or a mourning piece. In good health, the air is a cordial of incredible virtue. Crossing a bare common, in snow puddles, at twilight, under a clouded sky, without having in my thoughts any occurrence of special good fortune, I have enjoyed a perfect exhilaration. I am glad to the brink of fear. In the woods, too, a man casts off his years, as the snake his slough, and at what period soever of life is always a child. In the woods is perpetual youth. Within these plantations of God, a decorum and sanctity reign, a perennial festival is dressed, and the guest sees not how he should tire of them in a thousand years. In the woods, we return to reason and faith. There I feel that nothing can befall me in life,—no disgrace, no calamity (leaving me my eyes), which nature cannot repair. Standing on the bare ground,—my head bathed by the blithe air and uplifted into infinite space,—all mean egotism vanishes. I become a transparent eyeball; I am nothing; I see all;

the currents of the Universal Being circulate through me; I am part or parcel of God.

As well as containing the transparent eyeball, that best-known (or most notorious) of Emerson's images in this essay—indeed, in his entire oeuvre—this passage establishes numerous characteristic ideas and themes for the essay to follow. Students should keep these staples in mind and note when they reappear.

Emerson claims that as a subject nature can be equally "comic or mourning"—nature has an ambiguity; a heterogeneity, such that it can contain a mixture of registers and genres that seem to be—or are—contradictory. The paradox of binary opposites existing simultaneously, and the possible redemptive reconciliation or resolution of these oppositions, abounds in Emerson's writing.

Emerson's bland and seemingly inconsequential hyperbole of not tiring of the woods "in a thousand years" and his lauding of perpetual youth both foreground notions of time, timelessness, and eternity. Emerson's interest, from the start of the essay, is to propound an escape from history and our slavish debt to past and tradition. His ultimate transcendental aim in this essay is to go beyond conventions of space and time. Setting his scene in "the woods," Emerson transforms the scene of the American frontier from a place of darkness and savagery and gothic fear to a place of youth and reason. (Nathaniel Hawthorne would soon enough dramatize a similar transformation of the meaning of "the woods" in *The Scarlet Letter*.) Emerson's complex sense of what he means by "reason" will be refined as the essay develops.

Here, then, is the legendary "transparent eyeball." The grisly phrase that precedes it—"no calamity (leaving me my eyes)"—primes the reader's imagination, inevitably, to reflect on all the other "calamities" that remain possible. The separation of the eyes from the body instantly privileges the eyes above the other senses and the rest of the body—the division of the eyes from the body, the soul from the NOT-ME, which is reiterated by Emerson's transcendental metamorphosis into a giant (and notably transparent) eyeball. Eyes and seeing are paramount in Emerson's philosophy. The eyeball, we deduce, is spiritually (and, in Emerson's telling, literally) above and beyond the body. This image and this supposition will recur and flower over the essay's course. *Seeing* can mean literally "visualizing," but it can also connote "comprehension." This pun is at the core of the essay—the eye as that which sees (comprehends to the fullest). There is a well-known cartoon by Emerson's fellow transcendentalist Christopher Pearse Cranch, which comically crystallizes Emerson's image. It shows Emerson strolling abroad on distended legs, with an eyeball atop his cravat and under a beat-up top hat.

TOPICS AND STRATEGIES

The following section suggests several possible topics for essays on *Nature.* They can and should be used as starting points for your own, independent exploration of the essay.

Themes

"To a sound judgment, the most abstract truth is the most practical," Emerson writes in *Nature.* Emerson turns the earth into a metaphysical plane populated by "types." In this realm of the abstract, he has only occasional recourse to concrete objects. Even when he writes of nature, it is often Nature capitalized: the personification of Nature rather than its constituent fauna and flora, phyla and genera. When Emerson looks over the countryside, he takes in the larger vista—he sees the ultimate horizon, not the cubits apportioned to squires Miller, Locke, and Manning.

This refusal to descend to the concrete and a preference to remain in the realm of ultimate "types" means that both "themes" and "subjects" for Emerson are of the high Platonic order, and distinguishing one from the other is not a simple matter. Is "Nature" a subject or a theme? What about "Man," "Matter," or "Soul"? Or what about those chapter headings (Commodity, Beauty, Language, Discipline, Idealism, Spirit)? This problematic question at least illuminates one aspect of Emerson's writing—and his thesis. Things in this essay appear at times in their abstract forms and at others in their material forms.

These themes are broad and ubiquitous and so may swamp the reader. Other themes arise and recur in a more familiar way, similar to themes as they occur in a fictional narrative. Most glaring (literally) is the famous transparent eyeball, echoed by a recurring vocabulary referring to optical perception. Readers should jolt upright when Emerson makes any ocular reference. Finally, as much as Emerson concerns himself with matter and its physical existence in space, he also explores our construction of time, history, tradition, and a past. An inquiry—or a campaign—gesturing toward an escape from history pervades this essay to its (apocalyptic?) close.

Sample Topics:

1. **"Nature"**: What does Emerson mean by "nature"? Give more than one example.

   This question seems simple, and then it becomes clear that it is not. To use a nature-friendly illustration, so constant and present is nature in this essay you can not always "see the wood for the trees." Emerson defines nature in many different ways. From the "Introduction," Emerson distinguishes between two usages of the word: "in its common and in its philosophical import." What is the difference between the two? What problems arise from this? A question that might follow is, Why do you suppose Emerson capitalizes the word at times (*Nature*) and not at others (*nature*)? Find examples of each and compare Emerson's usages of the word. Is nature viewed as negative or positive, or both? Give examples.

2. **Perception**: "So shall we come to look at the world with new eyes." What is the significance of eyes and seeing in *Nature*?

   To answer this question, the reader should first ask: Why is the eye privileged by Emerson when the body is not? Why this conspicuous separation of the eye from the rest of the body? At one juncture, Emerson writes: "the eye,—the mind,—" as though the two are one. Later, he writes of "the eye of Reason." What precisely is the eyeball taken to represent? This question does not solely ask for a Freudian meditation on the significance of eyes and castration theory (although this is certainly admissible, if properly supported), but for what Emerson is trying to articulate when he invokes the image of the eye. To see means to understand as well as merely to observe.

"The eye is the best of artists," Emerson claims. What does this mean? For Emerson seeing is not passive, but properly *seeing* is an active thing and creates the world. What is the relation between seeing and being? Is that which we see all that exists? Is that which we see even real? This question, which clearly occupies Emerson, is a larger preoccupation of a vast philosophical tradition and can be found in writers from Plato through Immanuel Kant and beyond. Where does Emerson sit in this debate? Look out for all Emerson's references to seeing and eyes and associated language. You will begin to notice their frequency. Note these occurrences and build a profile of them. Are there inconsistencies among them? Is not the eye also the organ of misperception, deceiving the mind with illusions?

History and Context

Given Emerson's antagonism to history, declared at the essay's outset, and his subsequent idealist rejection of space, time, and matter, it is easy at first to regard *Nature* as an essay with little to say about history. Especially in its most philosophical passages, such as the "Idealism" chapter, the essay seems to hover above and outside time, "aloof, and, as it were, afloat." Emerson writes that "the world is a divine dream from which we may presently awake to the glories and certainties of day." Especially in a time of such political upheaval and turmoil, is this denial of the historical, the concrete, and substantial a sort of dreamy, apolitical lotus eating?

However, when Emerson rejects idealism and lists his "examples of Reason's momentary grasping of the sceptre," he also acknowledges admirable aspects of his own society and, as it were, reenters his own time and space. In a rush he praises:

religious and political revolutions ... the abolition of the slave-trade; the miracles of enthusiasm ... and the Shakers; many obscure and yet uncontested facts, now arranged under the name Animal Magnetism.

In this concession, Emerson identifies himself with religious enthusiasm in the wake of the wave known as the Second Great Awakening;

he allies himself furthermore with radical religious reform, here lauding the Shakers; he endorses the popular fascination with science and at
least one of the pseudosciences ("Animal Magnetism"); and of course, he
backs social reform (here, abolitionism).

One of the aspects of social reform under Jacksonian democracy was
the celebration and empowerment of the so-called common man. Emerson was always chary about this (and always critical of Jackson), but his
rhetoric in *Nature* nevertheless reflects such concerns. At one stage in
his comments he chooses a simile that refers to then-president Andrew
Jackson's "Bank War" (1832–36): "A paper currency is employed when
there is no bullion in the vaults." In "Prospects," concluding his essay,
Emerson is clearly reconciled with his time and place: "You also are a
man. Man and woman and their social life, poverty, labor, sleep, fortune,
are known to you."

Another reason for the seeming timelessness of the essay is Emerson's espousing of the rural over the urban. Despite appearances,
Emerson is very much *in* history in this respect. His desire for timelessness is, in fact, entirely of its time. His resentment of the city and
aspects of industrialism resembles Thomas Jefferson's objections, and
in his championing of the self-reliant yeoman farmer, Emerson seems
to reiterate Jefferson's corollary espousing of agrarianism. Two facets of
agrarianism were antiurbanism and anti-industrialism, both of which
are apparent in Emerson's essay. Such positions address the rapid birth
and growth of cities and the rise of the Industrial Revolution. Emerson occasionally addresses these directly, yet their tyranny informs his
essay throughout. Is Emerson's partial celebration of the new technology consistent, though, with his romanticizing of the agrarian life?

Sample Topics:

1. **The Industrial Revolution:** How is the rise of industrialism
   reflected in Emerson's essay?

   While one might expect *Nature* to be unstintingly green and
   environmentally exacting, Emerson's view of industrialism is
   ambiguous. Industrialism had advanced greatly in his lifetime,
   so it still had the shock of the new about it. Emerson does not
   simply condemn the advances in technology but places them

within a narrative still dominated by nature. Is this naïve? How do machinery, technology, and industry fit into his view of nature, then? Emerson is seldom categorical in his pronouncements, so contradictory attitudes may blithely sit close to each other. In one breath, Emerson may damn the "noxious work" of the urban "tradesman," before, only a few breaths later, praising the "new thoughts" that result from traveling through familiar terrain "in the rapid movement of a railroad car!" Is he lamenting or crowing when he exclaims, "By the aggregate of these aids, how is the face of the world changed, from the era of Noah to that of Napoleon!" Rally his various remarks and engage scrupulously the contradictions.

For example, Emerson notes how the "camera obscura" renders the familiar miraculously strange, so that "the butcher's cart, and the figure of one of our own family amuse us." But is such amusement advantageous or a further distortion of reality? Is it a distillation of the pure vision of the transparent eyeball? Challenge Emerson by his own standards. "The private poor man hath cities, ships, canals, bridges, built for him," he proclaims, before railing roundly against the corruption of the urban environment. Assemble a number of Emerson's statements regarding technology, industrialism, work, "art," and commerce, particularly those that seem incompatible. Weigh these statements and prosecute the inconsistencies.

2. **Agrarianism and the rise of cities:** Compare Emerson's portrayal of city and countryside. Does he show a bias? If so, is he fair?

Note when Emerson sets the city against the country. For instance, he remarks in the chapter "Language," "These facts may suggest the advantages that the country-life possesses, for a powerful mind, over the artificial and curtailed life of cities."

Emerson's view of agrarianism is grounded in an American tradition. Earlier examples can be found in the writings and thoughts of Thomas Jefferson and in texts such as

Crèvecœur's *Letters from an American Farmer* (1782). Farming has long been identified in American history and letters with autonomy and morality. What other books fit into this tradition? Come up with some further examples, and compare the responses of the authors. Does Emerson's portrait fit this tradition?

Likewise, Emerson's portrait of the city exists in a larger tradition (for example, Edgar Allan Poe's "The Man of the Crowd," published five years later). The city was viewed by many as corrupting and sinister (and worse, European). Is this true in *Nature*? At the time of Emerson's writing, there was a pronounced exodus of young, talented men out of the New England villages to New York and a sense of country culture dissipating. Does Emerson's portrait reflect this? Is Emerson's bias—if there is one—reflected in his philosophical argument? Is transcendence possible in the city?

3. **Social reform:** What, according to Emerson, are the social consequences of nature?

This question requires the reader to locate those instances in the essay where Emerson refers to society or elements with a political aspect. For example, he remarks how to be master or servant is, in the eyes of nature, "a trifle and a disturbance." Does he suggest, then, that social position is irrelevant? Is this a cavalier attitude?

When does Emerson's argument—which often takes place in the abstract, or on a metaphysical plane—enter the "actual" world, a world inhabited by men? Instances have been noted previously. In "Commodity" Emerson acknowledges that when enumerating the commercial uses of nature, the "catalogue is endless" and the "examples so obvious." How, then, is nature used less obviously, for uses more intellectual? To answer this question properly, the reader should review the later, more theoretical chapters, to clarify Emerson's subtler views and how they might reflect social considerations of the day (such as slavery, equality, democracy, westward expansion, rights of the individual).

Emerson remarks, "Give me health and a day, and I will make the pomp of emperors ridiculous." What does such a comment suggest of his political views? Are they revolutionary? Or this one: "The universe is the property of every individual in it." In particular, the student should scour the "Prospects" chapter, and Emerson's conclusions. Social reform and philosophy, for Emerson, should be inseparable. Are they? Should they be? Does philosophy have any place in politics?

Philosophy and Ideas

Emerson's own opening epigram to *Nature* was a replacement inserted into the 1849 revised edition. In the original book (1836), a quotation from the third-century philosopher Plotinus was in its place:

> Nature is but an image or imitation of wisdom, the last thing of the soul; nature being a thing which doth only do, but not know.

This switch of texts, from philosophy to poetry, highlights an ambivalence sensed by many readers of Emerson: Does he write poetry or philosophy? If *Nature* is not easily defined as a work of philosophy, it can certainly be conceded that it is a work indebted to philosophy. Despite his rejection of tradition and bookishness in the introduction, Emerson places himself firmly in a tradition, and it is a philosophical one. Emerson either alludes to or assimilates ideas from many thinkers, whether they are from antiquity (Heraclitus through Plato to Plotinus), from several centuries of British thought (Bishop Berkeley through the aesthetic theory of the English poet Coleridge and then to Thomas Carlyle), from the mystic Swedenborg, or from German idealism.

The reader of *Nature* does not need to study all these writers, by any means, to enjoy the essay. To understand it adequately, however, a passing knowledge of the tradition will prove beneficial. A good history of Western philosophy will provide a brief account of most of these thinkers. Such a history may, in turn, encourage the reader to read further and will offer directions for such research.

Sample Topics:

1. **Reason and understanding:** What is the difference between "reason" and "understanding"?

This question is central to Emerson's philosophy in *Nature* and in his later essays. Do not simply expect Emerson's understanding of the words to match the definition in Webster's dictionary. Words have different uses and meanings in philosophical discourse. It will take some research to find the context in which Emerson's usage of these words exists. Look also to the text for Emerson's explication of his use of the term. In the section titled "Language," Emerson elaborates on what he means by reason. What is understanding, then, and why are the two paired?

Other terms are auxiliary to these. What, for example, is meant by a fact?

2. **Idealism:** What is the "ideal theory"? Does Emerson support it or challenge it?

First, this question requires the reader to clarify Emerson's theory espoused in the "Language" and "Idealism" chapters. What does he mean by idealism? Where does this argument lead? Emerson's essay impressed Orestes Brownson, a friend in the "Transcendental Club," but one aspect unnerved Brownson: Emerson "seems seriously to doubt the existence of the external world except as a picture which God stamps on the mind." Do you agree with this reading? Does Emerson doubt the existence of the external world, and, if so, does this change your reading of the essay? Brownson's objections can be read as a contemporary (and sympathetic) response to Emerson's theory. Reviews of *Nature* by Emerson's contemporaries can help a student understand how the essay was received and comprehended in its own time.

"Spirit" is an important chapter for this question. Here, in one of his characteristic twists of position from chapter to chapter, Emerson seems to reevaluate the idealist theory:

> Yet, if it only deny the existence of matter, it does not satisfy the demands of the spirit. It leaves God out of me. It leaves me in the splendid labyrinth of my perceptions, to wander without end.

Does Emerson, then, reject idealism as the essay evolves? If so, why? And what does he propose in its stead?

You should research idealism, particularly following the reading Emerson himself indicates. When a name is dropped, however lightly, Emerson is providing clues to his sources. Most notably, inspiration is found in the work of the 18th-century Irish Christian philosopher Bishop George Berkeley. See especially *A Treatise Concerning the Principles of Human Knowledge* (1710). The German philosopher Immanuel Kant was another proponent of idealism, again influential on Emerson. By familiarizing yourself with the work of those who influenced Emerson, you can reflect on how well or poorly he modifies their thought.

3. **Man:** What is Emerson's view of man, and what is man's relation to nature?

Emerson calls his inquiry "A true theory of nature and of man." He elsewhere insists, "I only wish to indicate the true position of nature in regard to man." Is this aim realized? Questions to ask might include, Is Emerson always either negative or positive in his portrayal of man? Compare different views of man within the essay. For instance, of the following passages, does the first seem consistent with the last two?

> In the tranquil landscape, and especially in the distant line of the horizon, man beholds somewhat as beautiful as his own nature.

> Unfortunately, every one of them [humans] bears the marks as of some injury; is marred and superficially defective.

> Man is the dwarf of himself.

The context for these statements, then, is all-important. Is Emerson's attitude to man the same in the chapters "Beauty" or "Language" as it is "Discipline" or "Prospects"? What might explain any differences, and which version do you find more convincing?

This question also requires an explanation of what man's relation to nature is. Obvious examples are given in "Commodity," but in each subsequent chapter Emerson specifies a way in which man and nature harmonize or fail to. With each chapter an example should be found. Ask ancillary questions: Is the collaboration a success? Can it be? A final question might be asked, regarding Emerson's indulgence of the "ideal theory." In a theory that doubts the existence of external objects, where does man stand? Read Emerson's comments at the end of "Discipline." What is his attitude to friendship?

Form and Genre

Emerson writes: "Nature is a setting that fits equally well a comic or a mourning piece." With his variety of registers and tones, ranging from the casual and anecdotal to the highly loaded quasi-academic language of metaphysics and theology, Emerson switches genres within what is ostensibly an "essay." As Emerson's friend Henry David Thoreau wrote to a friend, *Nature* is "neither a song nor a sermon." It is something of a miscellany.

Emerson uses different forms of writing within the text. We may find several genres existing within this hybrid narrative. For instance, Emerson's high lauding of the rural life recalls a tradition of pastoral lyric and drama. His debt to the English romantic poets is likewise well established. Perhaps a less obvious influence on Emerson is that of the gothic tradition, which had absorbed and titillated readers of popular American fiction since the late 18th century, in the tales and novels of writers such as Charles Brockden Brown. Edgar Allan Poe's tales had begun to appear in print four years before *Nature,* and in some ways both writers partook of common imagery. Each form sheds a different light on Emerson's discourse, and, as such, form may edify the reader as much as content. As one critic remarks: "Our concern must then be not only with *what* Emerson's key words mean as such, but with *how* they act." How does Emerson's use of imagery or forms from other, nonessay genres, illuminate his present project?

Sample Topics:

1. **Pastoral:** Discuss pastoral elements in *Nature.* How does this essay fit the pastoral tradition, and how does it subvert the form?

First, this question clearly requires the reader to research the pastoral tradition. The pastoral form is an old one, emerging from third-century B.C.E. Greece. It has existed in poetic, dramatic, and prose forms. Good definitions can be found in a dictionary of literary terms, but such a definition will not suffice. Studies of the genre exist and should be consulted. Pinpoint conventions of the genre, find examples from literature, and compare these with Emerson's work. For example, 13 years before *Nature* was published, a young countryside-bound Emerson wrote a letter quoting from the ancient Roman poet Virgil's *Georgics,* a pastoral that celebrates a fictional, ideal "Arcadia." In his letter Emerson rants, "I am seeking to put myself on a footing of old acquaintance with nature, as a poet should." His self-construction, at this time, was in a pastoral tradition. How much of this endures in his more mature self, 13 years later?

Read some criticisms of the form for resonances with Emerson's essay. One critic remarks that from its inception the pastoral was intended for an urban audience, exploiting that tension between coastal town and the shepherd's mountainous countryside; a tension "between people and nature . . . retreat and return." How does Emerson mirror this form? Does he play to similar reader biases?

2. **Romantic (prose) poem:** What is Emerson's debt to the romantic poets?

Emerson openly avowed his debt to the English poets Samuel Taylor Coleridge and William Wordsworth. He went so far as to make a pilgrimage to meet them when he visited England in 1833. In their celebrated habitat, the Lake District, Emerson saw the rural settings that had inspired them to write the poetry he enjoyed. (Emerson's journal, recalling these meetings, provides an interesting biographical twist and some resolution to this influence.)

You should, of course, familiarize yourself with the principle poems of Coleridge and Wordsworth (to begin, their *Lyrical Ballads* of 1798). What are the similarities? What does Emerson take from them, and what does he reject? Do not simply read the poetry, but consult the prose and critical writings (Coleridge's work particularly; this had a huge influence on Emerson, particularly in the development of a philosophy in *Nature*). There are innumerable studies of the romantics as a group. Several should be consulted, to provide instances and explanations of the aesthetic theories expounded by the group's constituents. What, if anything, rings familiar to the reader of *Nature*? What clangs as discordant? Elizabeth Palmer Peabody, a crony of Emerson's, wrote a review of *Nature* in which she called the essay "A Prose Poem," the chapters "Cantos" and the whole a "song." How does recasting *Nature* in this light affect the reading of it? Does it lessen the significance of the treatise if you reenvision the essay as a poem? How do you think Emerson intended the essay to be read?

3. **Gothic/fantastic:** To what extent is *Nature* a gothic text?

Gothic and fantastic forms are not customarily associated with Emerson. Nevertheless, recent scholarship has found in Emerson some assimilation of imagery and language from incongruous sources. Debts to sensationalist fiction and frontier humor have both been identified in passages from *Nature* (see David Reynolds's study in the bibliography). It is little wonder—*Nature* particularly encourages such a reading, with its eye fixation. Eye mutilation (with its unsaid Freudian double, castration), obsessions with seeing, and distortions of perception alike are staples of gothic and fantastic fiction; for instance, E. T. A. Hoffmann's "The Sandman" plays with ideas of lenses, as do Nathaniel Hawthorne's "The Beauty Spot" and Fitz-James O'Brien's "The Diamond Lens." Violent brawls culminating in eye gougings were a stock feature of the frontier humor appearing in the sporting registers, newspapers, and almanacs.

To answer a question of this sort, the student should become familiar with the genres. Who are the gothic and fantastic writers? What are their works? Is there criticism about them? (Of course.) An obvious writer (but not the only one) is Edgar Allan Poe—who notably despised Emerson and the transcendentalists. Ostensibly, then, they were at opposite poles of interest. Consult some Poe (or Hawthorne, or Charles Brockden Brown) and note any themes, language, or images that occur in *Nature*. Conversely, what gothic staples show up in Emerson's essay? For instance, violent and grotesque imagery characterizes gothic fiction. Can examples of such possibly be found in *Nature*? Does Emerson sound like Poe when he remarks that "even the corpse has its own beauty"? The incongruous mixture of beauty and the grave has an unusual effect. Transformations and apparitions, differing planes of reality and unreality, arresting the very mechanics of time and space—all of these feature in *Nature*. Astute readers can find the instances. What explains Emerson's eerie gravitation to such imagery—what purpose might it serve? What historical factors may have prompted Emerson and Poe to share imagery? And what does this say about *Nature* and its more serious aims? Is this really a work about nature or about supernature?

Language, Symbols, and Imagery

Language is fundamental to Emerson's account of nature and man in harmony, since it is one of the principal uses man makes of nature. It is hardly surprising, then, that Emerson is so vigilant of the language he uses in this essay. Indeed, some readers have argued that he is over-watchful to the point of being strangled and unintelligible. Reading Emerson, a critic writes, "one feels that almost every noun and every verb should be put in quotation marks." Language is Emerson's subject and simultaneously his conduit. Inevitably, Emerson finds himself in the dizzying position of using language to show the inadequacies of language. Unsurprisingly then in "Discipline," Emerson favors actions over words:

> The central Unity is still more conspicuous in actions. Words are finite organs of the infinite mind. They cannot cover the dimensions of what is in truth. They break, chop, and impoverish it. An action is the perfection and publication of thought.

Language becomes corrupted as men do, Emerson avers, and therefore simplicity is the best model. A proximity to nature provides a constant reminder of what words refer to and illustrate. Thus the "strong-natured farmer" and the "backwoodsman" are the models for the writer or poet.

In the course of discussing language and writing, Emerson offers the reader an insight into his own writing processes. For instance, Emerson emphasizes the importance of allegory and analogy: "man is an analo-gist"; "good writing and brilliant discourse are perpetual allegories." Emerson also makes use of "typology" in the essay, drawing on a Puritan theological tradition. Typology was a means of allegorizing by which the Puritans viewed their own histories and biographies as retracing events in the Bible. When Emerson writes of "types," he denotes this specific use of the word. Rather than in biblical figures and stories, Emerson finds "types" for the present day in nature.

Such highly specialized and even obscure usage of broad words lit-ters *Nature*. Emerson's aversion to explaining or crystallizing his point means that there is no clear indication to the reader—particularly the

21st-century reader—as to the sense in which the words should be understood. For this reason, an annotated edition is helpful. The reader should ask, however: To what end is this apparently willful obscurity?

Sample Topics:

1. **Nature and language:** How is language related to nature?

   To answer this question, a thorough scrutiny of the chapter called "Language" is clearly required. In it, Emerson explains his version of the origin of words and their sources. This is a difficult passage in the essay—even Emerson concedes it—and yet it is vital to comprehending the essay overall. Within the chapter, in one of his transformative switches, Emerson goes from discussing nature as a source for language to discussing a "universal soul," reason and spirit. What is the relevance of spirit and reason to language?

   Here Emerson uses the term *type* as well. What is meant by a type? The doctrine is indeed abstruse and requires the student to have a good dictionary of terms—preferably several of them. Emerson's linguistic theory duly assimilated, the student might apply it to Emerson's own writing. Test the theory: When does Emerson use nature in analogy, allegory, or typology? One example occurs in the "Language" chapter: "We are like travellers using the cinders of a volcano to roast their eggs." Find other examples in the text, or indeed in other Emersonian texts (for example, the more florid poetry).

2. **Agriculture:** Discuss Emerson's use of farm and farmer imagery. What do they signify?

   Initially, the student must identify each mention or appearance of the farmer in Emerson's essay. Are they consistent? How is the farmer defined? What is he contrasted with? Does Emerson's image of the farmer seem real? Some research about the figure of the farmer in American history and literature might be useful, for instance, in the Jeffersonian view of the farmer as the ideal citizen. Is this how Emerson shows the farmer? Noah Webster, dogged linguist and compiler of the dictionary, claimed the same ideal in his crusade for American English: the yeoman farmer. Emerson sees simple straightforward language as allied with God and truth. The question is, How? And is this simplicity reflected in the language that Emerson himself uses? What, then, of the poet?

3. **The Orphic poet:** Who is the Orphic poet? How does he differ from the author of the rest of the essay?

Read superficially, this question seeks a fairly obvious answer. The Orphic poet is, as the most superficial research will show, Emerson himself. The more important corollary question is, Why does Emerson use this fiction to voice these particular words and this view? In a text ostensibly about truth, revelation, and denouncing masquerades, why have this pretense? This question is one concerning narratology—the critique of narrative. Not only does the question ask the reader to pay close attention to those passages written by the Orphic poet; it also draws the reader's closer attention to those parts not written by the poet. Who is the narrative voice during the larger body of the essay? How does he differ from the Orphic poet? Is it important that the 1836 edition of *Nature* was published anonymously? Can we identify Ralph Waldo Emerson properly as either "speaker"? Do we take one to be more authoritative than the other? Which one is to be trusted?

Last, look for clues in the allusion. Who is Orpheus? Why does Emerson name his poet after the orphic tradition? How does this reflect on Emerson's essay and its tenor? In the light of this cryptic hint, should we view his enterprise in a different way?

Compare and Contrast

It is valuable to be aware of the different versions of the text, which text you are working from, and the variants. *Nature* was originally published alone, as a book. Emerson conceived of this 1836 text as "my book on nature." Is there a difference in how we read a text, depending on how it is defined? *Nature* was subsequently revised and reprinted in its more familiar form as the essay "Nature" for the text in 1849. Of *Nature, Addresses, and Lectures,* Emerson wrote to his brother:

> I am just reprinting my first little book of "Nature" with various "Orations, lectures" &c. that have not been collected here before, into a volume the size of the Essays, and it gives me the chance to make many important corrections.

As Emerson noted, this volume was conceived in the light of his first collection of *Essays,* which required a reconfiguration and reenvisioning of the original book in the light of its successors. While the changes might seem slight enough, since Emerson chose every word with exacting care, imbuing each syllable with profound significance, each change and tweak is interesting to note. Furthermore, the change conceptually from book to essay alters the reader's perceptions. Note the context in which texts are packaged as well as the content itself.

Sample Topics:

1. **Editions of *Nature*:** Compare Emerson's 1836 version of *Nature* with the 1849 one. Discuss the changes made and their significance.

   This question requires the reader to be skillful in differentiating among different versions of a text. First, obviously, the student needs to locate editions of both versions. Identifying Emerson's changes between the texts should not entail a simple, dull listing of the alterations (this has already been done by previous editors). Rather, find those changes that seem most provocative and profound: the ones that seem to indicate a considerable change of view. This may involve Emerson's replacement of one extremely significant word or a whole phrase. For instance, why does the 1836 edition open with the Plotinus quotation and the 1849 version open with a poem written by Emerson? These are the quotations that frame the reading of the entire essay. Do both quotations suggest the same summary of the essay, or does one reframe the essay in a different light? Why do you think Emerson made the change?

What does it mean for a text to be published anonymously, or as a stand-alone text? Does such an extratextual (outside the text itself) consideration affect our reading experience? Does our perception of the author change when his name is revealed? Finally, further interesting illumination might be gained by comparing these two texts with Emerson's other reconsiderations of nature that occurred between the publication of each. In 1841, he gave the lecture "The Method of Nature," and he wrote a further essay called "Nature" in the second series of *Essays* (1844). Does the content of these essays influence the rewriting of the 1849 "Nature"?

Bibliography and Online Resources

Brownson, Orestes. "*Nature.*" Burkholder and Myerson 17–19.

Buell, Lawrence. *Emerson.* Cambridge, MA: Harvard UP, 2003.

Burke, Kenneth. "I, Eye, Ay—Concerning Emerson's Early Essay on 'Nature' and the Machinery of Transcendence." *Sewanee Review* 74 (Fall 1966): 875–895.

Burkholder, Robert E., and Joel Myerson, eds. *Critical Essays on Ralph Waldo Emerson.* Boston: G. K. Hall, 1983.

Coleridge, Samuel Taylor. "On the Difference in Kind between Reason and Understanding." *Selected Writings of the American Transcendentalists.* Ed. George Hochfield. New Haven, CT: Yale UP, 2004. 113–118.

Gifford, Terry. *Pastoral.* London: Routledge, 1999.

Hankins, Barry. *The Second Great Awakening and the Transcendentalists.* Westport, CT: Greenwood, 2004.

Hodder, Alan D. *Emerson's Rhetoric of Revelation: Nature, the Reader, and the Apocalypse Within.* University Park: Pennsylvania State UP, 1989.

Lauter, Paul. "Truth and Nature: Emerson's Use of Two Complex Words." *ELH* 27.1 (March 1960): 66–85.

Marx, Leo. *The Machine in the Garden: Technology and the Pastoral Ideal in America.* New York: Oxford UP, 1964.

Peabody, Elizabeth Palmer. "Nature—a Prose Poem." Burkholder and Myerson 24–31.

Reynolds, David. *Beneath the American Renaissance.* Cambridge, MA: Harvard UP, 1988.

Sealts, Merton M., Jr., and Alfred R. Ferguson. *Emerson's Nature: Origin, Growth, Meaning.* 2nd ed. Carbondale: Southern Illinois UP, 1979.

Stenerson, Douglas C. "Emerson and the Agrarian Tradition." *Journal of the History of Ideas* 14.1 (January 1953): 95–115.

THE AMERICAN
SCHOLAR

READING TO WRITE

IN *THE AMERICAN Scholar* Emerson observes, "Books are the best of things, well used; abused, among the worst." This essay is a discourse on how to read: how to use books and how not to abuse them. Emerson defines popular representations of the reader or scholar and considers how apt these are. He further discourses on how the reader should properly engage literature. He considers a question familiar to readers of Plato's *Republic*: how to balance life and art, thought and action, experience and learning.

In considering how to read all of Emerson's works, then, this essay provides important "insider" hints. Emerson is effectively telling his readers how he would like to be read, while recognizing that with time, inevitably, this advice becomes antiquated and unavoidably dated. More, he is telling how he himself writes: through reading. The essay is also about how to write, then. Reading is a creative act. "One must be an inventor to read well," he avers. "There is then creative reading as well as creative writing." Reading in this way, the text becomes alive: "Every sentence is doubly significant."

Emerson writes, at one point, about reading Chaucer, Marvell, and Dryden and experiencing "surprise" (or recognition) when he finds "that which lies close to my own soul." Here he is, surely, also writing for his own readers "two or three hundred years" later; anticipating them—us—insofar as he can. Thus the telepathy Emerson is describing is also occurring in the 21st century. Emerson broadcasts to the future—*The American Scholar* is a self-conscious time capsule. In the spirit of Emerson, then, to write on Emerson requires that you "read creatively." Endeavor to receive and interpret the text as telepathy, not as anesthetized, anthologized classic literature.

However, more important than reading to the writer is fully living (or: "action"). Emerson writes of the numerous authors "who have written out their vein." We might read this as coded autobiography; was Emerson himself flagging? Regarding divine inspiration, he wrote to his brother a month before giving the Phi Beta Kappa address that "we cannot get any word from Olympus." The solution for many writers, he remarks ironically, is to "sail for Greece or Palestine, follow the trapper into the prairie, or ramble round Algiers, to replenish their merchantable stock." No—for Emerson the solution (as in *Nature*) originates within the self and from his immediate surroundings. Education for the scholar has three sources: "by nature, by books, and by action."

The following passage occurs in the last paragraph of the address:

> Mr. President and Gentlemen, this confidence in the unsearched might of man belongs, by all motives, by all prophecy, by all preparation, to the American Scholar. We have listened too long to the courtly muses of Europe. The spirit of the American freeman is already suspected to be timid, imitative, tame. Public and private avarice make the air we breathe thick and fat. The scholar is decent, indolent, complaisant. See already the tragic consequence. The mind of this country, taught to aim at low objects, eats upon itself. There is no work for any but the decorous and the complaisant. Young men of the fairest promise, who begin life upon our shores, inflated by the mountain winds, shined upon by all the stars of God, find the earth below not in unison with these, but are hindered from action by the disgust which the principles on which business is managed aspire, and turn drudges, or die of disgust, some of them suicides. What is the remedy? They did not yet see, and thousands of young men as hopeful now crowding to the barriers for the career do not yet see, that if the single man plant himself indomitably on his instincts, and there abide, the huge world will come round to him.

In this excerpt Emerson returns to his sporadic (and within the Phi Beta Kappa tradition, thoroughly conventional) subject within the essay, that of American nationalism. Europe's influence has been excessive. Yet in the preceding paragraphs, Emerson has singled out for praise several eminent men of European letters: Goethe, Wordsworth, Carlyle, and Swedenborg. Convictions and allegiances are flying—the tone turns. Emerson's tenor is unusual in that it flips without warning between celebration and condemnation. This can happen even within a single, short sentence: "The scholar is decent, indolent, complaisant." What is the audience (or the reader) to make of this? While initially praising (the word *decent*), the speaker switches in a breath to denigrating the scholar. Can decency be complaisant and indolent—that is, overobliging and lazy? Emerson's address is as much denunciation as it is praise. He confounded the expectations of his audience on that day and of his readers today. By such means the text remains alive and engaging.

Emerson's language can be savage, grotesque, apocalyptic: "Public and private avarice make the air we breathe thick and fat. . . . The mind of this country, taught to aim at low objects, eats upon itself." He summons images of psychic self-cannibalism. The reader might be reminded of the apocalyptic close to *Nature* as well. What is the significance of such apocalyptic tones? Does the context of the poem seem to merit such a tone? Again, Emerson confounds expectation. He recalls the figurative style and the sensational imagery of the jeremiads of his Calvinist forebears. Is it significant that this was an address, to be delivered orally and like a sermon? Does the form, then, mold the content?

There follows another shift—again as in *Nature*—from damnation to redemption: "What is the remedy?" Emerson sees, amid the present wretched state of affairs, possible resolution (elsewhere, as in *Nature*'s close, he speaks of revolution) from which may follow the ascendancy of his messianic savior, the American Scholar. As the address recalls the ideas and language of *Nature*, it points also to the work to come, particularly "Self-Reliance." The remedy, Emerson says, resides in "the single man" who will "plant himself indomitably on his instincts, and there abide," so that "the huge world will come round to him." The American Scholar is Emerson's hero, the self-reliant man enduring through the essays and Emerson's developing philosophy.

TOPICS AND STRATEGIES

The following section suggests several possible topics for essays on *The American Scholar*. They can and should be used as starting points for your own, independent exploration of the essay.

Themes

Examining *The American Scholar* thematically we find sites of ambivalence. Emerson's subject is an American scholar, his call for a rejection of the past, yet as a model he summons Emanuel Swedenborg—a 17th-century Swedish mystic. Critics stress that the argument for a native, independent culture in *The American Scholar* has been overemphasized. How much does Emerson argue for a new culture, and how much is he in thrall of Europe and the past himself?

Emerson seems at similar odds with himself with reference to scholarship. Reading, he declares, is a waste: "When he can read God directly, the hour is too precious to be wasted in other men's transcripts of their readings." He further slams book learning (notably a popular target in the newspaper humor of the time). "Books," he says, "are for the scholar's idle times." What was Emerson himself, though, if not book learned? Emerson celebrates action—"Life is our dictionary," and "This is the way to learn grammar. Colleges and books only copy the language which the field and the work-yard made." Yet later he notes gravely how the "practical men" sneer at the scholar, which he challenges. Which side, then, is Emerson on?

Sample Topics:

1. **Influence and originality:** What are Emerson's views on influence and originality in *The American Scholar*?

   This question can (and should) be posed in reference to originality both in the art of writing and in the formation of an autonomous nation. That is, Emerson addresses anxieties about American literary originality and about American national identity. For him, the two are intimately connected. How? As with *Nature*, Emerson argues for creativity and originality, setting these high aims against slavish imitation and plodding deference to tradition. He states that "genius is always suffi-ciently the enemy of genius by over-influence." How does this view prevail in the light of Emerson's later eulogy to Sweden-borg? How can this eulogy—and Emerson's praise for Goethe and Carlyle—be consistent with a philosophy that is opposed to imitation?

Emerson—but also America—contends with what Har-old Bloom calls (in a book of the same name) the "anxiety of influence." Can this term also be used to describe American cultural identity in Emerson's essay? "The English poets have Shakespearized now for two hundred years," Emerson com-plains. What are Emerson's views, however, on Shakespeare? Use your knowledge of Emerson's writings to judge: Is this consistent with Emerson's own use of Shakespeare and other writers?

2. **Scholarship:** How does Emerson portray scholarship?

This question, seemingly straightforward enough, requires you to weigh statements from Emerson that are not necessar-ily consistent. There are numerous models of scholarship and scholars in this essay. "Meek young men grow up in libraries," Emerson rails at one stage, recoiling from the "bookworm." Yet the scholar is the "hero" of his declamation, refined and idealized, as "Man Thinking." Obviously, this is a more compli-cated question than clear, clumsy delineation of "sides" allows. Emerson is viewing the scholar from all sides. His audience should be remembered—they are an elite society of scholars. Emerson himself was a graduate of Harvard. How is his view couched for (or directed against) his audience? And how does it reflect his view of himself? What, in Emerson's own past, might contribute to this view? As a scholar and a churchman, does Emerson aim all his criticism outward? Readers should approach the text psychologically as well: How much is "the scholar" Emerson himself? And how much is this essay a self-rebuke, or a self-justification?

Examine closely Emerson's remarks concerning college, and its juxtaposition with the workplace or the farm or the field. "Colleges and books only copy the language which the field and the work-yard made." Is this anti-intellectualism? In his enumeration of the scholar's duties, Emerson describes the scholar as in a state of "virtual hostility" to society—especially "educated society." Does Emerson's idealized scholar even fit into institutionalized education, then?

3. **Action:** What does Emerson mean by action?

Does Emerson value action? Where and how is action demonstrated? For instance, is travel to far-off places action? Is manual labor action? Is scholarship action? And does Emerson recommend these? Action can be viewed from a Platonic view. Does Emerson value the lived life over the speculative life, or the written life? The most pertinent passage for the purposes of this question is that segment of the address numbered III by Emerson, explaining "the education of the scholar . . . by action." One critic reads this essay as Emerson's "problem" involving the opposition "Action versus Contemplation"—as an antagonistic dialogue between "actors" and "students," commitment and detachment. Do you agree? Another distinction, made by Emerson himself, is that between public and private acts. How does he differentiate between the two? Emerson was divided between a life of social commitment and one of removed meditation. How is this conflict expressed in *The American Scholar*?

A document of some interest to the student investigating the extent of Emerson's political "action" is his 1838 open letter to the president, Martin Van Buren, concerning the removal of the Cherokee from their Georgia territories. Emerson wrote this under pressure from reformer friends and subsequently came to regret the action, which he called "stirring in the philanthropic mud." The division between action and contemplation is stark when, reflecting on his protest, he writes in his journal, "The amount of it, be sure, is merely a scream but sometimes a scream is better than a thesis." Students interested in Emerson's political actions might well look into the letter and its fallout, following so soon as it does after *The American Scholar* address. Which does Emerson choose—scream or thesis?

History and Context

It is important to bear in mind the strict original context for Emerson's address when you read it. *The American Scholar* was composed expressly for a single occasion: the main address for the annual gathering of the learned Phi Beta Kappa society at the Harvard University commencement ceremony in August 1837. Emerson's 1837 subject, far from being spontaneous and unique, was decidedly in the tradition of the society's previous addresses. Among the audience were elder political dignitaries including John Quincy Adams and Daniel Webster, as well as the future writers, then students, Oliver Wendell Holmes, James Russell Lowell, and Richard Henry Dana. Thoreau was a member of the class of 1837, but he may have slipped out of Cambridge—somewhat characteristically—the previous day. The address was subsequently (50 years later) heralded by Holmes as "our literary Declaration of Independence," while Lowell pronounced of it:

> The Puritan revolt had made us ecclesiastically, and the Revolution politically independent, but we were still socially and intellectually moored to English thought, till Emerson cut the cable and gave us a chance at the dangers and the glories of blue water.

Since then *The American Scholar* has been long read, rightly or wrongly, as a vital document in establishing an American voice and project in literature. Previously, it is said, literature looked abroad for its influence and its subject. For instance, among all his many European and exotic tales, only one Edgar Allan Poe story takes place identifiably in America. Emerson argues for a literature that does not look to the distant horizon for inspiration, but to its own stoop: "Man is surprised to find that things near are not less beautiful than things remote."

To Emerson (or, to Emerson's idealized Scholar), the government is a "fetish" and wars are ephemeral: "a popgun is a popgun, though the ancient and honourable of the earth affirm it to be the crack of doom." The government at the time the address was read was under the new (Democratic) president Martin Van Buren, who succeeded Andrew Jackson in March of the year. The wars Emerson dismisses might have been the second Seminole War (1835–42) or the wars of the Texas Revolution (1835–36, including the battle of the Alamo in March 1836). In spring of that year, America had suffered a financial panic followed in turn by a severe depression that lasted through 1843. Emerson, however, was about to receive the first yearly installment from his first wife's estate.

Another target of Emerson's contempt is the professional American travel writer. The argument, for Emerson, is one of nationalism, of writing about the local. However, as Emerson's Harvard critic John Pierce noted of the address,

> he spoke severely of our dependence on British literature. Notwithstanding, I must question whether he himself would have written such an apparently incoherent and unintelligible address, had he not been familiar with the writings of [Swedenborg, Coleridge, and Carlyle].

The point is a fair one. Furthermore, Emerson had made a pilgrimage to Europe, from December 1832 through September 1833, traveling to Italy, France, England, and Scotland and meeting with Walter Savage Landor, Coleridge, Wordsworth, and Carlyle. Recently, the Emerson critic Laurence Buell has challenged the "myth" of *The American Scholar,* asking, "How American was Emerson's 'American Scholar'?"

Sample Topics:

1. **Nationalism:** What is American about *The American Scholar*?

The American Scholar is frequently and somewhat blithely cited as being the point of origin for a truly American literature, often on the strength of the Holmes and Lowell quotations cited previously. Useful when in shorthand as a commonplace, this summation is glib and dubious when examined in detail and context. Such legends require and invite critical challenges. The true test of this matter is in the text. Where is Emerson notably nationalistic? What is he saying in these passages? What, in your mind, constitutes being "American" anyway? Is it a stylistic tone, a subject, a choice of certain themes and images? Is it a particular choice of influences? What is "American literature"? Define this with textual examples and justification. Next, decide: Does Emerson meet these criteria?

Emerson's address existed in a specific history of orations—whether addresses or poems—given for the Phi Beta Kappa societies of American colleges. What was discussed in previous orations? What was the subject, and what was the tone? These addresses can be read and compared with Emerson's (see especially Carl F. Strauch's essay). Further questions to be asked concern the biases behind reading a text in a certain way. Why was a critical, nationalist mythology created about this essay? What purpose might this serve? Emerson himself speaks, in the essay, about the different readings of a text over time. What was Emerson's intention with the essay—was it nationalistic at all? (In his journal, for example, Emerson writes merely that he seeks "to offer the theory of the Scholar's function. He has an office to perform in society. What is it?")

2. **Democracy and elitism:** Is *The American Scholar* democratic or elitist? Is Emerson a snob?

The first question you might profitably ask is, What is the Phi Beta Kappa society? Phi Beta Kappa was a college fraternity dedicated to scholarship, founded in 1776 at William and Mary College. The Greek letters *Phi Beta Kappa* stand for "philosophy the guide of life." Within the four years of its existence at William and Mary College, the society granted affiliated chapters including one at Harvard. So, was the occasion exclusive? Was the audience an elite crowd? And was the address elitist? Emerson's address and those in attendance have been described in detail by scholars including Bliss Perry (see the bibliography). Consulting such accounts, as well as a history of the Phi Beta Kappa society, will elucidate a position on this question.

Define for yourself and your reader what constituted "democratic" values in the administration of Van Buren. Where did Emerson stand? In his journal, ruminating on "Vanburenism," Emerson explodes: "I hate persons who are nothing but persons. I hate numbers." Was Emerson a snob, and therefore undemocratic, for giving his address under the Phi Beta Kappa aegis? This question is best answered by analyzing the text itself for Emerson's remarks indicating thoughts on class. Is Emerson divisive, for instance, in separating the scholar from the "so-called 'practical men'"? Or for preaching a doctrine of self-trust, removed from the "mob"? The address exists in a time when Jacksonian principles—conspicuously celebrating the crowd and the common man—prevailed in the national culture. Is Emerson reacting against such an ideology when he rails that "men in the world of to-day, are bugs, are spawn, and are called 'the mass' and 'the herd.' In a century, in a millennium, one or two men"? Balance this, though, with other statements, such as when he asks, "Is not indeed every man a student, and do not all things exist for the student's behoof?" or when he heralds a "literature of the poor" and a "philosophy of the street?" Does Emerson write that literature, that philosophy? It is a question that remains open; Emerson scholars are not entirely confident yet about Emerson's position regarding "democracy."

Form and Genre

The American Scholar exists in a very specific tradition. Not only is it oratory, it is specifically the address to the Phi Beta Kappa society at Harvard. In his preamble, Emerson recognizes the conventional aspect of these addresses when he notes how "Year by year we come up hither to read one more chapter of [the American Scholar's] biography." Already, in his first breaths, there is a nagging irony to his tone. How does Emerson's subject matter comply with the conventions expected from the Phi Beta Kappa address? But as oratory how does Emerson's address exist in the larger tradition that was exploding around him? How does his subject differ by being delivered orally, before an audience?

The form of the address aside, Emerson's subject for a considerable portion of the whole concerns ways of writing and reading. In other words, it is literary theory. Emerson discusses canon formation. What is his opinion of defining and venerating a canon? He describes the processes that occur when we read. How does the process he describes clash and how does it coincide with contemporary theories of reading? Another renowned aspect of the Phi Beta Kappa address is its revolutionary tenor. Emerson shocked the older auditors at the gathering and inspired the younger ones. How is this a shocking text? What aspects clash with tradition? What in the subject defies convention? And, more importantly, how does the form of the address depart from conservative expectation? How does an address become a manifesto?

Sample Topics:

1. **Oratory:** How does the oratorical aspect of *The American Scholar* affect its content?

   Should we consider *The American Scholar*—and the Divinity School Address indeed—as essays first, addresses second, or vice versa? What is different about the two forms and their composition processes? What considerations does writing an address necessitate that an essay does not? This question requires the reader to consider how the form and context of a text might influence its content. For instance, oratory can be bombastic or compelling in a way that a literary essay need not be. Oratorical rhetoric is frequently employed. Does Emerson compromise his message with such concessions to oratory and audience?

   To answer this question, the reader should of course read *The American Scholar* with the aim of comparing it to Emerson's pieces written expressly for reading. The reader should notice those parts of the text where Emerson talks about oratory, for example when he remarks that "the orator distrusts at first the fitness of his frank confessions, his want of knowledge of the persons he addresses, until he finds that he is the complement of his hearers." Does this suggest Emerson's own feelings in the course of this address? Elsewhere, he remarks how "I might not carry with me the feeling of my audience in stating my belief." Would such anxieties exist for the essayist writing solely for a reader? Another consideration might be the historical one. Research oratory in 19th-century America. What sort of audience did it draw, and was it the same as the audience that read literary essays? Was Emerson viewed popularly as a lecturer or an essayist? Studies have been written on the popularity of lectures and addresses in Emerson's period. How was democracy furthered by the promulgation of public speech?

2. **Literary theory:** What, according to Emerson, is the purpose of literature? What are his views on literary canons and posterity?

This question requires the reader to identify the tenets of Emerson's critical view. The second section of the address, on "the theory of books," is key. Emerson lays out what he expects from great literature, including his view of canonization. Once his criteria and views are identified, we can ask: What would Emerson make of his own place within the American canon? Would he be pleased or horrified? Even in 1837, he writes of the institutions: "They pin me down. They look backward and not forward." Emerson's works are viewed by many critics as the foundation for the American canon. Does his own resistance to the notion subvert the concept? What was the established literary canon of Emerson's time? To answer this question will necessitate some amount of research. What were English and American critics of 1837 interested in? Was American literature, at this time, part of the canon or out of it? How might this alter Emerson's view? Canon formation is a controversial subject in literary theory to this day. Compare Emerson's views with those of a current commentator, for instance, Harold Bloom. Would Emerson agree with Bloom's views in *The Western Canon*?

In *The American Scholar* Emerson considers the position of the dead writer and so, implicitly, himself as dead writer. What does he say about posterity? He writes, "The books of an older period will not fit this." How does Emerson fail in our own time, then? Can literature transcend time? Does Emerson survive in his writings, or is he reinvented by each generation?

3. **Manifesto:** How does *The American Scholar* serve as a manifesto for an independent American culture?

The American Scholar has a place in American literary history as a call to arms—as a declaration of independence from English cultural mores: "I look upon the discontent of the literary class as a mere announcement of the fact that they find themselves not in the state of mind of their fathers, and regret the coming state as untried." What sort of language does one expect from a manifesto? Look at examples of other manifestos, literary, artistic, or political. There were many manifestos and tracts being written in the antebellum period, manifestos for religious enclaves, social utopias, and reform movements, from temperance to free love, extolling social panaceas ranging from anarchy to communism. "Not a reading man but has a draft of a new Community in his new pocket," Emerson wrote to Thomas Carlyle; "I am gently mad myself."

What do the different statements of the many creeds all share; what does the manifesto form have, consistently? Fiery, rousing language is one common constituent of many manifestos. Does Emerson comply with this? Look for words like *revolution*—when do they occur? Another question to ask is, What was Emerson's audience for this address? Harvard students, members of a scholarly fraternity. Is this the apt setting for a national revolution? Is this the correct audience? Apart from the language and the context, what about *The American Scholar's* content suggests a manifesto?

Language, Symbols, and Imagery

Emerson's address employs an array of literary devices to provide imagery and symbols. *The American Scholar* uses fables, proverbs, and narrative devices recalling the hero quest. The text was first delivered as an address, which is to say, as an oral communication. What distinguishes oral communications from literary ones? Does Emerson observe these conventions? While there is nothing obviously primitivistic about Emerson's text, his recourse to abstraction and to a fable of monolithic man reinforces our sense of the text as, in some ways, preliterate. Is this deliberate, in an essay that ostensibly praises scholarship? How does the fable of the One Man color our reading of the text that follows? Does it contain the key to the discourse? Is the dissolution of the One Man a biblical Fall, followed by the scholar's messianic hero quest for redemption?

Sample Topics:

1. **The fable:** What is the significance of the "old fable" of the One Man? How is it relevant to the address—and Emerson's philosophy—as a whole?

   The "old fable" and Emerson's ruminations on it occur in the third through the seventh paragraphs. This passage should be submitted to analysis in close detail. How does the fable anticipate the subsequent address? Is it a "microcosm" of the whole (a device found in the opening line of "Circles," for instance)? As well as interpreting the relevance of the fable to the overall essay, you should ask why Emerson uses this form to articulate his point. Does he prepare the reader (or listener) thematically and intellectually for the address to follow, or is it an aside? Sacvan Bercovitch argues that the fable introduces the "main theme" of the text and defines the underlying "meaning" of the address. Do you agree?

2. **The scholar as hero:** How does Emerson characterize the American scholar? Is he a hero?

Is it possible to consider the characterization of the scholar as a heroic figure—even as a character from fiction, or myth, and his mission something of a hero quest; or is he simply an abstract blur, a convenient cipher on which Emerson hangs his philosophy? What are the heroic traits of the scholar? Given the oral nature of Emerson's address, does Emerson's hero even have an aspect that recalls the heroes of oral epic? What classically distinguishes heroes in narratives, either in their experiences or in their characters? Does Emerson's Scholar share any of these traits or experiences?

As this essay has had enormous influence on later American literature, has the Scholar echoed as a figure in later literature? There is one critical tradition, for instance, that regards Thoreau as the actual realization of the "American Scholar." Do you agree with this? Using your knowledge of Thoreau, particularly his account in *Walden*, you might compare Emerson's archetype with the actual man. Literary comparisons might be made, too, such as with Plato's conception of the philosopher-ruler from the *Republic*. Emerson himself, meanwhile, makes the implicit comparison between his scholar and Hamlet ("The time is infected with Hamlet's unhappiness"). Can you find mutual characteristics in the two? One might even look at characters from contemporaneous American fiction or poetry, for instance, from the stories of Nathaniel Hawthorne (as both *The American Scholar* and *Twice-Told Tales* were published in 1837) or Edgar Allan Poe's *Arthur Gordon Pym* (1838). Was Emerson drawing on a character that already existed, in part, in other literature, or was his characterization wholly original?

Compare and Contrast

While *The American Scholar* may not be the literary call to arms some have claimed it to be, it nevertheless makes allegations about the American literature of the day and calls for reform. What, then, is the literature he finds objectionable? It is useful to have in mind what the literature of the time actually consisted of, rather than accept Emerson's plaint uncritically. Many of America's canonized authors were writing in this period—Poe, Cooper, Irving, Hawthorne, Longfellow. Native humor, exploring American vernacular and dialect, was surfacing in such notable works as Seba Smith's *Jack Downing*, Augustus Baldwin Longstreet's *Georgia Scenes*, the "Crockett Almanacks" with their tall tales of Davy Crockett. Was American letters found to be wanting or was it Emerson, who was all the while engrossed in Goethe and Carlyle?

Sample Topic:

1. **"American" literature:** "Authors we have, in numbers, who have written out their vein." Which American authors is Emerson criticizing? Is his criticism justified?

In those passages of *The American Scholar* devoted to literary critique, Emerson does not single out any one writer by name. Inferences are present, but these are cryptic to contemporary readers. This question first requires some detective work, so that you can identify the possible targets of Emerson's ire. Which American writers authored travel guides from Palestine, accompanied the trappers on the prairie, or toured Algiers for ideas? Authors such as Washington Irving were writing fiction and travelogues with English, French, German, and Spanish settings. Subsequently, Richard Henry Dana, Herman Melville, Bayard Taylor, and Mark Twain would all profit from literature set abroad. One writer Emerson probably had in mind was John Lloyd Stephens, whose *Incidents of Travel in Egypt, Arabia Petraea, and the Holy Land* was published in the same year as *The American Scholar* and was reprinted six times in 12 months, even in the fallout of the great financial panic. In an address given the following year (well worth consulting), "Literary Ethics," Emerson revisits his theme and gives further clues. One critic has divined in this text a criticism of the poet William Cullen Bryant. But look at the range of authors then writing, all implicitly found wanting by Emerson: It includes James Fenimore Cooper, Edgar Allan Poe, Henry Wadsworth Longfellow, and Nathaniel Hawthorne, all published in the years before *The American Scholar.*

When the author accused has been identified, look critically at the works in question. Do they lack the native quality Emerson is searching for? (What are these native qualities— "The meal in the firkin—the milk in the pan"?) What native qualities are lacking, for instance, in an account of the prairie trapper? Was Emerson's criticism fair and necessary, or neglectful? Is Emerson's definition of "native literature" a relevant one?

Bibliography and Online Resources

Bercovitch, Sacvan. "The Philosophical Background to the Fable of Emerson's 'American Scholar.'" *Journal of the History of Ideas* 28.1 (January–March 1967): 123–128.

Bloom, Harold. *The Anxiety of Influence: A Theory of Poetry.* New York: Oxford UP, 1973.

———. *The Western Canon: The Books and Schools of the Ages.* New York: Riverhead Books, 1994.

Cmiel, Kenneth. *Democratic Eloquence: The Fight over Popular Speech in Nineteenth-Century America.* New York: William Morrow, 1990.

Cole, Phyllis. "Emerson Father and Son: A Precedent for 'The American Scholar.'" *New England Quarterly* 78.1 (March 2005): 101–124.

Emerson, Ralph Waldo. "Letter: To Martin Van Buren, President of the United States." *The Portable Emerson.* Ed. Carl Bode and Malcolm Cowley. New York: Viking, 1981. 527–531.

Garvey, T. Gregory, ed. *The Emerson Dilemma: Essays on Emerson and Social Reform.* Athens: U of Georgia P, 2001.

Mead, David. "Emerson's Scholar and the Scholars." *Journal of Higher Education* 40.8 (November 1969): 649–660.

Perry, Bliss. "Emerson's Most Famous Speech." *Ralph Waldo Emerson: A Profile.* Ed. Carl Bode. New York: Hill & Wang, 1969. 52–65.

Rusk, Ralph L. *The Life of Ralph Waldo Emerson.* New York: Charles Scribner's Sons, 1949.

Sacks, Kenneth S. *Understanding Emerson: "The American Scholar" and His Struggle for Self-Reliance.* Princeton, NJ: Princeton UP, 2003.

Sealts, Merton M., Jr. "The American Scholar and Public Issues: The Case of Emerson." *Ariel: A Review of International English Literature* 7.3 (July 1976): 109–121.

———. *Emerson on the Scholar.* Columbia: U of Missouri P, 1992.

Smith, Henry Nash. "Emerson's Problem of Vocation: A Note on 'The American Scholar.'" *New England Quarterly* 12.1 (March 1939): 52–67.

Strauch, Carl F. "Emerson's Phi Beta Kappa Poem." *New England Quarterly* 23.1 (March 1950): 65–90.

West, Cornel. *The American Evasion of Philosophy: A Genealogy of Pragmatism.* Madison: U of Wisconsin P, 1989.

Whicher, Stephen. "The Question of Means." *Modern Critical Views: Ralph Waldo Emerson.* Ed. Harold Bloom. New York: Chelsea House, 1985. 13–28.

Web Sites
Phi Beta Kappa Society Official Web site. Available online. URL: http://staging.pbk.org/AM/Template.cfm?Section=Home3&Template=/Templates/Te mplateHomepage/PhiBetaKappaSociety_1504_20060223T20 1608_LayoutHomePage.cfm.

THE DIVINITY
SCHOOL ADDRESS

READING TO WRITE

APPEARING LESS than a year later, "An Address to the Senior Class in Divinity College, Cambridge July 15, 1838," or the Divinity School Address, as it is usually known, recalls *The American Scholar* in several ways. It was a return for Emerson to Cambridge, Massachusetts, where he had previously studied. Emerson had attended the Divinity School (which is attached to Harvard) from February 1825 until October 1826, when he was approbated to preach. His stinging consciousness of his earlier self, travailing to be a preacher, colors his words. By 1838, he had abandoned such a project. As with the earlier text, the Divinity School Address was first delivered orally rather than published as an essay. There are, accordingly, structural differences from the classic Emersonian essay. It is arranged to be more easily absorbed. One way a lecture differs from an essay is that difficult lines cannot be reread by the auditor. One chance is all the listeners get; they cannot pore over difficult passages in their own time. The reader of this essay, then, will detect a certain comfortable flow to it. Before he was a man of letters, it is to be remembered, Emerson was a preacher. He could construct sermons easily.

This address is coupled with *The American Scholar* also because each address precipitated its own storm of controversy. The Divinity School Address was the final straw for Emerson in the eyes of the orthodox. After this, he was not asked to read at Harvard—his alma mater—for another 20 years. Emerson's address was expressly intended for a smattering of theological students about to enter the ministry and preach to the community at large; it had consequences outside mere theory. Were his words justified or irresponsible? To 21st-century readers, the radicalism of the text may not be immediately apparent. Many of Emerson's tenets—self-trust, a "personal" relationship with God, rejection of institutional religion—have become almost conventional. Emerson writes, "By trusting your own heart, you shall gain more confidence in other men." Such a view, or similar words, would not be out of place in any contemporary spiritual gift book or self-help guide. Daytime talk shows and bumper stickers affirm similar slogans, although obviously with less philosophical and theological backing than Emerson's. For this reason, you would do well to attend to the supporting theory of Emerson's address, not simply the catchier sound bites.

The following excerpt from the address is from Emerson's examination of the "second defect of the traditionary and limited way of using the mind of Christ":

> To this holy office you propose to devote yourselves. I wish you may feel your call in throbs of desire and hope. The office is the first in the world. It is of that reality that it cannot suffer the deduction of any falsehood. And it is my duty to say to you that the need was never greater of new revelation than now. From the views I have already expressed, you will infer the sad conviction, which I share, I believe, with numbers, of the universal decay and now almost death of faith in society. The soul is not preached. The Church seems to totter to its fall, almost all life extinct. On this occasion, any complaisance would be criminal which told you, whose hope and commission it is to preach the faith of Christ, that the faith of Christ is preached.

Note first the tone of the text—this address remains very much a transcript of an oration. It is more clear when reading the Divinity School Address than *The American Scholar* that this was first intended for listeners. Why might this be? Is such "foregrounding" of the text's oral origins deliberate on Emerson's part? Notable references to Emerson's audience abound in direct exhortations to his listeners. Emerson is addressing the members of the Divinity School, and we as readers are receiving the address over their shoulders. What difference does this make to the reading experience? Is it alienating or intimate? Compare the imagery in this excerpt—language lamenting decay, death, extinction—with the opening vignette ("The grass grows, the buds burst, the meadow is spotted with fire and gold in the tint of flowers"). The contrast is striking. Why do you think Emerson employs such a stark juxtaposition? What rhetorical purpose does it serve?

What tone does Emerson strike in this passage? Do we imagine him as coaxing and gentle or furious and rousing? Is it cold and formal, or is it personal and fiery? What sort of preacher was Emerson? Is he a "formalist," a "bad preacher"? What is his purpose anyway? What is his target? "And it is my duty to say to you that the need was never greater of new revelation than now." His aim in the address, then, is revelation. What religious associations might the reader make with revelation? Does Emerson seem to be preaching against the "end times"? Is he apocalyptic? Millenarian religions—that is, religious sects that expected the imminent second coming of Christ followed by Christ's rule on earth for a thousand years—proliferated in New England in this period. In this address, as in *The American Scholar*, complaisance is charged as the worst failing. (Complaisance, not complacency; note the different meanings.) Look out for recurring, favored words in Emerson's lexicon. Where has he used such words before and in what context? Is Emerson's intent to shock the listener out of this overobliging state?

TOPICS AND STRATEGIES

The following section suggests several possible topics for essays on the Divinity School Address. They can and should be used as starting points for your own, independent exploration of the essay.

Themes

Having dealt with nature and the written arts, Emerson now turns his excoriating eye on religion. His essays blossomed organically from his journals, and there is inevitably a thematic resemblance they share. "Life consists in what a man is thinking of all day," Emerson wrote in one journal. Unsurprisingly, then, certain themes recur, albeit they are reexamined from a new angle, with a new emphasis. For instance, in the Divinity School Address, Emerson is still thinking about the role of action in the life of "Man Thinking." This time he applies it to the ministry rather than to the scholarly community. How can the minister engage in life?

Amid the familiar (nature, reason, understanding) and the reaffirmations of his position, the reader should also be alert for those terms and themes to which Emerson seems to pay particular attention. In the Divinity School Address, Christianity and the example of Christ are his main subjects. From this premise he thematically examines the nature of dogma, of faith, and of tradition and its opposite, spontaneity. He also examines virtue and how it fits into his evolving and expanding philosophy. One phrase, kaleidoscopically reconsidered, serves as a motto and symbol for the address: *He ought; I ought; the Ought.*

Sample Topics:

1. **Virtue and the problem of evil:** What is Emersonian virtue? Do you agree that such virtue is "the essence of all religion" or is Emerson naïve? Does Emerson face the "problem of evil"?

   What is the significance of virtue in the Divinity School Address? Where does it fit into Emerson's larger system of ideas? Emerson foregrounds virtue in the essay early on, speaking about it in the third paragraph of the address, so that much of the text is viewed in the light of this definition. As usual, Emerson's definitions are not concrete but poetic, and need to be puzzled out, analyzed, and rearticulated. "These laws refuse to be adequately stated," he writes. "They will not be written out on paper, or spoken by the tongue." Certain words recur: *sentiment, justice, energy, soul.* Do not be put off by the amorphous words, but engage them. To clarify for yourself, ask other questions: What is the relation of virtue to the self, to nature, to the soul, to God? What does Emerson mean by "that Law" and "the religious sentiment"? Locate virtue's place in Emerson's whole system.

Second, the student should critically evaluate Emerson's convictions about virtue. Is it "the essence of all religion"? Is this morally simplistic? Consider the tradition and history of religions—all religions. Is virtue always their essence, or are there other factors (fear, superstition, power)? Look also at Emerson's relation of virtue with justice. Is he naïve? This is a charge made by certain eminent commentators, including the Irish poet William Butler Yeats, who claimed that Emerson never adequately faced the "problem of evil." Do you agree? Is virtue always rewarded? Look in later essays and writings of Emerson (correspondence, journals). Does he persist in the beliefs held here? For instance, when he writes in his journal that "those who succeed in life, in civilized society, are beasts of prey," is it a view consistent with that held in the Divinity School Address?

2. **The ought:** What is "the ought"?

As in *The American Scholar*, action is Emerson's subject here, and the affirmation of saying "I Ought." With these two syllables the leap is made from lying low in "evil and weakness" to a state of knowing "that to the good, to the perfect, he is born." It is, if you like, 19th-century "shazam." But is "I ought" an affirmation or a vacillation? Why does Emerson employ this ambiguity? Why does he not say "I will" in its stead? What is the difference in saying the one or the other? *Ought* is said on the verge of a decision—the precipice of change, reform. Why is this liminal position preferable to Emerson to an outright affirmation?

To clarify the word's meaning (for Emerson) find each instance when he uses the word and regard closely the contexts. What does it achieve? Why is it said? How is it used? For example, why is the word italicized in the first instance? Why, in the final paragraph, is it capitalized? Why, indeed, is *ought* converted by Emerson into a proper noun? Consult the word's alternate meanings and even its etymology; after all, Emerson pointedly privileges the word in this essay. *Ought* as a noun means "duty"; it can also denote—as a variant of *aught*—"any-thing," and indeed—as a variant of *nought*—it can also mean "nothing." Emerson uses the word—"that grand word"—on multiple levels, and so must you.

3. **Christianity:** Is the Divinity School Address anti-Christian? Discuss Emerson's treatment of Christ and Christianity.

First, Emerson separates Christ and Christianity. For this question you should do the same. Is this division, of itself, anti-Christian? What does such a division signify? This ques-tion is at the heart of Emerson's inquiry. Emerson separates the man from the institution—and reason from understand-ing. If you have read Emerson's earlier essays, you will have already been presented his opinion of tradition, institutions, and "understanding."

Christ and Christianity are named surprisingly late in the address, after 10 lengthy paragraphs. Only in the 12th paragraph does Emerson properly (reluctantly?) leave these "general views." Look for the words Emerson uses to describe Christianity (*Cultus, Mythus*) and Christ (*prophet, true man*). Look at the images and anecdotes that illustrate them. What are the Church's "two errors in its administration"? Summa-rize these "defects" clearly, because they are the heart of the address. What does Emerson's statement "The soul knows no persons" mean, for instance? This remark continues to perplex and frustrate scholars to this day. Why? And what is the second complaint? "The soul is not preached." What does this mean? What is the connection between life (action) and preaching? (Look, for instance, to the example of the "formalist.")

Aside from theology, consider the question histori-cally—biographically. Theodore Parker, a friend of Emerson's, declared the Divinity School Address to be a "Sermon on the Mount." Does Emerson take Christ as his model, then, para-doxically to perform his own rejection of the church? Is there a "doubling" (deliberate or unconscious) between Emerson and Christ? To consider this possibility, you might investigate the reason behind Emerson's formal resignation from his position—his objection to the sacrament of the Last Supper. How does Emerson portray (or reinvent) Christ? Does Emerson's Christ tally with the Christ of the New Testament, for instance? If he differs, how does he?

History and Context

The context of the address and particularly the controversy that erupted in its wake characterize the address as much as the text itself. Familiarize yourself with what the Harvard Divinity School was and is. What was its tradition—what were the presiding ideas at the time of Emerson's address? New England theology has quite a tempestuous history, to say the least, and it has been written about plentifully.

For this annual address Emerson was invited by the graduating students—all seven of them—against the wishes of their teachers. The address was duly attended by several hundred, including those officers and teachers of the Divinity College. Emerson was not speaking at an underground meeting, to confirmed radicals, then, but at a solemn event within an orthodox institution. His audience was not baying iconoclasts, an intellectual avant garde, but custodians of the establishment Emerson was lambasting. Finally, his comments were immediately directed at those Divinity School students about to begin preaching in the wider community—his words would have reverberations beyond academic circles. Those seven students graduating (or half of them, at least) had deliberately chosen Emerson for the occasion, knowing full well his work and reputation. It was, then, a clash of generations. As Andrews Norton recounts, those notables and teachers "must have felt it not only as an insult to religion, but as a personal insult to themselves." The Divinity School Address was far more explosive and revolutionary than *The American Scholar* and enjoyed (if that is the word) a far greater notoriety beyond the realms of the college and the intellectual coteries (many responses are collected in Perry Miller's anthology, *The Transcendentalists*). It spoke as much of a generational divide as it did of a theological one. Was Emerson intending to ignite a controversy? If so, did he anticipate the furor he precipitated? What was his purpose—was it solely intellectual, or was there a personal aspect to it? Emerson had studied at the Divinity School, had entered the ministry, and had abandoned it too. The address and the flurry of vehement letters it prompted brought to notice a "new school" of thought that would in time become synonymous with transcendentalism.

The people of Massachusetts in the 1830s were no longer Puritans. A "liberal Christianity" existed in Massachusetts at this time under the Unitarian Church, and Emerson belonged to this faith. Nevertheless there remained a certain rigidity—albeit a "liberal" one—in society. It was in no small part through Emerson, and other proponents of religious reform, that this stiffness in American religious culture was—at least relatively—relaxed. Conversely, some critics point out that Unitarianism was a reforming religion, while—paradoxically—Emerson's criticism of Christianity recalled at times what sounds remarkably like Puritan rhetoric: a revisiting of angry Calvinism, rebuking a liberal Christianity for slackening.

Sample Topics:

1. **Unitarianism:** What is Unitarianism? Does Emerson fit into a Unitarian tradition?

   The tenets and history of the liberal Christian denomination Unitarianism are important in establishing a context for Emerson's ideas. He preached from a Unitarian pulpit, and the Divinity School at Harvard was Unitarian at the time of the address. What did Emerson take from this tradition, and how did he depart from its teachings? The church was by no means conservative, compared with other denominations of Christianity. Unitarianism has been described as "the most liberal wing of the New England ministry," its doctrines "all along . . . new and strange." Why? And what does it mean, then, for Emerson to be rejected by the Unitarians for radicalism? Studies of the church, its principal figures, and their writings exist. What, among their doctrines, resemble the subsequent ideas of Emerson? What, conversely, is Emerson reacting against among their tenets?

Despite his protestations against the Unitarian Church in the Divinity School Address and elsewhere (see his journal), Emerson may have been more indebted than he necessarily cared to admit. Would Emerson's philosophy have developed without this grounding, for instance? Or does he resemble more closely another, stricter branch of Christianity (even Calvinism)? Is Emerson more radical than Unitarianism or more orthodox?

2. **Personal history:** What in Emerson's personal history can explain the development of his philosophy in the Divinity School Address?

By reading about Emerson's personal history, particularly his education at the Divinity School and his brief career as a minister, the reader will gain useful insight into where Emerson's deductions—and possibly biases—originated. What was Emerson's experience at the Divinity School? What happened during his career as a preacher? Emerson's reason for quitting the ministry was an objection to the "Last Supper" sacrament. What is this ritual, and why did Emerson object to it?

Emerson's sermons can also be consulted, especially the later ones, written as he became increasingly disillusioned with the church. Sermons can and should be considered as literary texts just as any other textual form can. *Nature* was drawn in part from Emerson's sermons. As with his journals, Emerson found his sermons a valid source for self-cannibalizing and transformation into later "secular" essays and lectures. The journals are another source for such ruminations, the ones that Emerson did not necessarily intend to share with the public. Search the index. In one entry Emerson inventories the shortcomings of Christ as a lack of cheerfulness and as having no love for natural science or the arts. He pales next to Socrates or Shakespeare. "Do you ask me if I would rather resemble Jesus than any other man? If I say Yes I should suspect myself of superstition." Is such a philosophy already evident in the Divinity School Address?

3. **Audience:** Who was the intended audience for the Divinity School Address? How did Emerson intend it to be received?

This question pertains not simply to strict statistics of those in attendance but leads into questions of Emerson's narrative purpose with this address. First, who was the intended audience (or reader)? Second, how was the address intended to be received? For example, was this a deliberately provocative attention-grabbing coup, or did Emerson mildly stumble onto a hornets' nest? Extratextual clues indicating the extent of Emerson's culpability might be found in the journals and correspondence; for instance, he somewhat sheepishly sent a copy of the address to his aunt, Mary Moody Emerson, remarking that "if it offend you [it] brings at least this mitigation that it offended good men at Cambridge also." Do this admission and its tone suggest coyness and guilt or genuine surprise at the response?

Research into the historical facts of the Divinity School Address will shed light on Emerson's original designs. The actual audience proper for the address—those divinity students who were graduating—numbered only seven (of whom one student did not even attend). These students alone, not their attending friends and family nor the assembled faculty of the college, had formally invited Emerson to speak. Of the seven, only a small majority favored Emerson. Was the address written for three divinity students, then? How does its message answer to a larger audience? Emerson was loosed on those others in attendance (and from there, the Western canon) on the word of perhaps three students. What was *their* purpose? Was this a generational conflict? Who else was in attendance at the address? How did the content of the speech become disseminated so fast?

Search the text itself for inferences about the audience. When does Emerson address his auditors? Is his tone intimate or expansive? Was this text conceived for six divinity students or for a larger audience? This question requires you to research the history of the address, but also to be aware, within the text, of the different audiences that text may imply. Consider the identity of the "implied reader." Other narratological terms of use to analysis and worth exploring include *narratee* and *virtual reader*.

Philosophy and Ideas

Emerson's philosophy and ideas within the Divinity School Address fairly obviously pertain to religion, and specifically New England religion. This immediately explains their dangerousness and their rapid notoriety. His earlier works, although they contained the same fundamental notions, were not aimed at so hallowed an institution. Before it had any special cultural identity, Massachusetts had a religious identity. From the landing at Massachusetts Bay, New England was defined by its religion first, and this tempered any artistic, literary, or political development in the region. Consequently, Emerson's application of his ideas to religion exists in and challenges a much richer tradition than his thoughts on scholarship or poetry. This is a history composed of religious orthodoxy, debate, and heresy. Familiarity with the biography of Roger Williams or Anne Hutchinson, the beliefs of the Quakers and the Arminians, will inform the reader of the Divinity School Address well.

While the charge of Antinomianism was most frequently applied to Emerson, more peculiarly he also occasionally echoes Calvinism both here and, later, in "The Over-Soul." These are, unavoidably, the traditions he inherited, whether he absorbed and heeded them or not. What, precisely, is the debt? Where does the Divinity School Address sit in this tradition? Is it a mark of Emerson's independence of style and thought that he could be considered variously a heretic, an infidel, an atheist, an Antinomian, and a Puritan?

Sample Topics:

1. **Antinomianism:** Was Emerson an Antinomian?

The Antinomian heresy is one frequently raised in reference to Emerson's views on man's relations to God. First, then, it is important for you to identify and clarify Emerson's views in this regard. Isolate the passages where he speaks on this relationship and closely interpret them. For example, when Emerson faults the Church and "understanding" he voices their "error" thus: "This was Jehovah come down out of heaven. I will kill you, if you say he was a man." Rather, Emerson says, "God incarnates himself in man." How does Emerson differ from theological convention? Is this Antinomianism?

The question calls for knowledge of the Antinomian controversy. This subject is covered in most good histories of American colonial history, in varying degrees of detail. Some of the theology is difficult. Nevertheless, general studies of the first century of the Massachusetts Bay Colony will contain some discussion of Antinomianism and its chief proponent, Anne Hutchinson. Using such guides, you can be led to more detailed accounts by the bibliographies. In as close detail as you can, research the details and explain them. For example (broadly stated), Anne Hutchinson believed that she was in direct communication with God and regarded the dictates of this inner voice over any authority held by the ministry or the government or even the Bible. Where do Hutchinson's views coincide with Emerson's? Where do they differ? Weighing these similarities and differences, is it fair to call Emerson Antinomian, or is it a lazy and erroneous generalization?

2. **Puritanism:** Was Emerson a Puritan or a libertine?

What is the extent of Emerson's debt to radical liberalism, and what is his debt to Puritanism? This question suggests that both descriptions have some validity. Do they? Both possibilities should be addressed. In Emerson's time there was some anxiety about the New England intellectual inheritance from Puritanism. This anxiety is perhaps best expressed in the tales and novels of Nathaniel Hawthorne, but it exists also in Emerson's writing. Is there a wistfulness to Emerson's tone when he remarks of the austere Puritans, "But their creed is dying away, and none arises in its room"? This question requires research into the doctrines of Puritanism. Fortunately—and unfortunately—plenty has been written about American Puritanism. Good studies have been written by Edmund Morgan, Perry Miller, and Sacvan Bercovitch, among others. Miller also edited representative anthologies of Puritan writings containing sermons, poems, and histories. Look at writers such as Roger Williams, John Winthrop, or Cotton Mather. There is a broad spectrum, both in philosophy and theology and in the ways these ideas are formulated. Find the texts of most relevance to this topic, whether through resonance or dissonance with Emerson's ideas. For instance, the Puritans were repulsed by Catholicism and its vast tradition of Apocrypha and sacred commentaries; its "unscriptural ceremonies," rituals, and set prayers; its hierarchies of offices; its use of elaborate vestments; and its adherence to Latin. Puritans stressed the use of the Bible alone: no commentaries or interpretations but in preaching, which they emphasized. Puritans had been known, also, to object to the ritual of Communion. Does Emerson's statement "Dare to love God without mediator or veil" continue this tradition by minimizing the textual apparatus between worshiper and God, or does it reject it and fall into heresy?

Conversely, in the aftermath of the Divinity School Address and the furor it provoked, Emerson was called an "infidel" by Andrews Norton. He described himself to his former colleague and critic Henry Ware, Jr., as "a chartered libertine, free to worship and free to rail." Were these accurate appellations? Ideally, the reader will identify aspects of both extremes in Emerson's address and weigh them against each other to draw a reasoned and original conclusion.

3. **The New School:** What was the New School, and how did it influence Emerson's address?

The New School was the name given at the time to the grouping that was later called the transcendentalists. Historical surveys and anthologies of their writings exist. This question requires you to research the history of this group. Where did the name come from, and who first applied it to this group? If they were the New School, who made up the Old School, and how and why did the rift occur? Identify the key members of the group, and summarize their works and thoughts. Evaluate Emerson's work in this context. Does he share ideas with the other members of the New School (for instance, Orestes Brownson, Theodore Parker, George Ripley)?

Consult also those opponents of the movement who as much shaped the "school" as its proponents. As one critic has it, the "greatest and most formidable enemy to Transcendentalism" was Andrews Norton. He called the transcendentalists "infidels." Was he correct? Study Norton's criticisms of Emerson's address and transcendentalism, and weigh his grievances against the movement. Regardless of the later redemption and canonization of Emerson and transcendentalism, how were they received at the time? Is there merit to these criticisms? Do not disregard outright old and seemingly archaic criticisms simply because they are ostensibly outdated. Intuition remains in many of them, however much they may differ from the current critical consensus. Use criticism with sophistication: That is, judge all critics by their works and the integrity of their views. Critics such as Norton provide important cultural indicators, if nothing else, of how Emerson's address reverberated in wider society. His view that the transcendentalists were rehashing Carlyle, for instance, or that they were mouthing "common thoughts, sometimes true, oftener false" yet. What was the position of the New School as they set it out in the argument? A movement is often best defined in defense or protest of its critics.

Form and Genre

Is there a tone to Emerson's writing that remains from his time as a minister? Does he recall the sermon form in the Divinity School address? Is the address a form of sermon, then? Is it a religious discourse at all, or is it a political one? Does the address have literary value independent of its more volatile purpose? You should challenge overly bland suppositions about what this text is. Although he had left the ministry formally when he delivered the Divinity School Address,

Emerson was still preaching (and he continued to do so through January 1839).

More generally, this inquiry leads to questions regarding that which connects religion and writing. Are they, in Emerson's philosophy, necessarily connected? For Emerson, can there be a literature of any consequence without religious content? (Can there be a religion without poetry?)

Sample Topics:

1. **Sermon:** Is the Divinity School Address a sermon? If not, what is it?

Emerson was a writer of sermons before he was a writer of lectures or essays. Plenty of these have been published. Have a look at some of these, and note Emerson's rhetorical flourishes and tropes. Which ones reappear in the Divinity School Address? What differentiates a sermon from an address, anyway? Be ready to question easy assumptions about forms. Is a sermon an address that affirms Christianity or one that discusses Christian matters? Is a sermon anything preached from a pulpit? Is there any stylistic or structural reason to separate the sermons from the addresses—or the lectures, or the essays? What is the difference between a sermon and an Emersonian essay?

Beyond Emerson's sermons, consult other sermons to gain a sense of the form and its tradition. There are anthologies of classic American sermons. Consult the colonial writers (John Cotton, Thomas Hooker, and John Winthrop, author of the famous "A Modell of Christian Charity"), or try the 18th-century predecessors of Emerson such as Jonathan Edwards (for instance, "Sinners in the Hands of an Angry God"). Examine Emerson's contemporaries. The most successful preacher of Emerson's time was Henry Ward Beecher (1813–87), brother of Harriet Beecher Stowe. From this survey, can you deduce how sermons are constructed? Do they have a clear structure and subject, or are they fluid? Can sermons be political, for instance? Can they engage philosophy? Can the form be radical? How do sermons differ according to their authors, and what remains consistent in the form?

Is Emerson's address formally radical as well as in its doctrine, or is it conventional? Look to language and rhetoric in the address. Regard how Emerson punctuates and prefaces new paragraphs with exhortations: "My friends" or "My brothers." Look at the rhetorical tone of the essay—pleading, wheedling, and, in turn, excoriating. What form of oratory does this most closely resemble?

2. **Writing and religion:** How are writing and religion connected in Emerson's thinking?

For Emerson the scholar, the poet, and the priest are elevated, heroic figures in society. He is accustomed to using one or another as an exemplar of his philosophy. Is each a representation of Emerson himself? Do they all serve the same purpose? Are they used interchangeably, willy-nilly, or does each have a distinct identity?

Another question that might be asked is, Are literature and religion separable? Then, are they separable for Emerson? Without a church, Emerson writes, "Literature becomes frivolous." Why is this? What is the connection between the maintenance of the church and the well-being of the literary project? What sort of literature is there, without a church? Conversely, it might be asked, are literature and religion even compatible? Is Emerson a religious writer? One of Emerson's private problems with Jesus Christ was that "I see in him no kindness for Art." Is this view espoused in the Divinity School Address? Look also to Emerson's beliefs on language and religion. He finds fault with "the language that describes Christ to Europe and America," finds in historical Christianity a prevailing "error that corrupts all attempts to communicate religion." How, then, does he propose religion be communicated? How has the communication been "distorted"? And how are *understanding* and *reason*—opposed terms recurring from *Nature*—pertinent?

Language, Symbols, and Imagery

Emerson's language in the Divinity School Address is dependent on symbolism and imagery. How does the unusually serene opening scene of the address reflect the main body of the text? Is Emerson suggesting a biblical analogue to his discourse—beginning with the Garden of Eden and ending in apocalypse? Or is he relying on a series of oppositions to construct his narrative, balancing scenes of fertility and creation with their binary opposites, aridity and destruction? Critics claim that Emerson uses the dialectic form, in which questions and answers are used as a reasoning tool. How does Emerson apply his oppositions to the dialectic form?

Sample Topics:

1. **Prefatory vignette:** One critic has called the prefatory vignette to the Divinity School Address "the central theological point of the talk," suggesting that it defines the discourse to follow. Why do you think this is? Do you agree?

   What is the purpose of the opening paragraph of the Divinity School Address? Consider Emerson's other works, how they begin and how they end. Emerson is exacting with the overtures and the conclusions to his essays and addresses. Openings to essays can provide keys to the text to follow. Does this scene prepare the reader for the discourse ahead, or is it simply a scenic preamble? This question requires a close reading of the prefatory vignette, relating it to the body of the subsequent text. Since the paragraph is wholly descriptive and not didactic, one way of reading the text is symbolically. Engage the symbolism of the vignette. What is its predominating subject? Bounteous, sublime nature. Is Emerson reaffirming his doctrine from the 1836 essay? Or is he recalling a prelapsarian (meaning, before the biblical "Fall of Man")? What happens in the second paragraph, then, when "the mind opens"?

Look also at the end of the essay. In several instances Emerson closes his essays with grotesque images of apocalypse resolved by rapturous redemption, with a messianic central figure. You can provide examples of instances of these conventions. The Divinity School Address ends with a "smouldering, nigh quenched fire on the altar" and a clarion call for "the new Teacher" who shall "follow . . . the shining laws," so that they "come full circle." Does the Divinity School Address observe Emersonian conventions? Is Emerson writing according to an established, biblical, structure? What might this signify, in relation to the core argument of the essay? Is this a concession to his audience at the Divinity School? What does it mean if Emerson employs Christian symbolism in this address? Is this, as one critic describes it, "the use of scripture to deny scripture"?

2. **Symbolism:** Discuss the use of oppositions in the Divinity School Address.

"We have contrasted the Church with the Soul," Emerson announces in the address. Is this a summary of the address? What does it mean for Emerson to construct his essay around contrast? Is it an aggressive position? How does Emerson use oppositions in the Divinity School Address? Find some other instances of "polarity" in the address and study them closely. Oppositions used in the address include reason versus understanding, good versus evil, faith versus degradation, genesis and apocalypse, person versus soul. There are others. Perhaps the most elaborate opposition is the one described in the anecdote of the "formalist": the "sad contrast" of the preacher and the snowstorm. Emerson says that this is the contrast between the "real" and the "spectral"; what else is opposed? Is it significant, for instance, that Emerson makes his image of the "real" a force of nature? And that his symbol of the "spectral" is a preacher? What about his account of the Church's version of a miracle, described as "Monster" and contrasted with "the blowing clover and the falling rain"?

Find one such example of oppositional symbolism and submit it to close analysis. What might it mean that Emerson's narrative relies so heavily on oppositions? Is this rhetorical? Is it intentional or inadvertent? Compare the address with other works. Think, for instance, of the beginning of *Nature*: "Philosophically considered, the universe is composed of Nature and the Soul." Is the ordering principle of contrast or polarity an Emersonian convention? How does this relate to the dialectic method? And is any such reliance on convention Emersonian?

Compare and Contrast

While he was cryptic in exposition, Emerson was prone to revisit and revise earlier essays or addresses in later ones. Sometimes he would revisit the texts in the form of poetry. You might recall the poems that are used as epigraphs for the second edition of the first series of *Essays* (1847), which, in some ways, influence our readings of the essay that follows. While no such poem was written explicitly for the Divinity School Address, the poem "Uriel" is universally read as a commentary on that address.

Sample Topic:

1. **"Uriel"**: One critic has asserted that the poem "Uriel" "refights the Divinity School controversy." Do you agree?

The poem "Uriel" is unanimously read as Emerson's own ironic comment on the events surrounding the Divinity School Address and its attendant controversy. It is not known how soon after the fact it was written, but it was published in his first book of poems in 1846. One critic places its writing in 1845. There are seven years between the two. How does Emerson reenvision the events of the Divinity School Address?

First, provide a close reading of the poem. With whom is "Uriel" analogous? Who else is Emerson portraying, in celestial disguise? For example, who are the "stern old war-gods" who "shook their heads"? Who is Said? Most readers identify the war gods as Andrews Norton and his circle of high-ranking Unitarians. As you might deduce from this, the unraveling of the poem (and so the unraveling of the address) requires a knowledge of the aftermath of the address as well as the address itself. Nevertheless, attention and comparison to the address are important. How does the poem perhaps reveal Emerson's intent in the original text? One critic claims that Emerson admits here to a disruptive design to his original performance, one he never acknowledged otherwise. Do you agree? Why does Emerson commit his reflection to this particular genre and form?

Compare the symbolism of the two texts. Both play on imagery of the biblical Fall. Why? Why does Emerson equate the occasion of the address with the Fall of man? Why, also, does Emerson identify with deities? How might this affirm those transcendental theories in the address?

Bibliography and Online Resources

Arvin, Newton. "The House of Pain." *American Pantheon*. Ed. Daniel Aron and Sylvan Schendler. New York: Dell, 1966. 16–38.

Bloom, Harold. *The Ringers in the Tower: Studies in the Romantic Tradition*. Chicago: U of Chicago P, 1971.

Buell, Lawrence. *Emerson*. Cambridge: Harvard UP, 2003.

Burkholder, Robert E., and Joel Myerson. *Critical Essays on Ralph Waldo Emerson*. Boston: G. K. Hall, 1983.

Davis, G. T. "The Divinity School *Address*." Burkholder and Myerson 37–41.

Emerson, Ralph Waldo. *Young Emerson Speaks: Unpublished Discourses on Many Subjects*. Ed. Arthur Cushman McGiffert, Jr. Boston: Houghton Mifflin, 1938.

Foster, Charles Howell. "Emerson as American Scripture." *New England Quarterly* 16.1 (March 1943): 91–105.

Hall, David D., ed. *The Antinomian Controversy, 1636–1638: A Documentary History*. Middletown, CT: Wesleyan UP, 1968.

Hawthorne, Nathaniel. *Tales and Sketches*. New York: Library of America, 1982.

Johnston, Carol. "The Underlying Structure of the Divinity School Address: Emerson as Jeremiah." *Studies in the American Renaissance*. Ed. Joel Myerson. Boston: Twayne, 1980. 41–49.

Miller, Perry. *The Transcendentalists: Their Articles, Essays, Poems and Addresses.* Cambridge, MA: Harvard UP, 1950. See, particularly, the "Introduction." 3–15.

Morgan, Edmund. *Visible Saints: The History of a Puritan Idea.* Ithaca, NY: Cornell UP, 1963.

Mott, Wesley T. "Emerson and Antinomianism: The Legacy of the Sermons." *American Literature* 50.3 (November 1978): 369–397.

Norton, Andrews. "The New School in Literature and Religion." Burkholder and Myerson 31–34.

Parsons, Theophilus ["S.X."]. "The New School and Its Opponents." Burkholder and Myerson 35–37.

Porte, Joel, and Saundra Morris, eds. *Emerson's Prose and Poetry: Authoritative Texts, Contexts, Criticism.* New York: W. W. Norton, 2001.

Strauch, Carl. "Emerson as a Creator of Vignettes." *Modern Language Notes* 70.4 (April 1955): 274–278.

Thundyil, Zacharias. "Emerson and the Problem of Evil: Paradox and Resolution." *Harvard Theological Review* 62.1 (January 1969): 51–61.

Warner, Michael, ed. *American Sermons: The Pilgrims to Martin Luther King.* New York: Library of America, 1999.

Wright, Conrad Edick, ed. *American Unitarianism: 1805–1865.* Boston: Northeastern UP, 1989.

Yoder, R. A. *Emerson and the Orphic Tradition in America.* Berkeley: U of California P, 1978.

"SELF-RELIANCE"

READING TO WRITE

"**S**ELF-RELIANCE" DRAWS from a journal entry made as early as June 1839, while Emerson refined the essay in October 1840. It had a long gestation. While it was conceived earlier than other chapters in the first series of *Essays,* it was among the last to be completed. This complicated history is reflected in a complicated form. As with other essays in the series ("The Over-Soul," "Circles") it revisits ideas from the earlier works. The essay can reasonably be read as Emerson's considered response to the outcry that followed the Divinity School Address. There is a harsh tone to the essay ("God will not have his work made manifest by cowards"), and Emerson only compounds his earlier outrages; this is no olive branch held out to the orthodoxy. "We but half express ourselves, and are ashamed of that divine idea which each of us represents." His heresy remains. He revisits also questions of originality and imitation from *The American Scholar,* a theme that frames the essay with the first anecdote of the "eminent painter."

The sheer torrent of ideas and propositions in "Self-Reliance" recalls Benjamin Franklin's *Poor Richard's Almanac,* with its epigrams and aphorisms. The succession of Yankee notions can be dizzying. One critic has remarked of "Self-Reliance" that

> all those statements and many others in the same essay . . . are "sentences" in the Latin meaning of the words; they are what chiefly impress us at first reading. But if we read the essay again, this time more carefully, we see that each sentence belongs in its context, occurs at the inevitable moment, and contributes to the total effect that Emerson planned.

The difficulty with this essay is in trying to "sift through" what is, strictly, all significant matter. It is important to identify Emerson's different subjects; to impose order on what may seem at first, as the poet and critic James Russell Lowell termed it, a "chaos." The essay is not without structure, but it follows a tortuous and purposely whimsical structure. *Whim* is an important word to bear in mind; Emerson himself states, "I would write on the lintels of the door-post, *Whim*." He celebrates contradiction, and some of his statements within this essay may seem inconsistent. In his journal, only weeks before the essay's publication, Emerson confided, "My page about 'Consistency' would be better written thus: Damn Consistency!"

The following passage, from the first few pages of the essay, is famous for its shocking choice of images and words. It is a challenge to conformity and gentility.

> Whoso would be a man, must be a nonconformist. He who would gather immortal palms must not be hindered by the name of goodness, but must explore if it be goodness. Nothing is at last sacred but the integrity of your own mind. Absolve you to yourself, and you shall have the suffrage of the world. I remember an answer which when quite young I was prompted to make to a valued adviser who was wont to importune me with the dear old doctrines of the church. On my saying, "What have I to do with the sacredness of traditions, if I live wholly from within?" my friend suggested,—"But these impulses may be from below, not from above." I replied, "They do not seem to me to be such; but if I am the Devil's child, I will live then from the Devil." No law can be sacred to me but that of my nature. Good and bad are but names very readily transferable to that or this; the only right is what is after my constitution; the only wrong what is against it.

Instantly noticeable is Emerson's propensity for bluntness: "Whoso would be a man, must be a nonconformist." This is an uncompromising claim, almost a challenge. Here is Emerson braying and crowing like those southwestern frontiersmen featured in the newspapers of the time. Emerson's intention was to excite thought in his reader, to throw down an intellectual gauntlet. The radicalism of his message is matched by a forthright diction. While much has been made of Emerson's vagueness and obscurity, he could also be direct. The reader should take note of such shifting tones.

Emerson's anecdote is autobiographical—personalized. This is removed from the customary dry tone associated with "philosophy." Is "Self-Reliance" a philosophical work then? Was Emerson a philosopher or a poet? What genre can the text accurately be identified as? The essence of "Self-Reliance" is, indeed, to confound and subvert set roles for the individual. Contradiction and whim are the watchwords. In this extract, Emerson apparently recalls the rupture between him and the church following his Divinity School Address at Harvard in 1838, particularly the subsequent vituperation of Andrews Norton. Nevertheless, the anecdote is also symbolic of Emerson's more general severing of himself from the past and from all debts to society. Emerson places himself in a position violently opposed to the genteel, middle-class tenets of the day. In taking the side of the devil—perhaps the ultimate nonconformist—and calling himself "the Devil's child" his aim seems to be to upset delicate sensibilities.

Finally, Emerson states his underlying belief in this essay: "No law can be sacred to me but that of my nature." Is this reckless? Arrogant? Psychotic? Solipsistic? Taking his sense of morality from within rather than from without, Emerson seems again to hint at the Antinomian heresy that he invoked with the Divinity School Address. Does Emerson intend simply to outrage his readers? Is he favoring personal instinct over society's law? Because of his willingness to contradict himself, it is important to maintain a clear sense of Emerson's purpose as a writer as well as his philosophical one. Is truth his ultimate end or poetry?

TOPICS AND STRATEGIES

The following section suggests several possible topics for essays on "Self-Reliance." They can and should be used as starting points for your own, independent exploration of the essay.

Themes

The very title, "Self-Reliance," affirms the core theme of this essay: self and selfhood. Emerson says in the third paragraph, "Trust thyself: every heart vibrates to that iron string." This statement emerges as the motto of the essay. In *Nature*, Emerson defined the world as the soul and the NOT-ME. Here he defines further the soul and the self. Emerson provides models for the self in youth—the indulged infant, the adolescent, and the nonchalant boys, sure of dinner. Is this necessarily a positive model for the self, however? What sort of imagery does Emerson use and why? At what audience is such a version of selfhood aimed? How, equally, does Emerson characterize the opposing elements? One is surely tradition; another is society.

Sample Topics:

1. **Self:** How does Emerson understand "self"? Is it the same as "soul"?

   This is a tricky question, because it is so general. Self is the unifying theme in this essay, but so broad and abstract that it is not easily defined. The reader might first isolate those concrete instances when Emerson refers to the self. Note the language he uses—even if symbolic or metaphorical—for example, *aboriginal, childlike, latent, spontaneous,* and *innocent.* The self is defined also by its relation to God and society. How? Also, look for *self* and its synonyms in other essays by Emerson. Is self the same as soul? And what about mind? Emerson sometimes describes a fragmented and divided self. Unity and fragmentation are oppositions that recur in Emerson's rhetoric (remember, for instance, the "Fable" in *The American Scholar*). Mark instances of the divided self, such as when Emerson declares that "the man is as it were clapped into jail by his consciousness."

2. **Youth:** Youth is an important concept in "Self-Reliance." What does Emerson take it to represent? What favors youth over agedness?

   To answer this question you should first identify those passages where Emerson discusses "youth." Look also for references to boys, infants, and other paradigms of youth. Is Emerson using them simply as literal figures, or do they stand for something more? Similarly, how does he treat agedness and the aged? The celebration of youth had a pointed meaning to Emerson's audience when the essay was first published. What did youth symbolize—and what did the old and aged symbolize? Think of the "Old" and "New" Worlds, for instance. Research not only Emerson but also the history—both political and literary—of America in the 1830s.

The Young America movement, for instance, arose in the same year that Emerson was writing his essay. This was a self-conscious literary movement espousing Democratic politics in New York City, led by the editor Evert Duycinck and including among its adherents Herman Melville and (with less conviction) Edgar Allan Poe. Excellent studies of Young America have been written by Perry Miller (*The Raven and the Whale*, 1956) and Edward L. Widmer (*Young America*, 1999). Does Emerson draw on a common vein of imagery with writers in this movement? Is his a conscious identification? An inquiry such as this will lead into further fertile questions: What were Emerson's politics? What was the extent of his sympathies or familiarity with the New York literary scene? Indeed, how did New York writers perceive Boston and Concord?

3. **Tradition:** Emerson rejects tradition in his essay. Does he convince you? Is "Self-Reliance" wholly new, or does it too adhere to a tradition?

This topic requires you to locate those parts of the essay where Emerson rejects tradition and identifies his stated reason for doing so. Judge "self-reliance" by these same critical standards. Does Emerson meet them in his own work? Isolate those passages where Emerson seems to be referencing views of earlier thinkers; where he is himself maintaining a tradition. In which traditions does Emerson exist? The influence of romanticism—be it British (Coleridge, Wordsworth, Carlyle) or German (Goethe, Schiller)—is clearly present.

Emerson was well versed in the philosophers, and despite his antagonism to bookishness, he uses this reading often. In this essay he lists Pythagoras, Socrates, Anaxagoras, Zoroaster, Diogenes, Locke, Bentham, Fourier, Dante, Shakespeare, and Bacon, among others, as models. How is this brazen listing of influences consistent with the rejection of tradition?

Emerson's various beliefs can be traced to different sources, even when he does not declare them. In fact, those he does not declare can be as important as those he does. His New England tradition—Unitarianism, even Calvinism—is conspicuous in Emerson's thinking, even if he is reacting against it. Is Emerson any less in a tradition if he engages his forebears in a discourse, even if it is only to reject them?

History and Context

"Self-Reliance" was written during the presidency of Martin Van Buren (1837–41), who had previously served as vice president under Andrew Jackson (1829–37). Jackson, who had in his youth been scarred for life by a British soldier, held anti-European views. He challenged the prevailing American indebtedness to Europe for its fashions and customs. The first "log cabin" president, he also provided a voice and a uniting figure for lower born white, male Americans, previously neglected by American politics. This period also saw the rise in America of a reform movement, which over the next 30 years flared to a fever pitch abated only by the Civil War. Religious virtue was emphasized by its proponents, but so were liberal political causes. At the fore of these was abolitionism. In protesting slavery, reform could veer easily into radicalism (a progression perhaps best epitomized by the fate of John Brown and the events at Harpers Ferry). Does Emerson's thinking belong in this tradition of radicalism? For instance, were those "anarchist" beliefs held by Josiah Warren, who at his Long Island radical community Modern Times preached only the "sovereignty of the individual," comparable to Emersonian self-reliance?

Radical "utopias," each subscribing to (and sometimes practicing) its own form of "perfectionism"—ideal living—blossomed throughout America in this period. There had been a preponderance among the people for millennialism (and for millenarianism—the belief centering on the conviction that the second coming of Christ was imminent) in New England ever since the Puritans settled in the Massachusetts Bay Colony. Such hopes had swelled again in the flurry of the reform movement and Emerson's essay partakes of this feeling. "Our age yields no great and perfect persons," he complains. His words anticipate the apocalypse: "Our first thought is rendered back to us by the trumpets of the Last Judgment." Do his high expectations and radical demands on his audience ring more familiar when read in the context of millenarianism?

Sample Topics:

1. **Jacksonianism:** How does Emerson reflect the Jacksonian politics of his time?

The ideas for "Self-Reliance" were formulated in the years immediately after the "reign" of "King Andrew" Jackson (so called by his critics for his establishment of what they saw as an absolute autocracy). Emerson wrote and published the essay under the administration of Martin Van Buren, Jackson's former vice president and political heir. This topic requires the reader to research what broad traits colored and distinguished the character of politics under Jackson and Van Buren.

Jackson was a singular figure, with very identifiable beliefs, carried adamantly into his policies. He was a democratic champion of the so-called common man, a rough-and-ready frontiersman, opposed to patricians. Jackson was also fiercely nationalistic (arguably jingoistic). The reader should look for examples of such thought in Emerson's essay and show how they might match or contrast with other documents of the time, both political and literary. Is Emerson in accordance with or in revolt against such a vision? Does he celebrate "the mob" or condemn them? "Kingdom and lordship, power and estate, are a gaudier vocabulary than private John and Edward in a small house and common day's work," Emerson writes. He celebrates "the pit . . . in the playhouse" as "independent" and "irresponsible." He praises youth and implores his reader to emulate the young. Youth was celebrated as a national virtue, emblematic of the young country freed from an Old World, tyrannical father in the guise of Europe. Celebrated types in New York society of the time included vigorous, youthful types such as the "Bowery B'hoy."

Emerson is not clearly behind such a figure, however. Later in the essay he laments that "now we are a mob. Man does not stand in awe of man." Emerson's answers are never straightforward and need to be appraised with sophistication. Contradiction is, as he says, his prerogative and his bent.

2. **Radicalism:** Is Emerson a radical thinker in "Self-Reliance," or is he ultimately a conservative?

This question—bedeviling to critics to this day—calls for you to analyze and describe Emerson's political position. This is not easily done, given Emerson's resistance to ready identification. Critics find Emerson vacillating, perhaps willfully, between starkly opposed positions. You should measure these positions against each other and deduce a solution. Emerson makes little reference to party politics in this essay, notwithstanding a swipe at "the Whigs of Maine." The question calls rather for you to take note of when Emerson is speaking of a high metaphysical ideal and when he veers more into the social realm. The one often merges seamlessly into the other. At times, however, Emerson discusses abolitionism; on another occasion he clearly alludes to the radical and largely reviled challenge to the traditional form of marriage by champions of "free love":

> I will have no covenant but proximities. I shall endeavour to nourish my parents, to support my family, to be the chaste husband of one wife.

The reader should look out for broadly "political subjects" and scrutinize what Emerson's stance might be on them.

At other times, Emerson remains—to modern eyes especially—within a conventional framework, upholding family
and God, if not necessarily church. In his opposition to convention, Emerson can sound selfish, petulant, even nihilistic at
turns, and by no means radical. He holds up as an ideal "boys
who are sure of a dinner," "independent" and "irresponsible."
But are these positive models for "human nature"? You must
weigh these inconsistencies and come up with a definition of
radicalism. From here, an argument can be assembled.

3. **Personal history:** To what extent does "Self-Reliance" reflect
   Emerson's personal history?

This topic requires the reader to research Emerson's personal
background. For instance, how does Emerson's personal history reflect his opposition to inherited property? "Especially
he hates what he has if he see that it is accidental,—came to
him by inheritance, or gift, or crime." Emerson lived off a
yearly payment from his wife's estate. Did this grant him an
independence that allowed self-reliance—the flouting of convention and the rejection of institutions? Or does his criticism
of "accidental" inheritances suggest guilt about his situation?
What other factors in Emerson's personal history might contribute to seemingly purely intellectual attitudes?

There has been no shortage of good biographies of Emerson. Furthermore his journals and correspondence have been
scrupulously transcribed, annotated, and published (if anything, there is too much to choose easily). The reader should
then look particularly at the period around the writing of this
essay, picking with intelligence and discernment pertinent
excerpts from the journals and the correspondence (variously
noting using the index) and identifying possible references to
the essay and its inception.

Philosophy and Ideas

"Self-Reliance" revisits again the triumvirate—nature, the soul, and
God. It is, however, distinguished by a special emphasis on the self. This

emphasis borders on the willful at times; at other times, the humble. The will of God forms a major part of the discourse. Do humility and obeisance always haunt the tone of the essay, though? Is the Emerson who says that "when a man lives with God, his voice shall be as sweet as the murmur of the brook" identical to the one who spits, "I will live then from the Devil"? Self-centeredness and self-absorption, even solipsism, are dangers in this sort of rhetoric. Does Emerson fall into such a belief, already threatened in *Nature*? Darker aspects of "Self-Reliance" exist also in Emerson's cool acknowledgment of inconsistency and his celebration of whim. Are we to believe his pious exhortations on one hand and disbelieve them at others? When are we to believe Emerson, if at all?

Sample Topics:

1. **Self-reliance and God reliance:** Is Emersonian self-reliance in fact dependent on God? Does "Self-Reliance" affirm God's authority or challenge it? How is self-reliance consistent with religious deference?

   One critic has called Emerson's position one of "subjection," while Harold Bloom states that "Emersonian self-reliance is God-reliance." This fundamental and ambiguous antagonism between irresponsible autonomy and religious duty is the area to be negotiated and puzzled out. As radical as it was to his readers at the time, Emerson's essay is far from heresy to the contemporary reader. The reader should be mindful of how rigid religion was in Emerson's time. Isolate those passages where Emerson discusses God and the divine—paragraphs 22 through 28 in particular. Emerson has a firm idea of "the relations of the soul to the divine spirit."

   A useful essay to bear in mind in a question such as this is "The Over-Soul," which was published in the same book as "Self-Reliance" (the first series of *Essays,* 1841). How are transactions between God and self portrayed differently in one essay and the other? Additionally, when Emerson speaks against being carried backward "to the phraseology of some old mouldered nation in another country," he recalls the Divinity School Address. How much does "Self-Reliance" owe to that address?

2. **Selfishness and solipsism:** Is "Self-Reliance" essentially selfishness? Does its ultimate end lie in solipsism?

   First, you should define clearly the philosophical term *solipsism*. Solipsism is the belief that nothing exists or is real but
   the self. Such a conclusion can follow from Rene Descartes's
   famous statement, detailing the sum of all that can be known
   with any confidence, *Cogito, ergo sum* ("I think, therefore I
   am"). All that one can be sure of is oneself. Is this what Emerson is claiming? How are the views related? You may recall
   the doctrine of "idealism" somewhat vigorously expounded
   in *Nature,* wherein Emerson seems to consider the world as
   being illusory. Was this solipsism? How has Emerson's position
   in "Self-Reliance" developed from that proffered in *Nature*?
   Emerson writes of different "truths" existing simultaneously:
   "If you are true, but not in the same truth with me, cleave to
   your companions; I will seek my own." How is this so? Is there
   more than one truth? Emerson anticipates here the philosophical school of "pragmatism," as developed by William James.
   Might such a comparison clarify Emerson's essay?
       The question also asks about selfishness. Is Emerson—in
   championing the nonchalant, well-fed boys; in asking petu-
   lantly, "Are they *my* poor?"—espousing a reasoned, intellectual defense of selfishness? Is this the Emerson reinvented by
   businesspeople and professional pep talkers, or is this a misrepresentation of his message? And how might selfishness and
   solipsism be compatible?

3. **Consistency and whim:** What is wrong with consistency?
   What is to be celebrated about whim?

   Does an argument or philosophy need to be consistent? Is this
   compatible with reason? If Emerson proudly declares himself
   inconsistent and whimsical, how can we read him with any
   confidence or seriousness? This question requires the reader
   to focus first on Emerson's statements about whim (paragraph
   seven) and consistency and contradiction (paragraphs 12–17).

What is his reason for rejecting consistency? Second, the reader might look at the whole essay and identify sentences where Emerson does seem to contradict himself. Does this contradiction worsen or improve the essay? Why? And why do we expect consistency as a paramount requirement anyway? Consistency with what?

Should Emerson even be reasonable? Does he exist in a tradition that affirms tradition (say, that of Benjamin Franklin and the American Enlightenment), or one that affirms feeling and sentiment? There were two swells of religious "enthusiasm," in pronounced conflict with the scientifically based Enlightenment (the Great Awakening and the Second Awakening). To which is Emerson indebted? "That divided and rebel mind, that distrust of a sentiment because our arithmetic has computed the strength and means opposed to our purpose, these have not." Furthermore, what do we mean by *reason*, and what does Emerson mean by it?

Form and Genre

While Emerson has been viewed by some critics as a philosopher, other critics scoff at his inexactness and whimsy, his propensity for impressionistic obscurity. Can "whim" and boastful inconsistency be the basis for any philosophy? Philosophy is systematic and consistent, often tediously following its own logic. (Is it not?) Emerson rails against systems: "The pupil takes the same delight in subordinating every thing to the new terminology as a girl who has just learned botany in seeing a new earth and new seasons thereby." Is there, then, any reason why Emerson is viewed as a philosopher yet?

Another precedent, more malleable and variegated and so perhaps more easily applicable to "Self-Reliance," is the list of adages that readers found in the farmer's almanacs of the 18th and 19th centuries. Emerson includes fragments of diverse genres in "Self-Reliance," including poetry and an excerpt from a drama in his epigraph alone. As the critic David Reynolds has noted, Emerson also borrows imagery from the journalistic humor of his time. He peppers his narrative with autobiographical asides and personal anecdotes, as bases for philosophical speculation. Is this, then, autobiography?

Sample Topics:

1. **Philosophy:** Is "Self-Reliance" a work of philosophy? If not, what is it?

   To answer this question, you should delve into the history of philosophy, including its ancient origins. We expect philosophy—at least a certain branch of it—to be scientific. Some philosophers ally their work closely with mathematics, for instance, while in ancient Greece and Rome philosophers would equally write on matters of science and mathematics as well as the nature of thought. The subjects were deemed indistinguishable from one another. Does Emerson fit into this type? Consistency—surely an aim of strict science—is his bugbear.

   Conversely, other philosophers challenged the assertions of the scientists. There are more mystical philosophers, and the student might look into this tradition also. Read the thoughts and ideas of different philosophers and see whether you can find any that anticipate Emerson. Receiving particular notice should be those philosophers Emerson mentions in this essay. Does Emerson fit any of these types? What, finally, is "Self-Reliance" if not philosophy? If you were asked to describe it for a friend, what would you say it was about?

2. **The almanac:** Another form that was highly popular in New England in Emerson's time was the farmer's almanac. How does Emerson's essay owe its form to the almanac?

   This question requires the reader to research almanacs. There are several good studies, including George Lyman Kittredge's excellent *The Old Farmer and His Almanack,* centering especially on Robert Bailey Thomas's famous *Old Farmer's Almanack.* By far the best-known almanac is that one written and printed by Benjamin Franklin, for which he created the character Poor Richard. Familiarize yourself with Franklin's collection of sayings and advice from *Poor Richard's Almanac,* "The Way to Wealth" (1758). What similarities can be noted between this and Emerson's essay?

The almanac was a proletarian form of literature—it is said that every household in America had at least a copy of the Bible and an almanac. Why might Emerson have taken on the formal trappings of an almanac? What literary purpose would this perhaps serve? What might this suggest about Emerson's intended audience? Examine examples of the almanacs of Emerson's time. How would you describe them formally and in terms of style? The almanac is a fragmented, ragbag form, containing sage and practical advice, whimsical poetry, brief saws and skits, and occasionally pedantic, tedious didacticism. How does this style compare with "Self-Reliance"?

3. **Folk humor:** Critics have commented on Emerson's use of folk-lore and folk humor in his essays. Are there instances of folk materials in "Self-Reliance"? Why would Emerson use such a genre in his essay?

Categories of folk literature include folk humor, especially the tall tale, which might have the form of a traveler's hoax. Additionally, there are folk proverbs, aphorisms, and saws. In answering this question you should research 19th-century folklore and humor. What are the recurring motifs and types? Do they appear in Emerson's essay? One example might be Emerson's casual reference to the "popular fable of the sot who was picked up dead-drunk in the street, carried to the duke's house." Why does Emerson use such a tone and image for an ostensibly serious essay? Similarly, Emerson's vaunted "hero" in his philosophy is not the haughty Harvard scholar but the "sturdy lad from New Hampshire or Vermont," who "tries all the professions, who *teams it, farms it, peddles*"— the folk stereotype of the Yankee drawn from newspapers and almanacs.

Discover other examples of this sort. Studies of American humor by Constance Rourke and Walter Blair (see bibliography) discuss the popular history of the comic Yankee. Use these to lead you to exemplary writers such as Seba Smith (his Jack Downing letters), Thomas Chandler Haliburton ("Sam Slick"), and even Emerson's friend James Russell Lowell, whose dialect poem *The Biglow Papers* (1846–48) played with the notions of the folk Yankee to construct an incisive attack on America's war in Mexico. Does Emerson take imagery or rhetoric from these writers? If possible, the student can even find precedents of Emerson's fables in folklore studies. What is Emerson's purpose in using a jocular, folksy tone for an essay with a serious purpose? (Does "Self-Reliance" have a "serious purpose"?)

Language, Symbols, and Imagery

Can we discern Emerson's intent and purpose through his language and imagery? "Self-Reliance" uses starkly violent imagery at times, reflecting more the democratic literature of the day—the sensational novel, the violent frontier humor—than the scholarly or literary journals. At one juncture Emerson notes cheerfully:

> If the traveller tell us truly, strike the savage with a broad-axe and in a day or two the flesh shall unite and heal as if you struck the blow into soft pitch, and the same blow shall send the white to his grave.

This is hardly customary imagery for the salon or the drawing room. It is a peculiarly grotesque image. Why, then, would Emerson be employing such coarse illustrations in an intellectual discourse on "self-reliance"? What reaction does he desire from his readership? Is the image of the savage intended to shock? Is the violence necessary as an apt illustration, or is it sensational? What does the violence of the axe blow suggest about Emerson himself? Does he endorse the violence? Does Emerson pepper his essay with images both grotesque and sublime to draw in a broader audience than the Concord transcendentalist circle?

Sample Topic:

1. **"Grotesque and arabesque":** Discuss Emerson's use of grotesque and exotic images and language. Give examples, and explain why you think he uses them.

   Note those times when Emerson uses the grotesque, the exaggerated, and the exotic. Look for those phrases where he mentions the monstrous and the strange—any phrase that is punctuated by a sensational, unnatural image. For instance, "I will live then from the Devil." Is Emerson using gothic horror to portray defiance? Elsewhere he utilizes images or language evoking the Last Judgment, hobgoblins, and South Sea cannibals. When you have gathered a handful of examples, analyze why he is using such imagery. Would the sentence be any different without the grotesqueness? What does it add to his argument? Ask yourself what is the context or tradition in which such imagery is found. Frontier violence suggests American expansion and the corollary fear of the frontier, while apocalyptic images recall New England's Puritan past as portrayed in works such as Michael Wigglesworth's epic poem *The Day of Doom* (1662).

Look at the imagery of the literature of the time. Fiction writers were composing exaggeratedly grotesque and weird tales. Edgar Allan Poe's collection *Tales of the Grotesque and the Arabesque* was published in 1839, when Emerson began "Self-Reliance," and many of Nathaniel Hawthorne's tales of the Puritans, their anxieties and neuroses, were published in this period. Humorists like Augustus Baldwin Longstreet were writing comic sketches of the violent life on the frontier. Does Emerson's essay refer to this context, and should it be viewed within it? Does such inclusion illuminate the essay? How might this reflect Emerson's purpose in using the images he does?

Compare and Contrast

Two of the best sources for comparison are Emerson's own essays and the many writers he influenced. "Self-Reliance" particularly seems to anticipate two of the great works of the American literary canon: Henry David Thoreau's *Walden* (1854) and Whitman's *Leaves of Grass* (1855). Both Thoreau and Whitman have been read as followers if not disciples of Emerson. To some critics, they are the actual realizations of Emerson's prophesied American Scholar (Thoreau) and American poet (Whitman). Is this fair, however? What is the extent of their debt? And perhaps more importantly, how do they differ from Emerson? Discipleship aside, both writers became close to Emerson, eventually lapsing into antagonistic relations with him. Why?

Sample Topics:

1. **Whitman:** Emerson's work has been regarded as a major influence on the poetry of Walt Whitman. Reading from *Leaves of Grass,* discuss whether you agree.

   Famously, in "Song of Myself" (note the title) Whitman asks, "Do I contradict myself? / Very well then I contradict myself, / (I am large and contain multitudes.)" This provides an obvious and well-known example of a line influenced by Emerson's celebration of self-contradiction in "Self-Reliance." Read through Whitman's verse finding further lines that ring similar to Emerson's in both what they say and how they say it. What are recognizably Emersonian images? When does Whitman recall Emerson's philosophy? Provide examples and explain the similarity.

   You might also look into the long and sometimes comic private history between the two writers. How, temperamentally, did they differ? And is this reflected in their writings? For instance, Whitman's "sensuality" made many of Concord's freest thinkers queasy. What was Emerson's attitude to the sexual aspect of Whitman's writing? What does this suggest about the extent of Emerson's studied indifference to society's mores? Emerson wrote a private letter congratulating Whitman on his achievement in *Leaves of Grass,* which Whitman famously made very public—having it emblazoned on the spine of one edition of the book, precipitating a rift between the writers. Was such a gesture Emersonian? Was Emerson wrong to censure such self-promotion? Was Whitman's use of Emerson an act of inheritance or misreading?

2. **Thoreau:** Compare Henry David Thoreau's *Walden* with "Self-Reliance." What are the similarities and what are the differences? How might you explain each?

In answering this question, the reader should first mark those passages in *Walden* that recall passages in "Self-Reliance." How are they similar, and why do you think this might be? Equally important is to find those parts where Thoreau discusses subjects that Emerson has covered in "Self-Reliance" where the two writers differ. For a proper understanding of the relationship between Henry David Thoreau and Emerson, the student should certainly consult biographies of each man. It will soon become clear that they were, at least for a time, very close. Was there imitation of or collaboration with Emerson in Thoreau's work? Which writer do you prefer and why?

As with Whitman, inevitable rifts surfaced between Emerson and Thoreau. Again, why? Is there evidence of this rift in the writings? Does Thoreau take Emerson at his word and, in turn, outshine the master? Were Thoreau's social eccentricity and his propensity for solitude the ultimate manifestation of Emerson's teachings or an experiment gone wrong? After Thoreau's death, Emerson wrote an essay on his friend that was both revealing and—to some readers—strangely cool. Read this essay and decide whether you agree.

Bibliography and Online Resources

Blair, Walter. *Native American Humor* (1800–1900). New York: American Book Company, 1937.

Blair, Walter, and Hamlin Hill. *America's Humor: From Poor Richard to Doonesbury.* New York: Oxford UP, 1978.

Cowley, Malcolm. "A Note on the Selections." *The Portable Emerson.* Ed. Carl Bode and Malcolm Cowley. New York: Penguin, 1981. xxxiii–xxxv.

Eaton, Clement, ed. *The Leaven of Democracy: The Growth of the Democratic Spirit in the Time of Jackson.* New York: George Braziller, 1963.

Emerson, Ralph Waldo. "Thoreau." *The Portable Emerson.* Ed. Carl Bode and Malcolm Cowlet. New York: Penguin, 1981. 573–593.

Kittredge, George Lyman. *The Old Farmer and His Almanack.* Williamstown, MA: Corner House, 1974.

Ladu, Arthur I. "Emerson: Whig or Democrat?" *New England Quarterly* 13.3 (September 1840): 419–441.

Miller, Perry. *The Raven and the Whale: Poe, Melville, and the New York Literary Scene.* Baltimore: Johns Hopkins UP, 1997.

Newfield, Christopher. *The Emerson Effect: Individualism and Submission in America.* Chicago: U of Chicago P, 1996.

Pattee, Fred Lewis. "Critical Studies in American Literature III: An Essay on Emerson's 'Self-Reliance.'" *Chautauquan* 30 (March 1900): 628–633.

Reynolds, David. *Beneath the American Renaissance: The Subversive Imagination in the Age of Melville.* Cambridge, MA: Harvard UP, 1988.

Rourke, Constance. *American Humor: A Study of the National Character.* Tallahassee: Florida State UP, n.d.

Sagendorph, Robb. *America and Her Almanacs: Wit, Wisdom and Weather 1639–1970.* Boston: Little, Brown, 1970.

Schirmeister, Pamela J. *Less Legible Meanings: Between Poetry and Philosophy in the Work of Emerson.* Stanford, CA: Stanford UP, 1999.

Smith, Harmon. *My Friend, My Friend: The Story of Thoreau's Relationship with Emerson.* Amherst: U of Massachusetts P, 1999.

Widmer, Edward L. *Young America: The Flowering of Democracy in New York City.* New York: Oxford UP, 1999.

"THE OVER-SOUL"

READING TO WRITE

IN "THE Over-Soul" Emerson expands on his previous major essays. His vision and his project remain the same, but they unfold and adapt and revise, revealing new applications and shifts of emphasis. The subject of "revelation," referred to earlier, becomes one of Emerson's main topics here. "The Over-Soul" also shows a certain emotional maturity not present in the Divinity School Address. Man's communication with his fellow man becomes a significant subject, moving away from the haughty solitude vaunted in earlier essays. The defiance of the Divinity School Address gives way to a greater passivity to a higher force as Emerson describes the action of not simply God, but the Over-Soul.

"The Over-Soul," like "Self-Reliance" and "Circles" (alongside which it first appeared), should strictly be considered as a chapter rather than as a stand-alone essay. While *Nature, The American Scholar,* and the Divinity School Address were originally each conceived and published as independent works, "The Over-Soul" first appeared in print as chapter 9 in the first series of *Essays,* published in March 1841. However loosely, Emerson nevertheless conceived *Essays* as a unit. Which essays precede "The Over-Soul" in the book and which follow it? Is there a design in the ordering? Is there a logical development between one essay and the next that is lost in isolating the essays? Does this arbitrary mutilation, done frequently by anthologists and editors of surveys, alter our reading of the text? Be aware of the position of the essay in its correct context, howsoever you may read it. Emerson's essays are frequently jumbled and out of place in anthologies, leaving readers unaware of his original order and design.

"The Over-Soul" follows from ideas initiated in the Divinity School Address: "The simplest person who in his integrity worships God, becomes God." In this essay Emerson explores this dynamic further—how the godhead is transferred to man; how the "laws of the soul" and their existence are revealed to man. Again, Jesus Christ and his separation from historical Christianity inform part of Emerson's reading. Christ, he writes, "never . . . uttered a syllable concerning the duration of the soul. It was left to his disciples." Emerson's further meditation on Christ in this essay inevitably acknowledges and addresses the controversy that followed the Divinity School Address. Emerson clarifies his views, modifies them. Is the essay an olive branch to the orthodoxy, though, or a further flouting of their beliefs? Is this essay less inflammatory in content than the Divinity School Address, or was it simply less dangerous because it occurred between the pages of a collection of essays?

Emerson as a writer gives us signposts suggesting how he wishes to be viewed: "The great poet makes us feel our own wealth, and then we think less of his compositions. His best communication to our mind is to teach us to despise all he has done." This is a literature at war with its own words, a recoiling from its very self. What tradition does Emerson recall here? Is this the contented meditative state of a disciple of Eastern philosophy, or is it redolent of the self-hating, self-purging Calvinists of his ancestry? What is the significance of Emerson's passionate separation of body from soul? "What we commonly call man . . . Him we do not respect, but the soul whose organ he is . . . would make our knees bend." (Remember, in the Divinity School Address, "The soul knows no persons.")

The following excerpt shows a development in Emerson's attitude to others, a tentative nod to friendship. Perhaps it arose from his celebration of man's capacity for containing God in the Divinity School Address.

> One mode of the divine teaching is the incarnation of the spirit in a form,—in forms, like my own. I live in society; with persons who answer to thoughts in my own mind, or express a certain obedience to the great instincts to which I live. I see its presence to them. I am certified of a common nature; and these other souls, these separated selves, draw me

as nothing else can. They stir in me the new emotions we call passion; of love, hatred, fear, admiration, pity; thence come conversation, competition, persuasion, cities and war. Persons are supplementary to the primary teaching of the soul. In youth we are mad for persons. Childhood and youth see all the world in them. But the larger experience of man discovers the identical nature appearing through them all. Persons themselves acquaint us with the impersonal. In all conversation between two persons tacit reference is made, as to a third party, to a common nature. That third party or common nature is not social; it is impersonal; is God.

Emerson here turns his attention to the social self. While his earlier essays still smack of a somewhat pedantic solipsism, the idealism of a recluse, in "The Over-Soul" Emerson responds to his fellow man. In comparison to previous texts, he is positively "hail fellow well met"; he considers communication and friendship and recognition in its deepest sense—the communion between souls. A major break from his previous aloofness can be detected in a single dash: "in a form,—in forms, like my own." Here Emerson seems to make a leap of faith into committed company. No longer is the spirit in a single form, but in "forms," and Emerson humbles himself further by acknowledging that there are indeed other "forms, like my own." This seems to be the point at which Emerson acknowledges the possibility of sentient sharing of the Over-Soul.

There is almost a confessional tone when he states, "I live in society." By 1840 Emerson had established a circle of like-minded people. There is, nevertheless, a certain sadness to Emerson's surrendering of his soul's solitude. His language suggests again the Fall of Man and banishment from Eden, when he lists those factors good and bad that he has allowed in by acknowledging the existence of other sentient souls—"love, hatred, fear, admiration, pity"—leading inexorably to "conversation, competition, persuasion, cities and war." Emerson dramatizes solitude and solipsism as a prelapsarian state ruined by society.

The same writer who, in *Nature*, doubted whether the world as we see it is real, now concedes that "persons are supplementary to the primary teaching of the soul." How is this consistent with "Self-Reliance"? Another question that should be asked is whether Emerson's early philosophy is constructed on shyness or antisocial impulses, and his developing philosophy results from a softening of his attitude? The passage ends on an affirmation. While conversation leads inexorably to cities and war, it is also the means by which we summon that third party: God. The 20th-century French existentialist philosopher Jean-Paul Sartre said that "hell is other people." For Emerson, it was different. Through other people, we find God.

TOPICS AND STRATEGIES

The following section suggests several possible topics for essays on "The Over-Soul." They can and should be used as starting points for your own, independent exploration of the essay.

Themes

Theme and subject are one in this essay: Emerson discourses on souls and Over-Souls. Unlike some more dry philosophical inquiries, Emerson never doubts the existence of a soul nor its connection to God. He simply wishes to testify to the divine connection. In this sense, his is a work of visionary revelation. As in previous works, his subject is a seesawing mixture of man's abject lowness and his rare potential for holiness. "Our faith comes in moments; our vice is habitual." Faith and vice, the sacred and the profane, are the two nodes between which Emerson flits.

Sample Topics:
1. **The Over-Soul:** What is the Over-Soul?

   While Emerson reveals in the third paragraph what he takes the Over-Soul to be, as is customary he refines and augments his concept for the duration of the essay. Consider his statements on it at all points of the essay. How is the Over-Soul linked with the soul of every individual? Look at the imagery Emerson uses to express this attachment. When you have defined the concept, try to recall where you might have seen a similar idea used in Emerson's earlier works. Look at the language used—"Supreme critic," "Omniscience," "The universal mind," "The great soul," "divine unity." The concept, without necessarily being named, exists in his earlier works. How does the Over-Soul fit into Emerson's developing theory?

For instance, when Emerson writes of the soul as fragmented and seeking unity ("a spotted life of shreds and patches") he recalls the "old fable" of *The American Scholar.* What has he added to his conception of the "Over-Soul" since that earlier essay? Or how does the obeisance to an outside force tally with ideas of "Self-Reliance"? And if by "Over-Soul" Emerson means the Judeo-Christian God, why has he substituted a name of his own making?

2. **Friendship and communication—man's relations to man:** Is Emerson more humanized in "The Over-Soul" than in his earlier essays? How have his relations to "persons" developed?

This essay calls for the reader to note a change in tone and emphasis, specifically changes in Emerson's attitude to friendship and the possibilities of communication with other sentient "persons." Does "The Over-Soul" mark a move away from the solipsistic "idealism," in which Emerson is solely sure of himself, in isolation? Is friendship compatible with self-reliance? Compare Emerson's ideas about his fellow man in "The Over-Soul" with his philosophy as set out in *Nature* and "Self-Reliance." For example, in "The Over-Soul" Emerson writes that "more and more the surges of everlasting nature enter into me, and I become public and human in my regards and actions." What does it mean to "become public and human"? How does this change Emerson's philosophy? Does this compromise Emerson's idealist beliefs? Did Emerson become more politically motivated? How does friendship place us closer to self-knowledge? Why, then, does Emerson rail elsewhere against the "servile tone of conversation in the world" and "the mutual flattery" between authors?

You might look to Emerson's personal history to understand this change. What changes in Emerson's life, in the years

between *Nature* and "The Over-Soul," that might prompt him
to become more social? His biography shows an increase in
his social activities: the development of important friendships
that lasted his entire life and an intensification in the activities
of his intellectual circle. Look at his friendships with Margaret Fuller, Henry David Thoreau, and Amos Bronson Alcott.
What about the meetings of the Transcendental Club, which
began around the time of the publication of *Nature* and continued through 1840? Emerson also helped found and edit the
Dial magazine around this time (July 1840–April 1844). Do
you think such extratextual (meaning, occurring outside the
text discussed) collaborations find significant reflection in the
philosophy espoused in "The Over-Soul"? Locate other texts
that discuss friendship, such as "Friendship" and "Love," which
both appear in the text of the first series of *Essays,* before "The
Over-Soul."

3. **Time:** Discuss themes of time and infinity in "The Over-Soul."

Emerson positions man between sacred and profane, tending
toward the latter. How does time fit into this dynamic? Emerson views time as a construct of the senses, which he opposes
with the mind and the soul. His wish to escape history and
time was already established in *Nature,* which Emerson began
by lamenting, "Our age is retrospective." Examine Emerson's
pronouncements on time and evaluate them. For instance, if
time is a fallacy, what does it mean for Emerson to pronounce
elsewhere, "there is no profane history . . . all history is sacred
. . . the universe is represented in an atom, in a moment of
time." Emerson says that to view the "walls of time and space"
with "levity" is seen as a sign of insanity. What is there, if
there is not time or space? He writes of "another youth and
age than that which is measured from the year of our natural birth" (paragraph seven). What does this mean? Emerson
suggests that certain things transcend time, such as "a volume of Plato or Shakespeare." How do literature and poetry fit
into his alternative to time, then? (You might recall a previous

dissertation on literature and time in *The American Scholar*.) As well as considering the rejection of time from Emerson's own cosmology, the student might take a broader view of Emerson's society. What about his time and place might Emerson want to escape?

History and Context

Emerson begins this essay bemoaning an "uneasiness" and "discontent" in "us." On April 15, 1840, he had been working on the essay for two weeks. What, in 1840, might account for a national anxiety such as Emerson describes? For one thing, the antebellum American reform movement was at its height in the 1840s. This was social ferment at its most vigorous—brimming, almost hysterical, with ideas of a new age and society. Emerson's mysticism sits well in this context. Theories were abounding, such as Fourierism (the social theories of Charles Fourier, imported from France and extolled by the future newspaper magnate Horace Greeley) and other forms of communitarianism. Along with these wilder ideas appeared a downside: Confidence men, hucksters, hoaxes, table rappers, cult leaders, and sundry pseudoscience flim-flammers would exploit the reform movement and its excesses to their own advantage (sometimes monetary, sometimes sexual, often both). Emerson, even in his visionary ecstasy, aims bolts at these false prophets in "The Over-Soul" (in 1857, he would grumble in his journal against "this mummery of rapping & pseudo spiritualism"). With a sense of a golden age to come, then, appears a sense of a land needing reformation.

Second, in that hysteria were many presentiments of Armageddon. An apocalyptic tone is struck in Emerson's earlier essays also (*Nature, The American Scholar*). Hopes of a new age, then, are accompanied by presentiments of the necessary destruction of the old age. This frequent near-hysterical pitch of reform discourse can be traced to an earlier movement, rising in the 1820s, of religious revivalism—what was known as the Second Great Awakening. The original Great Awakening occurred in New England, peaking in the 1740s. Calvinism was dwindling and dry, reasoned intellectual Enlightenment values from Europe were penetrating the region and its thinkers (those Harvard-educated ministers, but also the likes of Benjamin Franklin). This Protestant movement arose then as a popular reaction. Certain preachers offered a more emotional, "enthusiastic," and zealous worship to the increasingly sedate, cerebral, and elite worship prescribed by their ministers. Such preachers enjoyed extensive lay support, although they were viewed as rowdy and controversial by the rationalist, orderly religious establishment. The Second Great Awakening, then, reiterated those values, and it is to such a tradition that Emerson refers when he vaunts "enthusiasm" in "The Over-Soul." Does this tradition—one marked often by hullabaloo, spectacle, and excess—seem consistent with the Emerson we have come to know? If not, what possibly precipitated such a transformation? And what does it mean for Emerson to include "the *revival* of the Calvinistic churches" among his examples of religious enthusiasm? Is Emerson praising Calvinism over the newer, more moderate Unitarianism?

Sample Topics:

1. **Enthusiasm:** What does Emerson mean by *enthusiasm*? Does he support it?

   In *Nature,* Emerson praises "the miracles of enthusiasm." In "The Over-Soul" he remarks that "a certain enthusiasm attends the individual's consciousness of that divine presence." What is enthusiasm? How closely does it, in its historical incidences, resemble Emerson's own thinking? The tradition of enthusiasm in New England Christianity is a long and contentious one. To answer this question, the student should research the history of the Great Awakening and its 19th-century sequel, and those tenets espoused by their proponents. What conflicts might this research expose in Emerson's thought? For example, siding with enthusiasm is to oppose the rationalist, Enlightenment view that rose to prevail throughout much of the 18th and 19th centuries. Is Emerson's philosophy anti-Enlightenment? One of the watchwords of the Enlightenment was *rationalism.* Is Emerson consciously favoring an irrational philosophy? He equates enthusiasm with that "certain tendency to insanity."

The student should examine Emerson's use of the word *reason*; is Emerson's reason compatible with the Enlightenment ideal of reason? Look at some of the writings of the American Enlightenment (the classic is, of course, Benjamin Franklin's *Autobiography*, but the writings of Thomas Jefferson were equally informed by the Enlightenment). Compare the Enlightenment texts and the "Over-Soul." Do you notice more similarities or disparities? List them and weigh them. Process your findings. It will also be helpful, of course, to look at texts of "enthusiasm." You might look to anthologies such as the one edited by Alan Heimert and Perry Miller (1966; see bibliography). What literary qualities characterize writings and sermons of the Great Awakening? Again, how do they compare with Emerson's text?

2. **Low curiosity and pseudoscience:** What does Emerson mean by "the popular notion of revelation"? Why does he oppose it?

In the 18th paragraph, Emerson rails against "the telling of fortunes" and those seeking the "answers to sensual questions"—"questions we lust to ask about the future." These he calls "low curiosity," charging that such inquiries are a "confession of sin." To answer these questions, the student needs to locate Emerson within a larger historical scene. What is Emerson referring to in these vehement, telling phrases, and why is he opposed to one form of revelation when he praises another so forcefully? Fortune telling and sensual questions about the future suggest the many pseudosciences that proliferated in Emerson's America. Pseudosciences are those theories not proved to be scientific but carrying the superficial appearance of science. Pseudoscience played on the same buoyant mood of enthusiasm and boundless hope that more noble reformers strived in their sermons and tracts.

Consulting historical texts shows also that William Miller, a self-appointed prophet who predicted the second coming of Christ in 1843, was at the height of his fame in 1840, when Emerson was writing his essay. Miller was a hugely successful lecturer, and his books went through several editions. Is it possible Miller was Emerson's target? Why would Emerson single him out for criticism? How does Miller fail Emerson's criteria for a visionary? Could Emerson's recoiling at such low spectacle betray a shock of self-recognition? Other useful comparisons may be found in American literature. In his novel *The Blithedale Romance* (1852), which loosely reimagines the events at the Brook Farm reformist community in 1841, Nathaniel Hawthorne includes a character who is enticed into giving performances at the local lyceum as "the Veiled Lady" and who predicts the future for a paying crowd. Could Hawthorne be ironically responding to Emerson's line "A veil shuts down on the facts of to-morrow"? Within seven years, Emerson's enemies would have multiplied. By 1848, a whole industry of spiritualism, or "table rapping" (staged communication, ostensibly with the spirits of the dead), would engulf the region, and several of the reform communities would be ruined by their gullible endorsement of the hoax. Is Emerson foreseeing this hysteria?

Philosophy and Ideas

The origin of Emerson's philosophical influence in "The Over-Soul"—if he has any—has proved difficult to determine. Some readers have recognized Eastern philosophy in it and—pricked by Emerson's later celebration of that tradition—assumed that he was reading the Bhagavad Gita, in some form, by 1840. However, this proves difficult to confirm. Other critics maintain that Emerson's ideas and terminology are his own, or drawn from Plato and the Neo-Platonists (those philosophers who succeeded and were influenced by Plato; the founder and principal was Plotinus). As well as possibly establishing Eastern philosophy on American soil—thereby initiating a new experiment that would continue as a tradition through the writings of Thoreau, Whitman, and on through the 20th century in the works of writers from Gary Snyder to J. D. Salinger—Emerson also foregrounds another source for creativity previously neglected in American literature: insanity. Emerson explores ideas of insanity and the now well-established link between madness and revelation, lunacy and creativity. In his visionary use of these wild and outsider sources and in his putative gestures toward a theory of the unconscious, Emerson is ultramodern in "The Over-Soul."

Sample Topics:

1. **Eastern philosophy and "The Over-Soul"**: Does "The Over-Soul" evidence the influence of Indian philosophy?

This question addresses a belief among some Emerson scholars that "The Over-Soul" shows the earliest evidence of Emerson's reading of Indian literature, particularly the ancient spiritual guide the Bhagavad Gita. Other scholars argue that Emerson did not discover Eastern philosophy until after the writing of "The Over-Soul." In one regard, this sort of question requires you to research the publication history of the chapter (by searching Emerson's journals and correspondence). Questions of influence can also be answered by studying these same documents. When does Emerson begin to write about Indian literature, even privately? Second, it might be helpful to look into the relevant Indian texts—principally the Bhagavad Gita—and to mark and cite those passages that seem to mirror Emerson's philosophy.

A further comparison that might benefit your reading of the essay would be with one of Emerson's later, consciously Eastern texts. Such works include the poem "Brahma" or the poem "The World-Soul." For example, Emerson's assertion in "The Over-Soul" that "the question and the answer are one" seems, with its blithe reconciliation of opposites, to lead logically to the well-known second verse of "Brahma":

> Far or forgot to me is near;
>   Shadow and sunlight are the same;
> The vanished gods to me appear;
>   And one to me are shame and fame.

What might explain any similarities between the earlier text and the later, Eastern-oriented works?

2. **Revelation and insanity:** Discuss the relation between insanity and revelation in "The Over-Soul."

Emerson first foregrounds perceptions of insanity in this essay when he discourses on the nonexistence of time and space. Are these concepts integral to a sane view of the world? Or are they arbitrary constructs with no reality? Is Emerson suggesting to the reader that he might be, by some standards, insane? If so, what are those standards? Such a question should naturally lead the student to questioning what we mean by "sanity." What does it mean for Emerson to identify himself with the insane? Is Emerson's identification another method of "unsettling" the reader and destabilizing a pat reading of the text? (See also "Self-Reliance," "Circles.") Research may be done into Emerson's own life for clues. How does insanity—or equivocations about mental normalcy—touch his biography? A younger brother, Robert Bulkely, was (in Emerson's words) "perfectly deranged" and possessed (in the words of one biographer) "a child's mind in a man's body." Another brother, Edward, lost his sanity for a time. Emerson was close to the poet Jones Very, who was almost the model of the half-lunatic visionary poet. Emerson edited a book of Very's verse. One might equally discern outward signs of mental instability in the extreme acts of figures like Thoreau and Emerson's aunt Mary Moody Emerson. By a perusal of biographical texts, get a sense of Emerson's own immediate milieu. See Emerson's meditations on the subject in his *Journals*, for instance, April 14, 1838: "Sanity is very rare: every man almost & every woman has a dash of madness." Is his view a universal one, though, or one very much governed by his position in the Emerson family and circle? Does he speak for man or for the Emersons? This question may also be viewed from a larger cultural—even political—context. In an age of conservatism, is Emerson speaking for the ultimate outsiders in society? In a declaration that kick-starts an American tradition that lasts to this day, the position of the romantic outsider is celebrated: "The great distinction

. . . between men of the world who are reckoned accomplished talkers, and here and there a fervent mystic, prophesying half-insane under the infinitude of his own thought." Is sanity even important if one would be self-reliant?

Form and Genre

"The Over-Soul" is an essay occurring within a book. Unlike some of Emerson's previous texts, which were delivered as orations and then published as pamphlets, it was originally published within a collection. Is it best considered, then, as a part of a whole (like a chapter in a novel) or an entity unto itself (like a short story)? Is it important to consider the context of texts, or does text remain identical irrespective of its form? A full awareness of a text's print history—even down to print runs and the color of the jacket cloth—benefits the student's knowledge of the text itself.

Regarding the content of the text, Emerson's essay also leads the reader into realms that might be called psychological. In discussing the workings of the mind, as well as in his significant use of water imagery, Emerson anticipates theories of psychology, such as the one developed later by the philosopher William James. It was in James's 1892 book, *Psychology: Briefer Course,* that the term *stream of consciousness* was first used. In Emerson, 50 years earlier, however, we find thought described as "a flowing river" and an "ethereal water" of which the thinker is only a "surprised spectator." James was always open about his philosophical debt to Emerson in the development of his theory of pragmatism. Is it possible that James's psychological theories—and his use of a similarly aqueous term to describe thought—were alike indebted in part to Emerson, who remarks here that "man is a stream whose source is hidden"?

Sample Topics:

1. **Psychology:** How does "The Over-Soul" anticipate 20th-century psychology?

   Psychology is the study of the way the mind works (and fails to work), especially the way the unconscious mind works (and fails). In "The Over-Soul" the mind, or the self, or that self's soul is discussed as an object unresolved and unknown ("We are wiser than we know"; "We know better than we do"). Emerson is groping toward a "natural history of man" that has "never been written," one that will search "the chambers and magazines of the soul." He writes of the dreaming mind and of the soul as unknowable to the self and seeks its revelation. How do these ideas presage those in later psychology? "Revelation is the disclosure of the soul," Emerson says. Can "revelation" be read as psychoanalysis?

For instance, Emerson remarks how "thoughts come into our minds by avenues which we never left open, and thoughts go out of our minds through avenues which we never voluntarily opened." The idea of the mind as removed from itself occurs repeatedly in the essay: "Character teaches over our head"; "somewhat higher in each of us overlooks this by-play, and Jove nods to Jove from behind each of us." What does this imagery mean? Look at the malaise described by Emerson; again, does it find later echoes in 20th-century anxieties? For instance: how does Emerson's complaint "We live in succession, in division, in parts, in particles" resemble later psychological complaints? The most obvious writer to explore the unconscious is, of course, the German psychoanalyst Sigmund Freud. What does Freud say about dreams? What other forms of subconscious thought and communication does Freud discuss, and can you identify echoes of Emerson in "The Over-Soul"? The reader might also look at associates of Freud, such as the Swiss Carl Jung. What in Jungian psychology sounds Emersonian? How, for instance, does Jung's idea of the collective unconscious tally with Emerson's Over-Soul?

Earlier theories of the mind were developed by a writer somewhat closer to Emerson within the American literary tradition: William James, the brother of the novelist Henry James. William James was a philosopher, espousing a theory of "pragmatism" that was clearly indebted to Emerson. He also wrote studies of how the mind works, including *The Principles of Psychology* (1890) and *The Varieties of Religious Experience* (1902). Explore the findings and writings of these psychologists and psychoanalysts and identify that which has antecedents in "The Over-Soul."

2. **Essay or chapter:** Is "The Over-Soul" best considered as a chapter of a larger work or as an isolated essay?

This question asks the reader about the context of the essay as much as either its content or its style. How is it best read and in what context? This question might seem a strange one, but it pertains very directly to authorial intent. To answer this question, the reader must become fully aware of the original form in which "The Over-Soul" appeared. What were the contents of the first series of *Essays*? Does "The Over-Soul" rely on ideas established in previous essays in the collection? Can the essay sit isolated—self-reliant—away from the other essays and still be the same? Is it fair to break up a book of essays and extract chapters willy-nilly? Would we do the same with a novel? Must the first series of *Essays* be read sequentially, as any other work would be, or are essay collections traditionally viewed differently from other forms?

Look at the other essays in the first series. For instance, essay 2 is "Self-Reliance." Does "The Over-Soul" complete, confirm, continue, compound, or trump this essay? Is there a gradual development of a philosophy over the course of the book? Are we missing this inner logic by reading essays in anthologies?

Language, Symbols, and Imagery

"The Over-Soul" reads more smoothly than other essays, reflecting the watery language and imagery that buoy it. It is variously afloat and gushing. Is it possible that Emerson structured the essay after the flow of water? Note as you read the essay all instances of water imagery so that you can return to them to choose the best examples for quotation. Within the essay Emerson articulates—or tries to articulate—a theory of revelation, inspiration, and communication. Does he fail to do so? As the essay is about the occasional, rarefied moments of "faith" (paragraph one) amid a life of habitual vice, are these moments in fact necessarily incommunicable?

Sample Topics:

1. **Water:** Discuss water imagery in "The Over-Soul."

The most striking imagery in "The Over-Soul" appears in the recurring references to water. Emerson articulates his philosophy primarily through the metaphor of water. How is this done? What is the advantage of this metaphor—is it convenient, or does it carry resonances beyond mere convenience? This question should not necessitate a monolithic answer; Emerson's use of imagery is often kaleidoscopic, ever evolving. Images work on a number of levels. They can be literal, they can be symbolic, or they can point to a literary allusion. Think, for example, of the use of water in myth and religion. In the biblical book of Genesis, to give one example, in the empty void before the world is created, the spirit of God is described moving "upon the face of the waters." A flood myth is one of the stories that recur in many religions. Water, then, has a mythical significance. How does Emerson use this? Water is also doubled by Emerson as blood. What potential effect is produced by this juxtaposition?

Second, the student might expound on how water reflects Emerson's interest in nature. However, how does water as a representative of nature differ from earlier uses of natural scenes and phenomena in Emerson's work? For instance, how did the use of the snowstorm in the Divinity School Address serve a different purpose from Emerson's use of water in the present text? A snowstorm, it can be argued, is more violent and aggressive; water flowing through its many tributaries into its many outlets is passive. How is Emerson's tone modified by his imagery?

2. **The crisis of language:** "Ineffable is the union of man and God in every act of the soul." Does Emerson's essay itself fail to communicate?

The ineffable is that which cannot be said or articulated. This is a famous paradox in literature: how to express that which is beyond words. Is Emerson's message conveyed across the watery divide, or does it plummet, and does he fail to communicate his intended point? To decide, find those examples in the text where Emerson writes self-consciously about the shortcomings of language. For example, in paragraph 18 Emerson rejects those who cheapen revelation for the purpose of tawdry prophecy. "An answer in words is delusive," he writes; "it is really no answer to the questions you ask." Look for language about language; later in the same paragraph he blasts the same targets: "Never a moment did that sublime spirit speak in their *patois.*"

We must return again and again to Emerson's differentiation between understanding and reason. What does Emerson say about language in his essay *Nature*? If language is a failure, why does Emerson persist in writing? For further illumination, look also to his allied views on literature elsewhere in this essay: "Converse with a mind that is grandly simple and literature looks like word-catching." Is Emerson being coy or voicing a paradox? In paragraph 22, Emerson differentiates between "teachers sacred or literary"—setting at one pole the poet George Herbert, at the other the poet Alexander Pope. How does Emerson oppose them? Compare their poetry yourself. Do you agree with this opposition?

Compare and Contrast

Given its position within a purposely composed collection of essays, the first comparison students should make is to view "The Over-Soul" within the first collection of *Essays.* The second essay is "Self-Reliance," the ninth "The Over-Soul." Do these two essays have a common thread to them, or are they bound together arbitrarily? One of Emerson's biographers sees no interrelationship between the essays within the collection, except inasmuch as passages from one essay could be cut and pasted into another without any discernible damage to the whole. Do you agree?

In addition, Emerson as usual offers enough citations and allusions for you to follow each reference, hunting down the source and making a textual comparison. These may well turn up precedents. One example is the opening quotation by Henry More. In the debate as to whether Emerson's sources were Eastern or Platonic, the quotation from More certainly points to the latter. However, the later addition of the Emersonian verse on the cuckoo seems to flout the first quote and recontextualize the essay in its entirety. Does the second epigraph seem to damn and abandon the essay as it was originally conceived?

Sample Topics:

1. **Epigraphs:** How do the epigraphs to "The Over-Soul" anticipate the essay that follows?

This question requires you to make a close reading of the opening verses. Read and analyze the poems word by word. Since these verses frame the essay, they color our reading of it. How though? In the case of the Henry More excerpt, further inquiry might be made into the large poem from which it is drawn, "Psychozoia, or, the life of the Soul," the first part of a collection called *Psychodia Platonica, or a Song of the Soul* (1642). Why does Emerson refer us to this poem? Does it contain materials relevant to the present inquiry? Such citations always have purpose; and this purpose can be investigated by reading further portions of the More poem. Why did Emerson choose the passage he did? The student might investigate what intellectual affinities Emerson shares with More.

The second poem, Emerson's own, was added for the 1847 edition of the first series of *Essays*. Why was this verse added? What does it contribute to the essay beneath it? Is it important, for instance, that Emerson added it at a later date? Does its presence alter your reading of the essay? Again, make a close reading of the poem. Look at the opening lines:

Space is ample, east and west,
But two cannot go abreast,
Cannot travel in it two . . .

Is this statement an affirmation or does it suggest something darker—failure? Look at the poem's subject—the cuckoo. How is the cuckoo perceived in folklore? Is it emblematic of the poem? Does this clash in tone or subject with the essay? Having already noted the fundamental themes, images, and arguments of "The Over-Soul," consider how this poem (re)addresses them. Always consider the text's place in history also. What occurred in America's history at the time of this addition to the text? America was midway through the Mexican War (1846–48). What were Emerson's feelings on the Mexican War and on American expansion in general? Might these later disappointments change his views of the Over-Soul and contribute to his darker portrait of the selfish cuckoo?

2. **Comparison with "Self-Reliance":** Compare "The Over-Soul" with "Self-Reliance."

The essays "Self-Reliance" and "The Over-Soul" appear together in the same collection of essays. How does the structure of this text—the order in which constituent essays are arranged—influence our perception of Emerson's overriding message? Does each essay necessarily have to be consistent with each of the other essays in the collection, or does each essay contain its own truths, incompatible with those others? If this is true, how can one take any essay seriously? This question requires the student to compare representations of the self in "Self-Reliance" and in "The Over-Soul." Find those passages in which Emerson especially addresses the subject of selfhood. For instance: "The weakness of the will begins when the individual would be something of himself." Measure this statement against Emerson's claim in "Self-Reliance": "To believe your own thought, to believe what is true for you in your private heart is true for all men, that is genius." Or consider the Over-Soul concept in the light of the epigraph to "Self-Reliance": "Do not seek yourself outside yourself." Does "The Over-Soul" revise the autonomy lauded in the earlier essay? If so, which view are we to take as Emerson's abiding, final one in *Essays*? Is there any such view?

Bibliography and Online Resources

Buell, Lawrence. "Reading Emerson for the Structures: The Coherence of the Essays." *Critical Essays on Ralph Waldo Emerson.* Ed. Robert E. Burkholder and Joel Myerson. Boston: G. K. Hall, 1983. 399–413.

Detweiler, Robert. "The Over-Rated 'Over-Soul.'" *American Literature* 36.1 (March 1964): 65–68.

Fromm, Harold. "Overcoming the Oversoul: Emerson's Evolutionary Existentialism." *Hudson Review* 57.1 (Spring 2004): 71–95.

Hankins, Barry. *The Second Great Awakening and the Transcendentalists.* Westport, CT: Greenwood Press, 2004.

Heimert, Alan. *Religion and the American Mind: From the Great Awakening to the Revolution.* Cambridge, MA: Harvard UP, 1966.

Heimert, Alan, and Perry Miller, eds. *The Great Awakening.* Indianapolis: Bobbs-Merrill, 1967.

Landsman, Ned C. *From Colonials to Provincials: American Thought and Culture, 1860–1760.* Ithaca, NY: Cornell UP, 1997.

Leidecker, Kurt F. "Emerson and East-West Synthesis." *Philosophy East and West* 1.2 (July 1951): 40–50.

Myerson, Joel. "A Calendar of Transcendental Club Meetings." *American Literature* 44.2 (May 1972): 197–207.

Pearsall, Ronald. *The Table-Rappers.* London: Michael Joseph, 1972.

Tyler, Alice Felt. *Freedom's Ferment: Phases of American Social History from the Colonial Period to the Outbreak of the Civil War.* New York: Harper & Row, 1962.

Walters, Ronald G. *American Reformers 1815–1860.* Revised ed. New York: Hill & Wang, 1997.

"CIRCLES"

READING TO WRITE

"C IRCLES," WHICH has been termed a "transitional essay" between two phases of Emerson's thinking, is strangely retrospective, which is particularly strange since Emerson condemns retrospection often. Yet here Emerson seems to be looking back on his own achievements of the last four years and predicting how he will be rendered obsolete. He advises his reader to ready himself for "the intrepid conviction that his laws, his relations to society, his Christianity, his world, may at any time be superseded and decease." "Self-doubt" might be an alternate title for this essay. The writer who celebrated youth in "Self-Reliance" speaks more from the side of age here: "The new statement is always hated by the old." Is he still smarting from the Divinity School Address fallout? Or is Emerson identifying, self-effacingly, with the old, assimilated and "generalized" by a newer philosophy. "Every man supposes himself not to be fully understood," Emerson remarks, prefacing 170 years of being misunderstood and not understood. There are intimations of personal failure too: "The last chamber . . . he must feel was never opened."

In another regard, "Circles" seems to be a summary of the essays that precede it in the first series of *Essays* ("Circles" is essay 10, immediately following "The Over-Soul"). Emerson revisits in brief those theses propounded in previous essays. It is almost a compendium—the edited highlights, remixed. Note especially, then, where ideas recur from earlier essays. There are intertextual cameos that seem to nod to earlier essays, recapping or revising "Compensation," "Friendship," "The Over-Soul," "Self-Reliance," the Divinity School Address, *Nature,* and *The American Scholar.* Ideas of nature and friendship are returned to in a more ruthless light. Emerson seems, by this change of tenor, to point to the later, darker essays of the second series of *Essays* ("Experience," "Fate").

The following excerpt from "Circles" is especially noteworthy for its narrative tone:

> And thus, O circular philosopher, I hear some reader exclaim, you have arrived at a fine Pyrrhonism, at an equivalence and indifferency of all actions, and would fain teach us that *if we are true,* forsooth, our crimes may be lively stones out of which we shall construct the temple of the true God!
>
> I am not careful to justify myself. I own I am gladdened by seeing the predominance of the saccharine principle throughout vegetable nature, and not less by beholding in morals that unrestrained inundation of the principle of good into every chink and hole that selfishness has left open, yea, into selfishness and sin itself; so that no evil is pure, nor hell itself without its extreme satisfactions. But lest I should mislead any when I have my own head and obey my whims, let me remind the reader that I am only an experimenter. Do not set the least value on what I do, or the least discredit on what I do not, as if I pretended to settle any thing as true or false. I unsettle all things. No facts are to me sacred; none are profane; I simply experiment, an endless seeker, with no Past at my back.

Emerson begins this refrain with a garrulous, almost comic address to the reader. Such an address recalls 18th-century British fiction, such as Laurence Sterne's *Tristram Shandy* or Henry Fielding's *Tom Jones* and could be read as intrusive by more genteel readers. It is certainly not a characteristic style of Emerson's, to address the reader so roundly; obscurity and lack of authorial leading are more his tendency. The incongruity of such a tenor in Emerson makes us wonder whether there is some irony in his present discourse. For this reason some critics have singled out the "speaker" of "Circles" and distinguished him (the "circular philosopher") pointedly from the "implied author" ("Ralph Waldo Emerson")—again, a flourish more usually used in comic fiction. Sensitivity to shifts in narrative tone is an important ability in any sophisticated interpretation of texts, as is the recognition that all literature, to some extent, lies. That we come to expect snow-white, incorruptible earnestness from Emerson only exposes our own failing as readers. In following a fictional tradition, of course, Emerson awakes us to possibilities of his employment of an "unreliable narrator." Conversely, other critics have found this to be Emerson unmasked—the man without his trappings, communicating directly. You should make your own intelligent judgment.

Pyrrhonyism (named after Pyrrho, a Greek philosopher of the third and fourth centuries B.C.E.) is a school of skeptical thought in which it is said nothing can be determined conclusively. Since nothing can be seen in its true nature, all judgment must be suspended and no firm facts stated. Is Emerson guilty of such a claim? Is he teasing the reader by suggesting such a model? The effect is unsettling—as is, as Emerson says later, his purpose: "I unsettle all things." Such a sinister boast almost conforms to the gothic tradition. Emerson's language here and elsewhere resembles that of a gothic novel. Towers collapse—worlds topple—he describes ruination and loss in bitter tones: "Beware when the great God lets loose a thinker on this planet," he rumbles elsewhere, sounding like a mislaid Edgar Allan Poe narrator. "Then all things are at risk. It is as when a conflagration has broken out in a great city, and no man knows what is safe, or where it will end." Is he any more (or less) serious here than Poe?

Emerson draws the reader back to analogies from nature when he compares the "saccharine principle throughout vegetable nature"— osmosis, in other words—with the movement of good throughout moral nature: how goodness finds its way into free pockets in the matter of selfishness and sin and even in hell itself. To prevent readers from becoming mollified by this qualification, Emerson (or the "circular philosopher") then assures them: "Do not set the least value on what I do, or the least discredit on what I do not, as if I pretended to settle any thing as true or false." Whim, that pivotal conceit to "Self-Reliance," is again invoked. Just as in that essay Emerson's gist was "damn consistency!" in "Circles" alike he pulls away any firm basis for the reader. Are we henceforward to believe anything the speaker says, or is it all ironic? Furthermore, does this experimenter's clause cover only this essay, or all of Emerson's work preceding it, and any to follow, perpetually? And is this "unsettling" liberating, or does it only leave us confounded?

TOPICS AND STRATEGIES

The following section suggests several possible topics for essays on "Circles." They can and should be used as starting points for your own, independent exploration of the essay.

Themes

Some readers of "Circles" see uncertainty and disillusionment in the essay, while others mark a sophisticated shift but do not view this as necessarily negating. "Circles" marks the transition between the first series of *Essays* (1841) and the second (1844). How do you read it? One way of gauging the modification of Emerson's thought is in his changing attitudes to certain perennials of his philosophical discourse. Most obvious are his perception and portrayal of nature. Are they in concord or discord with the earlier vision laid out in *Nature* four years earlier? A more recent subject of inquiry for Emerson is friendship. In "The Over-Soul" he viewed friendship hopefully, even ecstatically, as a site for religious experience. Does he maintain this position, or has the philosophy of his previous essays already been superseded, assimilated, generalized, and outdone, circled by a larger, more recent (negative) circle?

Sample Topics:

1. **Self-doubt:** To what extent is "Circles" a study in self-doubt?

   "Circles" is a divisive essay among critics. Some view it as ultimately affirming; others see it as negating and ringing in a new darker tone, one continued in essays like "Experience" and "Fate." Mark, then, the tenor of the essay. Does it recall previous essays—those essays that can confidently be identified as "affirming"? Ask yourself, in turn, which of Emerson's essays can be identified as affirming, and how is this affirmation articulated? Look at Emerson's rhetoric, his way of addressing the reader. Is he exhorting or scolding, lamenting or bragging? Does Emerson bemoan that he is not understood, that a "residuum" remains, "unknown, unanalyzable" (paragraph nine), or is this a celebration and a defiance? Look at the language and images.

What, for instance, is the meaning of the circular argument and the emphasis on flux? Are flux and regeneration necessarily either affirming or negating? When Emerson remarks, "I am God in nature; I am a weed by the wall," are these two statements compatible? Is Emerson mocking his earlier pronouncements, or is he reaffirming and refining them?

In plenty of his essays, Emerson fluctuates between dismay and ecstasy, optimism and skepticism, before he closes; how does "Circles" conclude? Is there a marked conclusion? Given the content of the essay, can there—ever—be a conclusion? Is Emerson fickle or does this changeability mark a readiness to reform? For other clues, look, for instance, at the motto to the essay, added for the edition of 1847. Does this qualify the tone of the essay and recast it? Emerson's mottoes can be mystifying, but they also provide a later commentary and index to the author's own reconsideration of the text.

2. **Nature:** How has Emerson's perception of nature changed since his 1836 study?

As a transition essay, "Circles" revisits and revises some of Emerson's earlier ideas as proposed in the essays. Central to Emerson's thought is nature. How is nature redefined in "Circles"? Obviously, look first to those statements directly about nature. For instance: "There are no fixtures in nature. The universe is fluid and volatile." Nature has become less assuring. "Nature abhors the old." Nature is a ruthless force. What is Emerson's composite depiction of nature now? Gather the disparate sentences together and construct an entire definition. Look also at Emerson's use of natural imagery, for example, the image of the farm (paragraph four). Compare this with Emerson's employment of farm imagery in *Nature*. Emerson also revisits the image of the eye to begin "Circles." Is this imagery consistent with his previous use of eye imagery? Is Emerson consciously responding to his own earlier work? Is he speaking to himself when he predicts that "the principle that seemed to explain nature will itself be included as one

example of a bolder generalization." Does this mark a concession that his earlier account was incomplete? Is he right?

3. **Friends and conversation:** How have Emerson's perceptions of
   friendship and conversation changed between "The Over-Soul"
   and "Circles"?

Having slowly and reluctantly let human intercourse into his
philosophy, Emerson reinvigorates the subject in "Circles."
Conversation is now "a game of circles" (paragraph 17). "Circles" immediately follows "The Over-Soul" in the first series
of *Essays.* Is there an intentional dialogue between these two
essays? Bearing in mind the argument of "Circles," does it
follow that each essay assimilates and supersedes its prede-
cessor within the book? Compare "Circles" with "The Over-
Soul." Find Emerson addressing the same issue in both essays
and compare each essay's—each Emerson's—findings. For
instance, in "Circles" Emerson writes that

> in conversation we pluck up the termini which bound the com-
> mon of silence on every side. The parties are not to be judged by
> the spirit they partake and even express under this Pentecost.

Compare this with "The Over-Soul" when, through inspired
conversation, the speakers summon a third party, God. The
same idea is considered further, differently—negatively?—here.
In "The Over-Soul," behind trivial conversation "Jove nods to
Jove from behind us." Now Emerson further reveals how, when
the speakers leave the group, "you shall find them stooping
under the old pack-saddles." He is left preferring silence.

In paragraph 11 Emerson discourses on friendship. "The
love of me accuses the other party," and "For every friend
whom he loses for truth, he gains a better." This time Emerson speaks of "limitations." What does he mean by limitation?
What in Emerson's biography might explain this disappointment? Look at the journals and the correspondence. Was this
"limitation" discovered in Thoreau, perhaps? In July 1840 he

was voicing disappointment with Thoreau's poetry in a letter to Margaret Fuller. Or was it Bronson Alcott, whose "Orphic Sayings," submitted for Emerson's new magazine the *Dial*, disappointed Emerson and when they were published—in 1840—were a public laughingstock. Counter to the celebration of friendship and intercourse is Emerson's espousing of philosophical "idealism" (first voiced in *Nature*), with its tendency toward solipsism. In "Circles" Emerson readdresses idealism. What are his findings this time? How might they relate to his evolved perception of human relations?

History and Context

Emerson was writing "Circles" on September 12, 1840, when he wrote to Elizabeth Hoar, "My chapter on 'Circles' begins to prosper and when it is October I shall write like a Latin Father." What does this mean? Whom does Emerson have in mind when he evokes the "Latin Father"? Is he intimating the fall of Rome? Images of destruction, towers fallen, empires forgotten, and cities burning punctuate "Circles." Why? While Emerson speaks figuratively, his images and presentiments are drawn from his surrounding world. What, historically, might have given him such presentiments? It is always useful to be aware, as closely as possible, when any essay was written, so that you can know precisely what the national and local events of the time were. Emerson's *Journals* provide some information as to when he was writing the different essays. One critic has suggested that the Whig "Log Cabin" presidential campaign for William Henry Harrison, which provided a background as Emerson wrote this essay, infiltrated his thinking fundamentally.

Another question arising from "Circles" is, Who, or what, prompted its writing? Emerson writes of being "generalized" by the next writer, being assimilated and superseded. Does he have a writer or thinker in mind? Equally, he later considers certain friends as failures, their limits reached. Who is meant here? Emerson's cryptic allusions can make a detective of the reader, trying to solve the puzzle. This is, of course, not strictly Emerson's point. Nevertheless, to situate the essay in its proper context, it is useful to give some thought to who might be meant and what events precipitated Emerson's change of heart. Most prominent perhaps, for the time when Emerson was writing "Circles," is the founding of the Brook Farm utopian community near Roxbury, Massachusetts. Although the founders were close friends of Emerson's and members of his Transcendental Club, Emerson did not join the community. He was seemingly content to visit the farm sporadically and leave at the end of the day. Was this perhaps a failure in Emerson's own eyes? Was he disappointing his own sense of political and philosophical commitment? Did he feel superseded by the denizens of Brook Farm? Does the sting of self-accusation inform the slightly savage tone of the essay?

Sample Topics:

1. **Modern anxiety:** What historical source might there be for Emerson's anxiety in "Circles"?

   In "Circles" there is a presiding air of uncertainty and doubt that is far from the boosterish tone of earlier essays such as *The American Scholar.* While this is due to a development in Emerson's philosophy, how might this change in philosophy have been influenced by outside—historical—events? Look for aspects of the essay that place it in its time. While *Nature* was so abstract it virtually ignored its concrete surroundings, is "Circles" the same? Think, for instance, of the following passage: "Then cometh the god, and converts the statues into fiery men, and by a flash of his eye burns up the veil which shrouded all things, and the meaning of the very furniture, of cup and saucer, of chair and clock and tester, is manifest." Emerson places the reader now among the trivial objects of life. Why does Emerson describe so many household objects? What does this suburban, domestic portrait suggest? Does Emerson's anxiety stem from industrial advancement, from the increasing tyranny of modern consumer goods in everyday life, from the growing emphasis on the middle-class family? Or can you locate his anxiety in other causes arising in his times?

2. **The log cabin campaign:** How might "Circles" be a response to Harrison's "Log Cabin" campaign?

The 1840 Whig candidate William Henry Harrison's campaign for the presidency (a position he duly won) was notable for the marked use of imagery and rhetoric previously used by his Democratic opponents. Most prominent in the campaign regalia and songs was the celebration of the "log cabin" and "hard cider," each of which smacked of classic Jacksonian iconography. As a further promotion for the campaign, a number of giant balls were rolled throughout the United States to draw attention to Harrison's policies. Emerson beheld one of these balls being rolled through Concord at the time when he was writing "Circles," and he notes it in his journal.

What, if anything, about the Harrison campaign resembles the content or argument of "Circles"? You might look, for instance, at the circular imagery of the ball itself. Do you believe this is a likely influence? (Note also the epigraph "Nature centers into balls.") More expansively, you might look at how the conspicuous changing of old values in the campaign might be reflected in the essay: the about-face of the Whigs and how they "generalized" Jacksonian ideas. Study histories of the campaign. What other iconography and rhetoric were abroad at this time that are reflected in the Emerson essay? Or does Emerson's essay exist outside this media hullabaloo, removed from history? (Is this perhaps why Emerson feels encroached upon by consumerism?) Look at Emerson's own politics. Was he sympathetic to the Whig or Democratic causes?

3. **Reform:** What is "the terror of reform"? How does "Circles" reflect Emerson's political position?

First, you should identify precisely where the quotation in the question occurs and what its full context is. From this, ascertain whether Emerson is speaking about reform as an abstract concept or as a specific political aspiration and movement of his time. How has Emerson used the word *reform* previously? Within the essay he uses the word several times. Find these and analyze them. You might further look at addresses such as "Man the Reformer," which Emerson delivered in Boston in January 1841—the same month in which he was editing the proofs of the first series of *Essays,* in which "Circles" was first published. Emerson gave another address in 1844 entitled "New England Reformers."

You might also look at some of the histories of the New England reform movement. What was transpiring as Emerson wrote "Circles"? Most prominent (for Emerson) was the founding of the Brook Farm community, which was composed of intellectuals and farmers trying to live in an ideal, "utopian" community, using philosophy drawn in no small part from Emerson. George Ripley, the community's founder, was a close Transcendental Club friend (also a cousin) of Emerson's. What was Emerson's attitude to Brook Farm? Was this what he meant by the "flying perfect"? If so, is this a derisive term? Look at his reflections in his journals and his correspondence (see, for instance, the telling letter to Thomas Carlyle of October 30, 1840). Might such a movement have been in Emerson's mind when he wrote of "the terror of reform"? Emerson never lived at Brook Farm, unlike his friends Ripley and Nathaniel Hawthorne. Is the terror his, and do his words address the communitarians at Brook Farm? What other reform movements were active at this time? Can Emerson's comments be taken as reflections on abolitionism, or antitemperance, for instance?

Philosophy and Ideas

As Emerson revisits certain themes of his earlier work in "Circles," so does he circle and consider again certain philosophical positions propounded in earlier studies. For instance, "Circles" returns to *Nature*'s earlier philosophical problem of "idealism." This mixture of retrospection and incessant self-renewal causes Emerson to look in turn at thought, and, perhaps to analyze his own thought. How does Emerson characterize his own philosophy within the essay? A further inquiry can be made into the darker aspects of Emerson's expanding philosophy. What is meant when Emerson, anticipating the reader, accuses himself of "Pyrrhonism"? Does he properly reject or parry the accusation?

Sample Topics:

1. **Thought and ideas:** "The key to every man is his thought." What is Emerson's "thought"—his "idea after which all his facts are classified"?

First, be clear about Emerson's language; what exactly does he mean here? For instance, *thought* can be one singular thought, or the process of thinking, or it could indicate the whole sum of an individual's thinking. What does the larger context of the quotation suggest? Emerson writes of a "helm," "the [singular] idea." This suggests, then, that Emerson is speaking of one characteristic idea to which any man can be reduced. In the next sentence, indeed, he writes that any man "can only be reformed by showing him a new idea which commands his own." First, you can consider whether you agree with this proposition. Challenge it on Emerson's own grounds. By Emerson's own philosophy, is this plausible? You might weigh this assertion by marshaling pertinent material from Emerson's own writings that seems to contradict such a monolithic thesis. Second, can Emerson be reduced to one single thought or idea? Presumably Emerson believed, when he wrote "Circles," that he could be so reduced. What, then, is Emerson's self-conscious "thought" within "Circles"? And if he cannot be reduced in this fashion, despite his thesis—why not?

2. **Pyrrhonism:** What is "Pyrrhonism"? Does Emerson take such a position in "Circles"?

Emerson voices the "reader" accusing him of Pyrrhonism. First, consider the context. Do you think Emerson is being ironic in this passage, with its exaggerated and uncharacteristic direct addressing of the reader? Second, research the terminology. Who was Pyrrho? A Greek philosopher of the fourth and third centuries B.C.E., he was the founder of the "skeptic" school of philosophy. Is Emerson, then, by his own "accusation" a skeptic? Research the philosophy; what are its tenets, and what are the best-known surviving works? Look at these and evaluate whether there is a resemblance between this philosophy and Emerson's. Does Emerson even deny the affinity? What is his response to his own question? Is it convincing?

Form and Genre

"Circles" is formally unusual, by Emerson's standards. It is shorter than many of his major essays. It has an unusual narrative tone and shape. The tone is teasing, slightly abandoned. There is an air of self-awareness to the essay. In his direct address to the reader and his conspicuous foregrounding of (or: drawing attention to) the relationship between reader and author, Emerson's narrator shows himself to be aware of himself as a writer and as a fiction. How does this change our reading experience? Some readers found such narrative tricks—familiar from fiction, particularly English comic fiction of the 18th-century—imposing and irritating. Do you? They also found that this methodology disrupted the willing suspension of disbelief in the unspoken reader-writer "contract." But is not disruption—or "unsettling"—Emerson's intent? How, then, does this narrative form tally with the content?

Further personal aspects to the essay may be less ironic or obvious. Is Emerson directing much of this critique inwardly; can we read in it a self-admonition? Many of those seemingly general aphorisms of "Circles" can be read as actually self-directed and specific, as though Emerson is taking stock of his own place so far. "The use of literature is to afford us a platform whence we may command a view of our present life," he writes. Is this performed introversion the purpose of "Circles"? Finally, the paradoxical aspect of "Circles" should be considered. A paradox is a statement or view that can occur in a variety of forms (poetry, humor) that seemingly contradicts itself and yet ("paradoxically") on closer scrutiny is found to express a truth. Is "Circles" a paradox, then?

Sample Topics:

1. **Self-awareness:** What is the purpose of Emerson's self-aware narrator? Is this self-awareness advantageous or hindering to the essay's tone and message?

The use of a self-aware narrator (or is it an authorial voice?) has a long history, occurring primarily in fiction but present in all literary forms. At the time Emerson was writing, William Makepeace Thackeray, the English humorist, was also coming in to his writing powers. Thackeray would prominently revive certain excesses of the self-aware narrator for the entertainment of both English and American audiences in the 19th century. Emerson's friend the Scotsman Thomas Carlyle also used narrative trickery and masques in his long essay *Sartor Resartus* (the tailor repatched), a work that had great influence on Emerson, who wrote the preface to the American edition in 1836. Look at contemporary uses of self-awareness. Is Emerson comparable? Books that study and theorize about narrative (the practice is "narratology") abound and can be consulted.

Some fiction writers use "unreliable narrators" deliberately to mislead their readers. Is Emerson doing this here? Why would he? Is this what the reader expects from an essay? Remember that Emerson's attested aim is to "disrupt." Are we, then, to believe anything Emerson (or his written persona) says? In "Self-Reliance" Emerson abandoned consistency and praised whim. Is "Circles" the same? How else is this essay self-aware? Think about Emerson's consciousness of his own reception by others—of not being understood—and of his own shortcomings as a writer. Think also of "intertextuality"—the relation between one text and another. Is "Circles" intertextual? Is Emerson responding to his earlier work, speaking to other essays, referring to them?

Another form of self-referentiality is the writer's discourse on literature: writing about writing. Emerson discourses on the disparity between his own art and self: "I shall wonder who he was that wrote so many continuous pages." Which Emerson, then, are we reading? Emerson speaks as a man in two different minds, the writer and the Emerson who exists off the page: "In my daily work I incline to repeat my old steps, and do not believe in remedial force, in the power of change and reform." Is this unsettling of the reader useful or merely confounding? What might be the advantages of unsettling the reader? For instance, does the form of the essay reinforce the content?

2. **Autobiography:** Can "Circles" be read as an essay in autobiography?

Autobiography is not an obvious generic description to apply to Emerson's essays. But why not? What do you expect from the genre autobiography (and what do you expect from Emerson)? Clarify for yourself what biography and autobiography are and do. Important studies of biography have been made by Leon Edel (*Literary Biography*, Indiana University Press, 1973) and Richard Ellmann (*Golden Codgers*, Oxford University Press, 1973). What in "Circles" resembles autobiography? In other words, when is Emerson talking about his life rather than life in the abstract? Evaluate when Emerson is speaking personally and when he is speaking in the abstract. It is not always obvious. What, indeed, is the difference? In "History," Emerson remarks that "the trivial experience of every day is always verifying some old prediction to us"—and in "Circles" he speaks of the "transcendentalism of common life."

Examine, for example, when Emerson asks, "Does the fact look crass and material, threatening to degrade thy theory of spirit?" Is this question directed at the reader or at Emerson himself? Emerson had developed a "theory of spirit"—one that had recently been set down and refined in "The Over-Soul." When he writes of the "young philosopher whose breeding had fallen into the Christian church," is he speaking of himself? Directly before this, he remarks that "cleansed by the elemental light and wind . . . we may chance to cast a right glance back upon biography." Where else does Emerson write about biography, and matters autobiographical? Look at other essays such as "History," in which Emerson compares history and biography and remarks that "man is explicable by nothing less than all his history." Does this suggest to you that Emerson's own history is integral—even essential—to understanding his writing?

3. **Paradox:** Is "Circles" a paradox?

First, define *paradox* clearly, providing examples. The term can be easily found in any good dictionary of literary terms and phraseology. This will lead you to useful instances of paradox. Having defined paradox, evaluate "Circles." What opposing ideas might be in simultaneous use here? One critic has described the essay as "aspiring at once to closure and continuity," for instance. Do you agree? Locate other oppositions that arguably exist simultaneously in the essay: Is it static or developing? Positive or negative? What might be Emerson's purpose in unsettling these binary oppositions by conflating them in one essay?

Language, Symbols, and Imagery

In essays written prior to "Circles," Emerson is prone to using sensational images, whether they draw on a religious tradition (intimations and iconography of apocalypse) or recall popular culture and sensational literature (the grotesque and gothic images of free-floating body parts and mutilation). "Circles" uses images of a destroyed world (paragraph three) that seem apocalyptic. "New arts destroy the old," however, and the old civilizations are burned to allow regeneration. Is this ritual rebirth still symbolic of a religious apocalyptic tradition?

The dominating image of "Circles" is, of course, the circle. The image is so omnipresent in the essay that the reader becomes numbed to its meaning. God (or "the nature of God") is, according to St. Augustine, a circle whose center is everywhere and circumference is nowhere. Emerson's crowning image, the eye (recall nature's transparent eyeball), meanwhile, is the "first circle," and "the horizon which it forms is the second." Emerson's infinite fable of men drawing circles around each other illustrates vividly his theme of generalization and assimilation, succession and reform.

Sample Topics:

1. **Images of destruction:** Discuss Emerson's imagery of destruction in "Circles." Does such imagery reflect Emerson's philosophy?

This question requires you first to isolate the instances of destructive imagery in "Circles," then to interpret their purpose in Emerson's argument. One prominent example is in the third paragraph, when the Greek sculpture and Greek letters are described melting. What does such an image evoke? What do we commonly associate classical Greek sculpture with, for instance? Democratic Athens stands as a model for civilization: Emerson himself celebrates Plato and his philosophical predecessors and successors in sundry other essays. What does this image of destruction signify? Is it an image of decline, or a celebration of reform? What is the difference? Does Emerson herald anarchy or civilization, entropy or perfectionism? Does he deliberately mix up this imagery, in the name of paradox and disruption?

2. **Circles:** What is the "circular" philosophy? How do the structure and the imagery of the essay reflect this?

This question does not solely call for you to tick off every instance of a circle image appearing in the essay. Regard, for instance, the opening sentence: "The eye is the first circle; the horizon which it forms is the second; and throughout nature this primary figure is repeated without end." Why is the eye first, before the horizon? And why does the eye "form" the horizon? This sentence has been discussed as a "microcosm" of the whole essay. What might this mean? A microcosm is a world in miniature, or a large body epitomized in a smaller one. In other words, the opening sentence purportedly summarizes the essay as a whole. Do you agree? From this central circle, Emerson's consecutive ideas emerge. Is there a circular motion to this emergence? How? Study the structure of the essay as well as its content. Emerson's ideas transcend one another; within the essay, one idea supersedes and resonates beyond the previous one.

One critic writes that even Emerson's punctuation replicates a circular rippling motion. How might this be? Attend to the essay in these different regards. Emerson employs puns as well. He writes: "It is the highest emblem in the cipher of the world." *Cipher* means "zero" in Arabic (so a circle), but *cipher* also means a message in code, a secret message in disguise. What might such a pun mean? And what does the employment of double meanings imply for our understanding of "Circles"? Is Emerson's aim revelation or a mere exercise in abandoned wordplay?

Compare and Contrast

Emerson's "Circles" can be compared with any of his other essays to some profit, since it marks a departure from those that preceded it and anticipates that which is to follow. It is useful as a benchmark, a transition between phases of his thought. What, though, is the social response to a reading of "Circles"? Emerson writes, "The way of life is wonderful; it is by abandonment." Was Emerson pointing to a dropout culture? Much of his social rhetoric in "Circles" seems—at least superficially—to anticipate the counterculture of the next century. However, is this simply a broad observation that folds under scrutiny? Is anything conclusive about an essay whose author—or narrator—states his explicit aim as to unsettle? Emerson says there is no anchor in life; is there an anchor to the narrative? Can we differentiate between the Emerson who wrote "Circles" and the narrator—the "circular philosopher" or "Latin Father"?

Sample Topics:

1. **Emerson and the counterculture:** How does the Emerson of "Circles" anticipate a later American "counterculture"?

This question of comparison requires you to isolate areas of the essay where Emerson considers social matters and reform. It also requires you to have a clear and well-supported definition of the 1960s American counterculture to compare with

Emerson's vision. What, then, were the defining tenets of that counterculture? Think, for instance, of the rejection of capitalism, a withdrawal from society, and a return to nature. Are there corresponding proposals in "Circles"? "For me, commerce is of trivial import," Emerson states, identifying his enemies. Then: "Nature abhors the old . . . conservatism." Was Emerson influenced by the establishment of reform communities like Brook Farm, in turn influencing the revival of such utopian "communes" in the following century?

Beyond the social suggestions, how does Emerson's rhetoric compare to the rhetoric of the counterculture? Look at key documents of the counterculture—the "Port Huron Statement" by Tom Hayden, for instance. Textual comparisons can be made. Similarities, at least broad ones, can be found. However, evaluate them critically. How does Emerson's philosophy run counter to the counterculture? An obvious example is in the essay's final, spontaneous rejection of "the use of opium and alcohol." Equally, while Emerson speaks many times, as we know, about nature and societal withdrawal, does his view of nature in "Circles" tally with the hippie view of nature? And is his social withdrawal—the way of "abandonment"—the same as Timothy Leary's sage advice to "drop out"?

2. **"The circular philosopher"**: Emerson's narrative voice has been read by some critics as a conscious "character," separate from Ralph Waldo Emerson, the "implied author" of the essay. Do you agree with this thesis? Can you distinguish the "circular philosopher" of "Circles" from the "speaker" of Emerson's other essays? How?

To make this comparison, choose another Emerson essay in which you feel Emerson's tone is perhaps less ironic—less guileful and guarded—and compare narrative techniques. (One critic has contended that "Circles" is the counteressay to "Compensation," for instance, and calls it a companion piece.) The speaker, the critics claim, is coaxing, proud, prone to retractions, bullying, qualifying, and evangelizing. Do you agree? Do you have any confidence in the "speaker" of the essay? Is this switching unsettling? How might such a reaction in the reader reflect Emerson's subject? Is this unnerving quality deliberate, then? Harold Bloom has called this voice "balefully ironic" and finds it so uncharacteristic that he does not "know how to read it." Another critic calls this persona the "Latin Father," taking the cue from Emerson's letter to Elizabeth Hoar (mentioned earlier).

Do you find this voice unsettling? And is this the purpose? Is it plausible, you may ask, that Emerson would assume a fictional or grotesque persona? What in his previous work suggests that this would or would not be likely? You might look for earlier addresses to the readers (or auditors) and previous use of exaggerated, grotesque rhetoric.

3. **Conclusion:** Is the conclusion of "Circles" typical for Emerson? Is it satisfactory?

This question requires you to evaluate whether Emerson follows any custom in concluding his essays. Is there usually resolution to them? Look at other examples and, by detailed analysis, discern whether they are convincingly resolved. How, for instance, does *Nature* conclude? Emerson uses apocalyptic language, both in describing the "disagreeable appearances" of the world and in prophesying a glorious rebirth—"to look at the world with new eyes." Other essays of Emerson's end with cataclysmic imagery coupled with messages of hope, striving for perfection and redemption and resolution. Does "Circles" follow this pattern? Or does it subvert such a tradition? How does "Circles" differ from these endings? Look also at the central "message" of "Circles"—it seems to contradict the possibility of any ending. Is, then, Emerson's essay structured in a way to reflect this? Is the ending sudden, arbitrary? And if so, is this deliberate, replicating the flux Emerson has found in life?

Bibliography and Online Resources

Crowe, Charles. *George Ripley: Transcendentalist and Utopian Socialist.* Athens: U of Georgia P, 1967.

Curtis, Edith Roelker. *A Season in Utopia: The Story of Brook Farm.* New York: Thomas Nelson, 1961.

Delano, Sterling F. *Brook Farm: The Dark Side of Utopia.* Cambridge, MA: Harvard UP, 2004.

Emerson, Ralph Waldo. "Compensation."

———. "Man the Reformer: A Lecture Read before the Mechanics' Apprentices' Library Association, Boston, January 25, 1841." *Emerson: Essays and Lectures.* Ed. Joel Porte. New York: Library of America, 1983. 133–150.

———. "New England Reformers: A Lecture Read before the Society in Amory Hall, on Sunday, March 3, 1844." *The Portable Emerson.* Ed. Mark Van Doren. New York: Viking, 1946. 110–133.

Hopkins, Vivian C. *Spires of Form: A Study of Emerson's Aesthetic Theory.* Cambridge, MA: Harvard UP, 1951.

Moss, William M. "'So Many Promising Youths': Emerson's Disappointing Discoveries of New England Poet-Seers." *New England Quarterly* 49.1 (March 1976): 46–64.

Myerson, Joel. "'In the Transcendental Emporium': Bronson Alcott's 'Orphic Sayings' in the *Dial.*" *English Language Notes* 10.1 (September 1972): 31–38.

Neufeldt, Leonard N., and Christopher Barr. "'I Shall Write like a Latin Father': Emerson's 'Circles.'" *New England Quarterly* 59.1 (March 1986): 92–108.

Porte, Joel. *Consciousness and Culture: Emerson and Thoreau Reviewed.* New Haven, CT: Yale UP, 2004.

Robinson, David. *Apostle of Culture: Emerson as Preacher and Lecturer.* Philadelphia: U of Pennsylvania P, 1982. Esp. 166–174.

———. "Emerson and the Challenge of the Future: The Paradox of the Unachieved in 'Circles.'" *Philological Quarterly* 57.2 (Spring 1978): 243–253.

Sams, Henry W., ed. *Autobiography of Brook Farm.* Englewood Cliffs, NJ: Prentice-Hall, 1958.

Swift, Lindsay. *Brook Farm.* New York: Corinth Books, 1961.

Wyatt, David M. "Spelling Time: The Reader in Emerson's 'Circles.'" *American Literature* 48.2 (May 1976): 140–151.

"THE
TRANSCENDENTALIST"

READING TO WRITE

"THE TRANSCENDENTALIST" would be important if only for its position in Emerson's bibliography and his developing philosophy, falling between the first and second series of *Essays*—or between those central chapters "Circles" and "Experience." It is furthermore important because it is the text in which Emerson meets fully the outward perception of himself and his work. Where else does Emerson bandy about the word *transcendentalism*? It is hardly a staple of his lexicon. Yet here he gamely meets the perceptions of him and his "party," if only to challenge, upend, and even parody those perceptions. Pay attention to Emerson's tenor. When does he speak of *them,* and when of *we,* and when does he speak of *I?* When is he in earnest, and when does he assume a guise? As "Circles" and "Experience" show, Emerson is not above fictionalizing stances for the advancement of an ultimate resolution.

In "The Transcendentalist," the "generalization" of Emerson's ideas discussed in "Circles" has happened: Emerson now surveys how this generalization represents and misrepresents his own, current thought. "I do not love routine," he says. He prefers not to repeat "four or forty thousand" applications of the same principle: "When he has hit the white, the rest may shatter the target." This address is about "the rest"—those who follow Emerson, imitating and misquoting him (one critic calls them "groupies"). Misrepresentation and misreading of his philosophy form a good part of the text. Writing to Margaret Fuller from New York, where he was lecturing with the series containing "The Transcendentalist," Emerson recalled how he was drawn into wearisome conversations about transcendentalism with the journalist Horace Greeley and the social theorist Albert Brisbane. "For me was nothing but disclaimers & still disclaimers," he wrote. Does this describe the aim of "The Transcendentalist"?

Is "The Transcendentalist" also aimed at Emerson's younger self? While the Divinity School Address set Emerson against the Unitarian orthodoxy and made him an outcast in the eyes of genteel, intellectual Boston, it also gained him adulation and imitation from the "new generation." By the time of "The Transcendentalist" four years later, Emerson is bucking his own "cultus" and followers. Recognition of his own tenets in the mouths of others causes him to readdress those tenets, more savagely. "Where are the old idealists?" he asks. "Are they dead,—taken in early ripeness to the gods,—as ancient wisdom foretold their fate? Or did the high idea die out of them . . . ?"

"The Transcendentalist" also anticipates "Experience" in its self-doubt. "What am I?" Emerson asks here. He complains of a "double consciousness" that is never reconciled: "the two lives, of the understanding and of the soul . . . never meet and measure each other." Tone changes from apology to self-parody, anticipating the changing "moods" of "Experience." These are "days of derision." After seeing the printing and publication of his first series of *Essays,* Emerson remarked, "I shall one day write something better than those poor cramp arid 'Essays' which I almost hate the sight of." Is "The Transcendentalist" a recantation, a justification, or a rationalization?

The following discusses the "new generation" of transcendentalist:

> But their solitary and fastidious manners not only withdraw them from the conversation, but from the labors of the world; they are not good citizens, not good members of society; unwillingly they bear their part of the public and private burdens; they do not willingly share in the public charities, in the public religious rites, in the enterprises of education, of missions foreign and domestic, in the abolition of the slave-trade, or in the temperance society. They do not even like to vote. The philanthropists inquire whether Transcendentalism does not mean sloth; they had as lief hear that their friend is dead, as that he is a Transcendentalist;

for then he is paralyzed, and can never do anything for humanity. What right, cries the good world, has the man of genius to retreat from work, and indulge himself? The popular literary creed seems to be, "I am a sublime genius; I ought not therefore to labor." But genius is the power to labor better and more availably. Deserve thy genius: exalt it. The good, the illuminated, sit apart from the rest, censuring their dulness and vices, as if they thought that by sitting very grand in their chairs, the very brokers, attorneys, and congressmen would see the error of their ways and flock to them. But the good and wise must learn to act, and carry salvation to the combatants and demagogues in the dusty arena below.

When reading this excerpt, try to identify Emerson's tenor. Is it disdainful? Is it proud? Is it defiant? Or is it apologetic? Emerson increasingly experiments with narrative tone at this time—in Emerson's bibliography, "The Transcendentalist" sits between "Circles" and "Experience," two texts with complex narrative tones. Elsewhere, Emerson proclaims, "We easily predict a fair future to each new candidate who enters the lists, but we are frivolous and volatile, and by low aims and ill example do what we can to defeat this hope." Is this an Emersonian unsettling? Can the speaker be trusted? For instance, is Emerson condemning the transcendentalists for being bad citizens, or is he praising them for their withdrawal? He has, previously, espoused withdrawal, and if he has not necessarily vaunted bad citizenship, he has previously taken pointedly antisocial and iconoclastic positions ("I will live then from the Devil"). Are there, perhaps, elements of self-parody in this account? "I am a sublime genius; I ought not therefore to labor" sounds exaggerated. Later, Emerson notes that his transcendentalists are "still liable to that slight taint of burlesque which . . . attaches to the zealot." Does Emerson, alike, burlesque himself and his followers? In some regards, this lecture is a disarming, revealing, even compromising gesture to the wider world. It—finally—explains plainly a philosophy that was previously famously obscure. Is Emerson's portrait of the transcendentalists, then, equally couched for a popular audience, playing on the mainstream portrait of transcendentalism, all "lampoons" and "moonshine"?

TOPICS AND STRATEGIES

The following section suggests several possible topics for essays on "The Transcendentalist." They can and should be used as starting points for your own, independent exploration of the essay.

Themes

In 1840 Emerson had begun to venture outside Boston to give lectures in New York and Providence, Rhode Island. By lecturing farther afield, did he necessarily temper his writing for a broader audience? Many of the best-known, earliest addresses were composed (at least ostensibly) for very specific, elite audiences. "The Transcendentalist" addresses the public perception of transcendentalism and its practitioners. Emerson seeks to reassure at times ("These persons are not by nature melancholy, sour, and unsocial"); at others he seems to pander to popular derision ("Like fairies, they do not wish to be spoken of"). Does he count himself among the transcendentalists, or is he a mediator between the audience and the secretive, elusive transcendentalists? Does Emerson truly believe in the term, even, or are his acceptance and use of it here an implicit admission of his more populist aims with this lecture? In the light of this change in Emerson's audience, and four years after *The American Scholar,* how does Emerson now view society and the place of the self in it?

Sample Topics:

1. **Transcendentalism:** What is transcendentalism?

   This question does not seek only a dry formulation of the term as evidenced either in the dictionary or indeed solely from the first paragraph of this lecture. It requires you to recognize the complexity and vagueness of the term, at least as it was used in New England. One critic, for instance, finds that there is both a "philosophical" and a "popular" definition of *transcendentalism* applied in this lecture. What do you think he means? Primed for multiplicity of meaning, gather the variety of uses employed here by Emerson and then locate and scrutinize any disparities between these definitions. Is New England transcendentalism identical with the philosophy of the German thinkers Kant, Fichte, and Jacobi? If not, why does it employ their terminology? Or is transcendentalism a "Saturnalia or excess of faith"? (And what does this mean?) Is it "sloth"? Can these all be "true" accounts?

Can you think of any occasions in earlier essays or addresses where Emerson uses the term? In the reviews that followed *Nature* (1836), the word *transcendentalism* was applied to the philosophy of Emerson and his followers by figures from outside his circle. Emerson later recalled how his circle was "surprised at this rumor of a school or sect, and certainly at the name of Transcendentalism, given nobody knows by whom, or when it was first applied" ("Historic Notes of Life and Letters in New England"). You might find these earliest applications of the name and evaluate their tone. Are these positive or negative? If the term *transcendentalism* was neither self-applied nor complimentary, why would Emerson identify himself with the term five years later? Emerson speaks of "transcendentalism" and then "transcendentalists." Does he maintain the same tone for discussing each, or does he alter his register depending on his subject?

2. **The transcendentalists:** How are the transcendentalists characterized in Emerson's lecture? Is Emerson's portrait of the transcendentalists a positive one? Is Emerson a transcendentalist?

Look for the adjectives Emerson uses to describe his subjects (*aloof, lonely, susceptible, affectionate*); mark those terms used to define them (*like fairies, bad citizens, lovers and worshippers of Beauty, novices*) but also take note of Emerson's tone. Is it disapproving or admiring? Does he take the position of the "grave seniors," for instance, who find the transcendentalists "very perverse"? Or is he defending his disciples and heirs? Is there a sense that he identifies himself among them, or is he conspicuously distant from them? Look for when Emerson writes speaking as we, as I, and then of them. What different positions does he take? Emerson says that there is no "pure Transcendentalist." Why not? Is pure transcendentalism impossible to sustain, or are its current practitioners incapable? Is the transcendentalist bound to fail?

You might compare the characteristics of the transcendentalists with views voiced by Emerson in earlier essays and addresses. How much do they recall *The American Scholar,* for instance? How does their reclusiveness mimic the words of *Nature*? How might the development of these transcendentalists follow from the "generalization" of "Circles"? Does Emerson use them as a conduit—or lens—for viewing and revising his earlier writings, perhaps? Are the unnamed transcendentalists of this lecture substitutes for the young Emerson? And does he count himself, now, among them? Or with his audience? Is Emerson's identification with (or his distancing from) the transcendentalists consistent in his published works and in his private journals?

3. **Self and society:** How is society depicted in "The Transcendentalist"?

In "The Transcendentalist" Emerson remarks that his subjects are "not good members of society." Is this intended as a rebuke, or a boast? How is society now portrayed? What are the symbols of society, and what sort of language does Emerson use to describe them? For instance, he describes all society in one passage as a "Mechanics' Fair." What might the significance of this emblem be? A good text to check developments in Emerson's view against is *Nature* (1836), which first established many of his enduring subjects. One opposition Emerson uses to explore the division between self and society is that between the rural and the urban. In *Nature,* Emerson argued for "the advantage that the country-life possesses, for a powerful mind, over the artificial and curtailed life of cities." Does this remain the same in the later lecture? Do not simply record any disparities; interpret them. What did a rural stance signify for Emerson? Has

Emerson's thought matured between the two works? Has his philosophy developed? Has America changed?

Another opposition that develops from the core polarity between self and society is the one between withdrawal and engagement, particularly (but not exclusively) political engagement. How has Emerson's view of political engagement changed since *Nature*, or *The American Scholar*, or "Self-Reliance"? What does Emerson say about abolition, temperance, and philanthropy? Does the self belong within society, or without?

History and Context

"The Transcendentalist," its subtitle notwithstanding, was read at the Masonic Temple in Boston on December 23, 1841. It was the fourth in a series of lectures on "The Times." Emerson gave the lecture again in Providence, Rhode Island, in February 1842, and again in New York in March. A text was first published in the *Dial*, the short-lived journal of Emerson's circle, in January 1843. Thus the text was prominent for Emerson soon after the death of his five-year-old son, Waldo, in late January 1842. While Emerson's later chapter "Experience" is commonly understood to be the text that first and most reacts to the death of Waldo, "The Transcendentalist" was among the lectures he read over that hard period. Are the pessimistic refrains of the later essay already legible in this address?

At the New York lecture series, Emerson recorded, he was received as

> very fine & poetical but a little puzzling. One thought it "as good as a kaleidoscope." Another, a good Staten Islander, would go hear, "for he had heard I was a *rattler*."

When Emerson was writing this lecture Henry David Thoreau was living in the Emerson family home, earning his keep as a handyman and gardener. Inevitably, each grated somewhat on the other's nerves, and critics have argued that Thoreau is the model for the wayward excesses of the Emersonian "groupies" of "The Transcendentalist." Critics are apt, of course, to see Thoreau in many of Emerson's ciphers (for instance, the American Scholar). Other models have been suggested, including the poets William Ellery Channing II and Jones Very, as well as Christopher Pearse Cranch and Charles King Newcomb. This last disciple, Newcomb, was a boarder at Brook Farm, which also forms a backdrop to the lecture and can perhaps be detected in Emerson's comment that "they have made the experiment." At the same time as Emerson looked critically on the Brook Farm experiment, abolitionism continued to disrupt the equanimity of the country. Did Emerson find more virtue in such political engagement than he did at "Education Farm," where "the noblest theory of life . . . would not rake or pitch a ton of hay" ("Experience")?

Sample Topics:

1. **"So many promising youths":** Who are the "many promising youths"? How did they disappoint Emerson?

    While deducing the identities of models for the text is not necessarily the primary job of literary criticism, in a text such as "The Transcendentalist" it can help inform an interpretation of the text. If in the first half of his discourse Emerson tries to explain transcendentalism, the latter half of the lecture—paragraphs 15 through 30—concerns itself with a description of its practitioners. Much rests, then, on the actual practice of transcendentalism in the world. While Emerson's comments give us one side of the story, identifying possible subjects and researching their own lives and writings can give us an insight into how transcendentalism was lived. Did these "promising youths" fail? Is Emerson the best source to evaluate their achievements, or is he biased?

    Informed keys as to who might be meant by this text exist, but you might equally note the characteristics of Emerson's nameless transcendentalists and construct a portrait yourself from these details. After the Divinity School Address and *The American Scholar,* Emerson attracted the attention of acolytes. In the years of "The Transcendentalist" he was also editing the *Dial,* which entailed looking for contributors—new young poets who almost invariably disappointed him. By researching such keys and Emerson's biography and journals from the period of "The Transcendentalist," possible candidates can be intelligently established and representative works analyzed. How do these youths fit Emerson's description and criticism? To what extent is Emerson accurate, his disappointment fair? Conversely, how far is "The Transcendentalist" a satire or misrepresentation of its subject?

2. **Abolitionism revisited:** How is political reform represented in "The Transcendentalist"? Is transcendentalism political? Should it be?

What was the larger political picture while Emerson was discoursing on the delicate and sensitive quirks and qualms of the transcendentalists? How does such a larger view change your view of the transcendentalist position (if there is any position)? This question asks you to show an awareness of the political situation at the time of Emerson's writing. "Slave narratives," such as the well-known autobiography of Frederick Douglass (1845), describe a larger picture well and were appearing within years of Emerson's lecture. Abolitionist figures such as William Lloyd Garrison and Wendell Phillips were vigorously active and writing at this time. They should be consulted. Does Emerson's account reflect the country in these lives and books? Should it? If so, are Emerson's transcendentalists amoral aesthetes?

How are the transcendentalists defined, politically? Can bad citizens who "do not even like to vote" be admired by Emerson's audience? The transcendentalists are opposed, in Emerson's discourse, by the "philanthropists" and "the good world." But whom and what does Emerson mean by this? Is this still an Emerson who (as in "Self-Reliance") calls philanthropists fools and scoffs, "Are they *my* poor"? How are the "zealot" and the "speculative reformer" described in this lecture? Society is best "when it is likest to solitude," and beauty is paramount in "the moral movements of the time," according to Emerson. "The justice which is now claimed for the black, and the pauper . . . is for Beauty." What does this mean? Do you agree? Clarify Emerson's position (distinguishing it from the transcendentalists', if a difference can be discerned) and compare it with the history of the day—as he says, "the moral movements of the time." One source of use might be Emerson's "Introductory Lecture on the Times," which framed the series of which "The Transcendentalist" was a part.

Philosophy and Ideas

"The Transcendentalist" revisits and explains, somewhat lately and with deceptive simplicity, what some of the philosophy behind *Nature* was. With unaccustomed directness Emerson explains his view of idealism and materialism. He also introduces a new term, *double consciousness*, which captures succinctly the divided, polarized struggle that has colored many of his previous discourses. What is Emerson's solution to this double consciousness, beyond waiting patiently?

Sample Topics:

1. **Materialism and idealism; double consciousness:** What is double consciousness? How is it related to materialism and idealism?

   While Emerson's explanation of double consciousness occurs comparatively late in the lecture, it is presaged in Emerson's opening definition of transcendentalism. "As thinkers," Emerson writes, "mankind have ever divided into two sects, Materialists and Idealists." As he has before, Emerson constructs a polarized system. What is "idealism" and what is "materialism"? While you should show your awareness of Emerson's early definitions given in this lecture, they can and should be challenged. Several critics have found Emerson's definitions— and his leaden division into sects—too breezy, even suggesting that he is being deliberately simplistic. Do you agree? Emerson discusses idealism in a number of his works, starting from *Nature*. What, though, is materialism? Emerson gives the example of the capitalist banker. Furthermore, as a balance in the same series as "The Transcendentalist" Emerson wrote a lecture called "The Conservative" in which he pitched conservatism against innovation, past against future, memory against hope, and understanding against reason. How does materialism fit in among these terms?

With the two terms fully and critically defined, you can now ask, How is the tension between these polar opposites manifested in life? How are materialism and idealism connected with the "two states of thought," the "two lives" connected with "double consciousness"? Why is double consciousness especially an attribute of the transcendentalists, and not, say, the "man of the world" (paragraph 24)? How is double consciousness to be resolved? Can it be?

2. **Waiting and patience:** What is the significance of waiting and patience in "The Transcendentalist" and elsewhere in Emerson's writing?

One upshot of the "double consciousness" is a state of "mere waiting." What are Emerson and his transcendentalists waiting for? Waiting is discussed both in the dialectic (or dialogue) between the transcendentalist and "the world" (paragraph 23) and in the exposition of paragraph 25. What does it mean, for example, for the transcendentalists to "await our turn of action in the Infinite Counsels"? One critic suggests that Emerson cultivated a "Philosophy of Waiting" (Sealts, 136). What might this mean? How is waiting represented in other works by Emerson? What might waiting signify in the time when Emerson was writing? Does waiting point to millennial anticipations of the end of the world—or political anxieties (presentiments, even, of the Civil War)?

What is Emerson's solution to this waiting? In "The Transcendentalist" he says: "Patience, then, is for us, is it not?" Is patience any solution at all, or a compromise? Where does patience occur in other texts by Emerson? In the conclusion to *The American Scholar,* for example, Emerson asks, "What is the remedy?" and cautions, "Patience,—patience." In "Experience," alike, he counsels, "Patience and patience, we shall win at the last." What does "patience" symbolize for Emerson? It is a state of being between things. How is this relevant to Emerson's thoughts on contact, reality, time, and religion?

Form and Genre

"The Transcendentalist" was one of a series of eight lectures given at the Boston Masonic Hall on "The Times." Along with an introductory "Lecture on the Times," the other subjects in this series were "The Conservative," "The Poet," "Manners," "Character," "The Relation of Man to Nature," and "Prospects." The series was completed by January 1842 (exactly a week before Emerson's son Waldo died of scarlatina). A year later the lecture was published in essay form in the *Dial,* a magazine begun by Emerson and his circle in 1840 that Emerson was now—reluctantly—editing. In Emerson's lifetime, "The Transcendentalist" was at least as well known as *The American Scholar.* Is this because it explains, succinctly and clearly, what Emerson said more expansively (and confusingly) in *Nature*? Is "The Transcendentalist" Emerson's primer—a self-conscious introduction to his thought for a wider audience?

If "The Transcendentalist" is a primer, is the characterization of the transcendentalists in it couched for a wider audience? Is Emerson apologetic as he describes the eccentricities of the transcendentalist brethren? Or is his a slight satire of the group—even a satire aimed at Emerson himself in his earlier works? In "The Transcendentalist" one hears echoes of previous works by Emerson, revisited with a certain narrative detachment. He speaks of others—followers—where before he spoke of himself. What he wrote in solitude is now taken up as a doctrine by a certain circle. Theory is put into practice, and "The Transcendentalist" reflects this, its first half propounding theory, its second half regarding—possibly in amusement, possibly in embarrassment—its practice. Perhaps most surprising is Emerson's acceptance of a term not chosen by him, *Transcendentalism.* Is this acceptance sincere? If not, is it a key to Emerson's subsequent tone—an ironic one? Tone is all, and—as with other works by Emerson—hard to read at times. Equally, is it possible that the work is apology and self-parody combined?

Sample Topics:

1. **Primer or introduction:** How well does "The Transcendentalist" serve as a primer or introduction to Emersonian

transcendentalism? Does it clarify Emerson's philosophy or mislead the reader?

You should first consider and define the purpose of a primer: to simplify and state clearly its subject for the benefit of those who are uninitiated in that subject. Can this be done with Emerson's philosophy without compromising the more nuanced aspects of his work? For instance, how does "The Transcendentalist" clarify a work like *Nature*? Compare passages from each text that have a common subject, such as Emerson's treatment of "idealism"—or "beauty," or indeed "nature." Each forms a whole subchapter in *Nature.* How are these ideas converted in "The Transcendentalist"? Is simplification—or compromise—evident? Does simplification improve Emerson's work, or does it neglect essential matter? In "The Transcendentalist," Emerson only seems to remark on nature as an afterthought: "They are lovers of nature also, and find an indemnity in the inviolable order of the world for the violated order and grace of man." Is this a sufficient précis?

The second prong of this question asks you whether the text clarifies or misleads. You should consider both options and if possible find instances of each. Does Emerson clarify what he means by transcendentalism, idealism, materialism? Conversely, is his portrait of the transcendentalist entirely reliable, or does it only lead you to more questions? The author admits to being "frivolous and volatile," his tone difficult to read. Is this appropriate in a work of an introductory nature? Weigh the respective instances and find a solution.

2. **Satire and self-parody:** Does "The Transcendentalist" contain elements of satire and self-parody?

Critics have written on Emerson's use of humor and found it throughout his essays and poetry. Reading Emerson's tone can be difficult. New Englanders were masters of the deadpan—straight-faced, unannounced humor. They were also, however, the descendents of the Puritans. However, even the Puritan divine Cotton Mather wrote, "The heart may be *Pleasant* when the face is not *Airy.*" Should we expect humor or self-mockery from Emerson? Was humor a way for Emerson to identify with the nontranscendentalist world, as one critic has argued (Porte 2004, 18)? One gauge for assessing tone and sincerity is to look at Emerson's private writings—his journals and his letters. What does Emerson say about transcendentalism and its practitioners in the journal? For instance, in October 1840 Emerson writes of a meeting with George Ripley, Margaret Fuller, and Bronson Alcott to discuss the Brook Farm social experiment. Emerson quips, "It was not the cave of persecution which is the palace of spiritual power, but only a room in the Astor House hired for the Transcendentalists." Does this resemble the tone of "The Transcendentalist"? Think, for example, of the passage where Emerson aligns the transcendentalists with the martyrs, "sawn asunder, or hung alive on meat-hooks."

Locate those passages in "The Transcendentalist" where Emerson discourses on familiar, favorite subjects. How has his tone changed over the years? Here Emerson writes of his subjects: "Like the young Mozart, they are rather ready to cry ten times a day, 'But are you sure you love me?'" "Love me, they say, but do not ask who is my cousin and my uncle." Does this resemble the muscular intellectual of *The American Scholar,* for whom "Life lies behind us as the quarry from whence we get tiles and copestones for the masonry of to-day"? More, is Emerson mocking his former self—an "old idealist" with the "high idea out of him"? There is no "pure Transcendentalist" who has "leaned entirely on his character, and eaten angels' food." You can find other comments such as these; are they making fun of Emerson's own "excesses of Faith"? And what would the possible purpose of such a self-parody be? Does it point toward the skepticism to follow in later works?

3. **Apology:** Is "The Transcendentalist" an apology for the transcendentalists or a defense?

Several scholars have noted the apologetic quality of "The Transcendentalist." Do you agree with this reading? It is useful, in considering this question, to determine who Emerson's audience was: Whom was he apologizing to and for what? Look for passages where Emerson identifies his audience, such as when he claims that "it is well known to most of my audience that the Idealism of the present day acquired the name of Transcendental from the use of that term by Immanuel Kant." Is this an accurate account of his audience? Look at imagery he uses. Emerson describes a "Mechanics' Fair" to represent society; at whom might such an image be aimed? Further information on Emerson's audiences can be found from sundry studies reviewing contemporary accounts of his lectures, some of which record the reactions of the audience (the bibliography lists a few). Were Emerson's lectures geared toward a specific audience?

Look also at the language and tone in the text, for instance, Emerson's closing remarks, when he seems to plead, "will you not tolerate one or two solitary voices in the land, speaking for thoughts and principles not marketable or perishable?" Is this compatible with the Emerson who snaps, "We perish of rest and rust: but we do not like your work." By studying such varying signals alongside each other, you can resolve this ambivalent tone and decipher what you take to be Emerson's ultimate position.

Language, Symbols, and Imagery

In "The Transcendentalist" Emerson asks: "From whence am I?" "Am I in harmony with myself? my position will seem to you just and commanding. Am I vicious and insane? my fortunes will seem to you obscure and descending." The audience and reader are flummoxed. Emerson's experimentation with the "circular philosopher" in "Circles" can be read as an announcement that Emerson is not above misleading and unsettling within his texts. "I am the doubter and the doubt," he announces in "Brahma." Does Emerson speak for the transcendentalists, the audience, or himself?

Sample Topic:

1. **Narrative position: *We* and *I* and *Them*:** What is the narrative position of "The Transcendentalist"? Who is the *I* of the lecture?

"The Transcendentalist" was a lecture before it was an essay. Does lecturing—appearing in person before an audience as the author of the text to be read—presuppose that the text is sincere? When Emerson stands on a stage to read, is the *I* taken to be the man before the audience? This question asks you to consider the complexities of Emerson's narrative position in "The Transcendentalist," questions an audience would ask alike. Compare "The Transcendentalist" with another lecture text, like the Divinity School Address. Are they similar in the construction of their narratives? What differentiates the two lectures, both within the text and outside the text? The Divinity School Address, like *The American Scholar,* was written for a specific occasion and an elite audience. In both cases Emerson was an insider—an alumnus of the institutions at which he spoke. Is the same true of "The Transcendentalist"? How might Emerson vary his narrative form according to his audience?

In the first line of the lecture, Emerson takes the narrative position of "we." Whom does he speak for here? Himself and the transcendentalists, or himself and the audience? When he speaks for the transcendentalists, is it as a member of the circle or as a mediator for them? Mark in the text how the narrative is constructed, and mark where it shifts. When might he be "acting" the role of the paradigmatic transcendentalist? Elsewhere he speaks as *we* and other times he speaks resolutely of *them*. For instance, in the 21st paragraph Emerson addresses *you*: "What you call your fundamental institutions." Who is the you? In the 22d paragraph there comes the remark "I do not love routine." Who is the I? Emerson (the speaker) articulates "the world" in the 23d paragraph and speaks of "this class" in the 26th. What might be the purpose of such a dizzying array of positions and their willful confusion? How might this text anticipate the later, even more divided (or fragmented) philosophy of "Experience"?

Bibliography and Online Resources

Allen, Gay Wilson. *Waldo Emerson: A Biography*. New York: Viking, 1981.

Barnes, Daniel R. "Emerson, Transcendentalism, and the Methodist Ladies." *Emerson Society Quarterly* 47 (197): 62–65.

Bubner, Rüdinger, ed. *German Idealist Philosophy*. Harmondsworth, England: Penguin, 1997.

Buell, Laurence. *Emerson*. Cambridge, MA: Harvard UP, 2003.

Cayton, Mary Kupiec. "The Making of an American Prophet: Emerson, His Audiences, and the Rise of the Culture Industry in Nineteenth-Century America." *American Historical Review* 92.3 (June 1987): 597–620.

Emerson, Ralph Waldo. "The Conservative: A Lecture Delivered at the Masonic Temple, Boston, December 9, 1841." *Essays and Lectures*. Ed. Joel Porte. New York: Library of America, 1983. 171–189.

———. "Historic Notes of Life and Letters in New England." (1868) *The Portable Emerson*. Ed. Mark Van Doren. New York: Viking, 1946. 513–543.

———. "Lecture on the Times. Read at Masonic Temple, Boston, December 2, 1841." *Essays and Lectures*. Ed. Joel Porte. New York: Library of America, 1983. 151–170.

———. "Transcendentalism." *Uncollected Writings*. Port Washington, NY: Kennikat Press, 1971. 60–64.

Field, Peter S. "'The Transformation of Genius into Practical Power': Ralph Waldo Emerson and the Public Lecture." *Journal of the Early Republic* 21.3 (Autumn 2001): 467–493.

Goddard, Harold Clarke. *Studies in New England Transcendentalism*. New York: Hillary House, 1960.

Griffin, C. S. *The Ferment of Reform, 1830–1860*. New York: Thomas Y. Crowell, 1968.

Lloyd, Henry Demarest. "Emerson's Wit and Humor." *Critical Essays on Ralph Waldo Emerson*. Ed. Robert E. Burkholder and Joel Myerson. Boston: G. K. Hall, 1983. 248–258.

Lowance, Mason, ed. *Against Slavery: An Abolitionist Reader*. New York: Penguin, 2000.

Nickels, Cameron C. "'Roaring Ralph': Emerson as Lecturer." *New England Quarterly* 76.1 (March 2003): 116–123.

Nye, Russel B. *William Lloyd Garrison and the Humanitarian Reformers*. Boston: Little, Brown, 1955.

Porte, Joel. "Emerson, Thoreau and the Double Consciousness." *New England Quarterly* 41.1 (March 1968): 40–50.

———. "Transcendental Antics." In *Consciousness and Culture: Emerson and Thoreau Reviewed.* New Haven, CT: Yale UP, 2004. 11–27.

Schorer, C. E. "Emerson and the Wisconsin Lyceum." *American Literature* 24 (1952): 462–475.

Scott, Eleanor Bryce. "Emerson Wins the Nine Hundred Dollars." *American Literature* 17 (1945): 78–85.

Sealts, Merton M., Jr. *Emerson on the Scholar.* Columbia: U of Missouri P, 1992.

Teichgraeber, Richard F. *Sublime Thoughts/Penny Wisdom: Situating Emerson and Thoreau in the American Market.* Baltimore: Johns Hopkins UP, 1995.

Vogel, Stanley M. *German Literary Influences on the American Transcendentalists.* New Haven, CT: Yale UP, 1955.

Wellek, René. "Emerson and German Philosophy." *New England Quarterly* 16.1 (March 1943): 41–62.

"EXPERIENCE"

READING TO WRITE

"THE ONE thing which we seek with insatiable desire is to forget ourselves," Emerson concludes at the end of "Circles," "in short to draw a new circle." "Experience" might be read as a sequel, where the longed-for forgetfulness and disorientation are won. Now, though, the cup of "lethe"—that water which according to legend brings forgetfulness—has been mixed too strongly, "and we cannot shake off the lethargy at noonday." What has changed in the interim between the two texts?

"I have set my heart on honesty in this chapter," Emerson writes in "Experience" (note, incidentally, Emerson's own definition of the work as a chapter and not an essay). Is he always honest? Mark well the tenor of different parts of the essay. Do you find marked shifts in tone and even opinion? "Experience" unfolds rather like a "whodunit," with clues to understanding it embedded in it only tangentially, even cryptically. Can you identify when the tonal shifts occur, and what mood they signify? For instance, is the "Mid-World" portion of the chapter (paragraphs 11 through 14) Emerson's honest voice, or the trying on of an alternative (easier, superficial) worldview? "I thus express the law as it is read from the platform of ordinary life," Emerson writes here. But is this a persona—like the "circular philosopher" of "Circles," or the "Orphic Poet" of *Nature*? Describing himself (ironically?) as one "free from dyspepsia," Emerson proceeds to drub many of his stalwart models and tenets from earlier essays. Criticism is now deemed futile, while the "young people"—those hopes of *The American Scholar*—are found to have "written much on reform" but reformed nothing. Emerson readdresses his former hero sneeringly: "Thou, dearest scholar, stick to thy foolish task." Artists, poets and orators are in turn "quacks," their works "disease." Then—strangely—he abandons this position for a new one.

"So it is with us," Emerson admits, "now skeptical, or without unity, because immersed in forms and effects all seeming to be of equal yet hostile value, and now religious, whilst in the reception of spiritual law." Be sensitive, then, to flips in tenor, and those places where argument upends (or, transcends) itself to try a new tack. As "Circles" described life as an ever-evolving, unsettled narrative, always generalizing, always superseding, "Experience" experimentally gives voices to this process: "a flux of moods." What governs these changes? Emerson provides a solution at the end, and (cryptically) at the beginning. The "lords of life" are perhaps all-important as a key to the narrative.

The following extract is perhaps the best known from this chapter, referring directly to the of Emerson's five-year-old son, Waldo, in 1842. Surely the core text of the dark phase, this snippet does not typify the entire chapter, although it is frequently taken to represent it. It is best not to see the death of Waldo in every sentence of "Experience"—indeed, the chapter draws on many journal entries that predate the death of Emerson's son.

> People grieve and bemoan themselves, but it is not half so bad with them as they say. There are moods in which we court suffering, in the hope that here, at least, we shall find reality, sharp peaks and edges of truth. But it turns out to be scene-painting and counterfeit. The only thing grief has taught me, is to know how shallow it is. That, like all the rest, plays about the surface, and never introduces me into the reality, for contact with which, we would even pay the costly price of sons and lovers. Was it Boscovich who found out that bodies never come in contact? Well, souls never touch their objects. An innavigable sea washes with silent waves between us and the things we aim at and converse with. Grief too will make us idealists. In the death of my son, now more than two years ago, I seem to have lost a beautiful estate,—no more. I cannot get it nearer to me. If tomorrow I should be informed of the bankruptcy of my principal debtors, the loss of my property would be a great inconvenience to me, perhaps, for many years; but it would leave me as it found me,—neither

better nor worse. So is it with this calamity; it does not touch me: some
thing which I fancied was a part of me, which could not be torn away
without tearing me, nor enlarged without enriching me, falls off from
me and leaves no scar.

This excerpt, from the third paragraph, is not (theoretically) written under the influence of any of the "lords of life." Emerson assumes
these voices and tones, emblematic of different lessons or ideas, only in
the fifth paragraph. So under what influence is this passage written? Is
this the "honest" Emerson? The author quickly introduces the defining
theme of "moods"—including that one, familiar to readers of Emerson's
earlier essays, "in which we court suffering," in the quest for "reality,
sharp peaks and edges of truth." This Emersonian grail is abandoned as
a fool's errand after "scene-painting and counterfeit."

This author is defeated and numbed. Unusually for Emerson, he
directly addresses his private life beyond mere anecdote. His grief is
found to be "shallow" and finite. Is the reader shocked by his coolness?
(Is the reader intended to be?) Is Emerson's use of his own "calamity" as an illustration brave or cynical or morbid? Here, Emerson uses
Waldo's death to personify the essential remoteness of the soul and
its objects. Failure to connect or to touch, and—perhaps worse, in
Emerson's hierarchy—failure to see clearly, are themes that will domi-
nate this discourse. Not the least of these failures to connect is, perhaps, that communication between author and reader. As Emerson
notes later—in a passage written under the influence of the "lord"
"Subjectiveness"—

A subject and an object,—it takes so much to make the galvanic circuit
complete, but magnitude adds nothing. What imports it whether it is
Kepler and the sphere; Columbus and America; a reader and his book; or
puss with her tail?

TOPICS AND STRATEGIES

The following section suggests several possible topics for essays on
"Experience." They can and should be used as starting points for your
own, independent exploration of the essay.

Themes

Each of the seven "lords of life" might be seen as providing a "theme" for "Experience," and the perception of what the central theme for this chapter is unsurprisingly varies from reader to reader. For some, Emerson's grief over the death of his son Waldo defines the subsequent inquiry. For others, this is almost incidental, and "Experience" collects ideas Emerson presaged in "Circles" and the journals years before Waldo's death. Themes of perception and vision are prominent from *Nature* (1836), indeed, and are revisited—albeit "through a glass darkly"—here. The chapter begins in doubt of the vision, emphasizing the illusions and obstacles to proper seeing. But it is "the Genius" that ushers us into the discourse, mixing too strongly the draft of lethe. Who is this framing figure? And why does the chapter end with a further meditation on genius (with a small *g*)? Fourth, the ultimate frame for the discourse is the title. Is this essay truly about "experience"?

Sample Topics:

1. **Perception revisited (misperception):** How is perception "threatened" in "Experience"? What are the consequences?

Emerson promptly warns the reader, "Our life is not so much threatened as our perception." How does Emerson use and revise themes of perception (and misperception) in "Experience," and what are the threats to it? Establish first the larger significance of seeing in Emerson's earlier philosophy (such as the transparent eyeball, the eye as the "first circle"). Remember, in *Nature*, Emerson's bold affirmation that "nothing can befall me in life,—no disgrace, no calamity," with its corollary qualification, "(leaving me my eyes)." Why is vision so central and vital to Emerson—and how has it failed now?

Threats abound; the apparent "sharp peaks and edges of truth" are just "scene-painting and counterfeit"; gone is the transparent eyeball—we are "subject-lenses," "colored and distorting," and so "we suspect our instruments." There are many other examples. Can perception still be trusted? If not, what is left? Illusion, surface, reality, and subjectiveness are all among the "lords of life." Consider each in turn. How does

Emerson overcome them and restore perception? Or does he overcome them?

2. **Grief:** How is grief depicted in "Experience"? Is grief the central motivation of this chapter?

"Experience" was, famously, composed over the two years following the death of Emerson's firstborn son, Waldo, aged five. This question asks you to evaluate how far the chapter is motivated by grief, and how that grief is used and represented. Does grief heighten or distort the argument itself? Is grief the impetus for the essay, or is it the absence of grief—the inability to feel it? The central text for such a query is, of course, Emerson's reflections on Waldo's death in the third paragraph, although you can and should locate grief in many other places. What do we expect from traditional (literary) expressions of grief? How does Emerson satisfy such conventions, and how does he subvert them?

Is Emerson's use of Waldo's death as an illustration ruthless or exploitative? Does he write, as one scholar argues, with "deliberate vulgarity," and, if so, why? Does Emerson's commitment to philosophy exceed his devotion to family? Look at Emerson's various responses under different "temperaments." For example, at one stage he declares himself "grown by sympathy, a little eager and sentimental," while elsewhere he broods that his is "a cold and defective nature." Look at his *Journal*—was Emerson's reaction always so cool? How is grief related to Emerson's dislocation from reality?

3. **Genius:** Who is the Genius of "Experience"? And what is the importance of "genius" to the chapter?

In "Experience" Emerson makes the pointed pun "Ah that our Genius were a little more of a genius!" What does this pun mean? What is a "Genius" (note the capitalized *G*)? Is it another unlisted "lord of life"? Where has Emerson used this term previously? Look, for instance, in "The Transcendentalist," with its redeeming, rallying cry: "Let them obey the Genius then most when his impulse is wildest." Is Emerson answering his own text? Look also to studies of Roman mythology. A genius was a doublelike spirit within a man that gave him powers of generation. How is "generation" important to "Experience"? It is Emerson's "Genius" of "experience" that prepares the cup of "lethe" for him that leaves him numb and disoriented. In parts of the chapter, Emerson addresses his Genius directly. Is this chapter a "dialectic" between Emerson and his Genius? How might this play on traditional themes of the "double" in fantastic and Gothic literature?

Second, how does "genius" (with a small *g*) feature in the chapter? Find instances such as paragraph five ("Of what use is genius, if the organ is too convex or too concave"; "some unfriendly excess . . . neutralizes the promise of genius"). What is the place of genius in Emerson's philosophy? What is the meaning of the final line of the essay—that final aim—"the transformation of genius into practical power"?

4. **Experience:** Why is this chapter titled "Experience"? How does Emerson view experience?

It is useful to know when answering this question that Emerson had originally intended to title this essay "Life." Why do you think the change was made? How—in Emersonian terms—does life differ from experience? Think about Emerson's earlier essays; is experience something to be valued in them? In "The Transcendentalist," for instance, Emerson favors "the intuitions" over "our experience." Does this chapter show an increased acceptance of experience or a further repudiation of it? One critic tallies Emerson's "vision" against his experience, "faith" against "facts." Does this, again, recall Emerson's perennial opposition of reason with understanding (see *Nature*)? "Experience is hands and feet to every enterprise," Emerson claims, "and yet, he who should do his business on this understanding, would be quickly bankrupt."

In an empiricist philosophy, experience is argued to be the only source of knowledge: that point where subject and object meet. Does this resemble Emerson's thought as you know it? Does any sign of Emerson's earlier philosophy of idealism remain in this chapter? If so, how does it relate to experience?

History and Context

While the death of Emerson's son Waldo in January 1842 is, of course, the predominant historical event overshadowing the writing of "Experience," it is easy to let this event crowd out the wider world and forget that Emerson wrote the chapter from the world, not a mausoleum. It is, indeed, illuminating to look at the wider world as well as the vividly internalized world of Emerson at this time. The wide world is, after all, an important part of this essay, albeit viewed through Emerson's colored lenses. Aspects that characterize that wide world include illusion, counterfeit, and surface. How is this reflected in the American republic?

By 1844, the showman impresario Phineas Taylor Barnum had run his American Museum on Broadway in New York for three years, in which time he had caught the nation's imagination and defined an obsession. His best-known hoax had involved the exhibition of an elderly African-American woman who was alleged to be George Washington's 161-year-old nursemaid. When this was challenged by skeptical pressmen, Barnum spread the rumor that she was in fact made of rubber and coils. In 1842, he exhibited the so-called Feejee Mermaid—supposedly a real mermaid, caught and stuffed—reveling in the doubt and confusion it spread. Barnum's name became ubiquitous, and synonymous with fraud. When the Mermaid was not on show in New York, it was displayed at the Boston museum of Barnum's friend and co-conspirator Moses Kimball. Could Emerson have avoided this popular furor? The craze lasted through 1843, as the Mermaid was toured through the southern United States. Thirteen years later, Emerson grumbled in his journal, "Men had rather be deceived than not; witness the secure road to riches of Barnum and the quacks."

Among these quacks, and another reflection of American mores and the presiding preoccupation with surface over substance, was the pseudoscience phrenology. Emerson writes explicitly about phrenology in

"Experience," in a passage that reflects his historical time. These popular amusements and distractions—tokens of an industry of leisure—in turn reflected the changing face of America. A middle-class was forming, and with it middle-class tastes. Is this what Emerson means by the "mid-world"? Emerson was lecturing in New York shortly after Waldo's death, and he remarked in his journal:

> In New York lately, as in cities generally, one seems to lose all substance, & become surface in a world of surfaces. Every thing is external, and I remember my hat & coat, and all my other surfaces, & nothing else. . . . I visited twice & parted with a most polite lady without giving her reason to believe that she had met any other in me than a worshipper of surfaces, like all Broadway. It stings me yet.

Sample Topics:

1. **The mid-world:** What does Emerson mean by "the mid-world"? Is it really best?

"The mid-world is best," Emerson avers at the beginning of the 13th paragraph. What does he mean by "mid-world"? And since this portion of the chapter is written under the influence of the "lord of life" called "surface," how are we intended to receive this assertion? Is this Emerson's compromise (or surrender) to the superficial world of manners above ideas? How might the "mid-world" reflect the rise of a middle-class culture? How does the Emerson of the "mid-world" express himself socially? For instance, what might his change of attitude about literature reflect? Abandoning the hard-to-find Goethe, Emerson celebrates the schoolboy with his Hamlet. What, too, of Emerson's celebrating the world of the footman in the Louvre? Is his "mid-world" persona a democratic Emerson?

One critic calls this view a "serious alternative" to reason. Do you agree? What are the shortcomings of this view? What about, for instance, Emerson's abandonment and denunciation of Brook Farm ("Education Farm"). Or how, in the mid-world view, does Emerson regard his own past works? "Nature hates peeping"; "We live amid surfaces, and the true art of life is to skate well on them." Is this a preferable position? Does Emerson suggest it bitterly, ironically, or earnestly? Is it a narrative conceit (like the "circular philosopher" of "Circles") or a defeated solution after the death of his son? Notice how several times Emerson describes a view only to smash it in due course. Is the mid-world, then, just Emerson's sarcastic masquerade? Is this just a trying out, the assumption of a disguise, scenery and counterfeit?

2. **Barnumism:** How does Emerson reflect the "age of Barnum" in "Experience"?

P. T. Barnum was synonymous with illusion and "humbugs"—amusements and hoaxes for popular entertainment—by the time Emerson wrote "Experience." How is this reflected in the language and imagery and even the arguments of "Experience"? The student should first familiarize himself well with Barnum, his biography, and his works. What were some of Barnum's hoaxes? How might such hoaxes and impositions inform the age? Why was society, at that time, so fascinated with doubting their own senses? Look at the history of American amusements, such as the panoramas and dioramas, the "Moon Hoax," and the chess-playing "automaton."

How is such a world manifested in "Experience"? Is Barnumism the source of the "system of illusions"? Is this an intensely private and inwardly turned discourse, or a historical reflection of the popular obsessions of Emerson's time? Look at the images Emerson uses. He rails against "this vertigo of shows and politics" and describes a "masquerade . . . of tamborines, laughter and shouting." Mark the language used, words such as *tricks, deception, games, counterfeit.* Emerson describes "diplomatists, and doctors, and considerate people" as "dupes." Dupes of what? Equally, how might the structure of "Experience" itself replicate a hoax?

3. **Chuckling phrenologists:** What is phrenology? What is Emerson's view of phrenology in "Experience"?

Phrenology was what is now dismissed as a "pseudoscience," but it was nevertheless popular in the period of Emerson's writing "Experience." What did it involve? Establish a definition to proceed from. When Emerson writes, "I saw a gracious gentleman who adapts his conversation to the form of the head of the man he talks with," is this a fair or an accurate description of phrenology? Research can be done into the history of phrenology. Prominent among its exponents were the Fowler brothers, who provided phrenological studies of Emerson's friends and associates Margaret Fuller and Walt Whitman. The Fowlers also published those two writers. What might these friendships and affinities suggest? Did Whitman and Fuller see similar projects in Emerson's work and in the Fowlers' work? Is phrenology conducive to transcendental ideas? Is Emerson's portrait of "chuckling phrenologists" fair?

How much does such a practice conform to those ideas in "Experience"? Both phrenology and "Experience" are experimental inquiries into identity, for instance. What is the context for Emerson's meditation on phrenology? What does he use phrenology to illustrate? It appears in the section of the chapter written under the influence of "temperament." How is phrenology connected to temperament?

Philosophy and Ideas

"Experience" is commonly understood to mark a transition to a darker view of life in Emerson's work. While it undoubtedly pays to be aware of prevailing interpretations, you should always think critically about such assertions and draw your own conclusion. Is "Experience" any "darker" than *Nature*, with its presentiments of apocalypse? Is its treatment of intellectual endeavor any harsher than the treatment of scholarship in parts of *The American Scholar*? Furthermore, ask yourself whether it is clear that Emerson truly endorses a certain position, or whether he is "trying out" a contrary position in order to synthesize a new amalgamated position: "Bear with these distractions, with this coetaneous growth of the parts: they will one day be *members*, and obey one will." In the same spirit of revision, does Emerson renounce his earlier tentative solipsism? He longs for contact where, previously, he disdained it. Can you reconcile this Emerson who gropes for a connection, to feel grief, and the one who snaps that "a preoccupied attention is the only answer to the importunate frivolity of other people."

Sample Topics:

1. **"Dark" Emerson:** "Experience" is considered by many to be the beginning of Emerson's "dark" phase. What does this mean? Do you agree?

   Do you think that "Experience" is pronouncedly "darker" or more pessimistic than Emerson's earlier writing? If so, why? What, for a start, defines "darkness"? Is it pessimism, or morbidity, or admission of defeat? Such an allegation should be demonstrated by textual comparison. Choose an essay that, placed in comparison with "Experience," best highlights those aspects that you find particularly pertinent to this question. Different scholars have isolated *Nature*, "Self-Reliance," "Circles," and "The Poet" each as countertexts to "Experience." Do you agree?
      Where in the text are the negations? Are they truly negations, or are they—eventually—dismissed, or contradicted? For instance, Emerson claims that "Nothing is left us now but death. We look to that with a grim satisfaction, saying, there at least is reality that will not dodge us." By the end of the essay, however, he coaches himself, "Up again, old heart!" Does the chapter end with an affirmation? And even if this is so, does the ending color the ultimate reading of the chapter or is order abandoned and irrelevant? Which of the moods carries the chapter? Or are they each—in part—representative of "Experience"? Note the larger context of the negations—and the affirmations. Are they always proffered in earnest, or is Emerson demonstrating a case, the view through a lens or filtered by a "lord of life"?

2. **Contact and touch:** Is contact impossible for Emerson? How are touching and connection central to "Experience"?

More perhaps than it is concerned with grief, "Experience" is concerned with Emerson's inability to feel grief. From the first paragraph of "Experience," Emerson drinks his draft of lethe and forgets himself. He is made remote from himself. In the third paragraph, he recites the findings of Boscovich: "Bodies never come in contact . . . souls never touch their objects." How does this frame the chapter? Numbness, division, distance, coldness, and the failure to touch are recurring ideas. Contact can be physical, or it can relate to a visual connection, even to contact of a psychic variety. Locate different forms of this numbness and analyze them. The "Curse of Kehama" is one dramatic realization of the problem; the Para coats that protect the wearer from the rain of "dearest events" provide another.

Ask, also, What does this remoteness suggest, philosophically? In previous writings Emerson has investigated the extent of man's connection with nature (*Nature*) and with sentient others ("The Over-Soul"). Has he revised these ideas in "Experience"? How is the regrettable lack of contact in "Experience" related to Emerson's earlier celebration of self-reliance? Does Emerson still tend toward philosophical skepticism, idealism, even solipsism (that belief that the thinker and perceiver is, alone, real)? And if so, does he still celebrate his state of solitude? Here he writes, "Let us treat the men and women well: treat them as if they were real: perhaps they are." What does this—"accepting our actual companions and circumstances"—signify? Does Emerson accept the immediate, material world more now or less?

3. **Anti-intellectualism:** Is the Emerson of "Experience" anti-intellectual? How does "Experience" reimagine *The American Scholar*?

How does Emerson reenvision his Scholar? "Here, among the farms, we adduce the scholars as examples of this treachery," he writes. "They are nature's victims of expression." What does this mean? The scholar's task is "foolish" and criticism is "futile." Is this Emerson's ultimate conclusion about scholarship in "Experience," or does he redeem the scholar later in the discourse? Finding similar pronouncements on scholarship, reform, and poetry (Emerson's frequent emblems for intellectual endeavor), compare the chapter, particularly the Surface section, with *The American Scholar*. Can you find resonances or departures? For instance, action was vaunted over pure bookishness in *The American Scholar* and the Divinity School Address. Is the same claim made in "Experience"? "Colleges and books only copy the language which the field and the work-yard made," Emerson wrote in *The American Scholar*. "Life is not intellectual or critical, but sturdy," he writes here.

Can a vein of anti-intellectualism be traced through Emerson's thought? Is "experience" its culmination? Or do you think Emerson is being ironic—or experimenting in dialectic (and so voicing both sides of a conflict)? "Life is . . . for well-mixed people who can enjoy what they find, without question." "To fill the hour—that is happiness." Does this sound like the Emerson you have read before? Is this a betrayal of the life of the mind: refuge in conservatism, the triumph of "old, mouldy convention," and a desertion of all Emerson's preceding work? Or does it suggest maturity and pragmatism?

Form and Genre

The form of "Experience" is protean, changing regularly and evolving. Under the influence of the "lords of life" Emerson follows his narrative through seven different registers, tones, and voices. Some critics have compared it to the Platonic "dialectic," then, denoting the question-and-answer form favored by Socrates. One lord of life questions its antithesis, and so a new, synthesized solution follows, again to be challenged. And so on.

The description *protean* is doubly apt, since the term is drawn from classical myth (after Proteus, a shape-changing sea deity in Homer's *Odyssey*). Almost as many mythic narratives underlie "Experience" as there are lords of life. The "Curse of Kehama" is cited, as is the Fall of

Man. For the better part, however, Emerson points the reader toward the classical mythology—and tragedy—of ancient Greece and Rome. To some critics, the citation of Flaxman's drawing of Orestes before the Eumenides and Apollo is paramount: the key to the essay. Emerson drops other hints in reference to Sophocles' *Antigone.* His discourse takes place in a semiclassical scene. *"Ate Dea* is gentle," he remarks, early in the chapter. Ate was the goddess of vengeance, but the word *atē* also signified the punishment received for hubris—pridefully flouting the will of the gods. Does Emerson reimagine his family drama as a classical tragedy, with his son Waldo as sacrifice for the father's hubris? In the later essay "Fate," Emerson would submit: "Wise men feel that there is something which cannot be talked or voted away.... The Greek Tragedy expressed the same sense." He would again intone words from Aeschylus: "Whatever is fated, that will take place. The great immense mind of Jove is not to be transgressed."

Sample Topics:

1. **Classical myth and tragedy:** How much is "Experience" modeled on classical myth and tragedy? Why is this influence important?

   This question requires the reader to be familiar enough with classical (that is, Greek and Roman) myth at least to recognize allusions when they occur. When there is a word or image that you do not understand, research it, and it may well be from classical mythology. The chapter opens with "deluges of lethe," for instance. What does the Lethe signify? It means "oblivion." Souls of the dead supped from the river Lethe to forget their lives before they died. How is this significant to "Experience"? Are Emerson's wavering moods—between guilt, steely indifference, grief, and almost cheerful complacency—indications of willful forgetfulness?

   Note the several times Emerson draws the reader's attention to Greek tragedy. He quotes from the *Antigone* of the Greek dramatist Sophocles. (Antigone was the daughter of Oedipus, condemned for burying her brother against the king's

orders.) Toward the close of the chapter, Emerson conspicuously recalls a drawing of the "Eumenides" from the drama
of that name, the finale of the *Oresteia* trilogy by the Greek
tragic poet Aeschylus. (The Eumenides were Furies sent to
punish Orestes for the unnatural crime of matricide.) Examine these particular dramas and their themes and ideas, but
also examine the premises of Greek tragedy generally. How
is "Experience" comparable to classical myth or Greek tragedy? Is Emerson providing a key, or solution, to "Experience"
in these classical allusions? The death of Waldo, for instance,
recalls the curse on the House of Atreus that precipitates the
events of the *Oresteia*. Does Emerson frame the death of his
son in mythic narrative? What alternative underlying (non-
classical) mythic narratives does Emerson offer us? Consider,
for instance, the Fall of Man, or the "Curse of Kehama." Why
does Emerson frame the discourse in mythic narratives?

2. **The lords of life:** Who—or what—are the "lords of life"? How
do they influence the form—and meaning—of the essay?

The "lords of life" are referred to both in the opening verse
to "Experience" and in its (supposed) summing-up. Is such
positioning significant? What are the lords of life, exactly?
Are the texts—verse and summing-up—consistent with each
other? Different "lords" are listed in the verse, including "Use,"
"Dream," and "Wrong." And who is the "inventor of the game"?
Critics have agreed that the chapter is divided up according to
the "lords," but how? Is it clear from Emerson's text when he is
under the influence of one lord or another? One way of detect-
ing an influence is provided when Emerson refers to one of the
listed "lords" within the discourse. He names Temperament in
paragraphs five through seven, for example, while other lords
are not announced but implied.

What is the purpose of such a fragmentation? "In the
growth of the embryo," Emerson writes, "evolution was not
from one central point, but coactive from three or more
points." Is there any time, in this melange, when "Emer-

son"—the "actual author"—is speaking to us, or is each voice (or "lord") a masque (or mood, or lens)? Does he ever (in the words of Melville) "strike through the mask"? Identify which voice sounds closer to the Emerson expressed in earlier essays. Are these effectively fictional narrative constructs or is each Emerson himself? Does Emerson even suggest that there is ultimately a "right" lord—a solution to this essay? What is the voice at the beginning—and what is the voice at the end? Is that final voice a successful and triumphant synthesis of all the voices and lessons that precede him, or a testimony of defeat? Does the ordering of these "lords" have any significance at all, indeed, or are they—as Emerson claims—unordered and incomplete?

3. **Dialectic:** Is "Experience" a dialectic?

This question requires first the definition of *dialectic* and second the application of the term to "Experience." Different forms of philosophical dialectic occur over the ages. The term is applied to the Platonic dialogues, in which the truth is sought by a series of questions and answers. Is this applicable to Emerson's project in "Experience"? In "Plato; or the Philosopher" (*Representative Men*, 1850) Emerson called dialectic "the Intellect discriminating the false and the true." For the German philosopher Immanuel Kant, dialectic used—necessarily—self-contradictory ideas to work toward the truth. Is this comparable with Emerson's project in "Experience"? "The new statement will comprise the skepticisms, as well as the faiths of society, and out of unbeliefs a creed shall be formed," he writes here; "the new philosophy must take them in, and make affirmations outside of them, just as much as it must include the oldest beliefs." "They will one day . . . obey one will."

Language, Symbols, and Imagery

In "Experience" Emerson recalls key images of his early works, with new—perhaps negative—emphases. As noted, imagery of perception—

previously a sign of clarity and focus—is now inverted to depict blindness, illusion, and misperception. Similarly, the imagery of youth in *The American Scholar* is here colored differently. Does the death of Waldo determine Emerson's images? While youth was used, in part, to represent the young republic of America in pronounced contrast with the Old World, how does Emerson represent youth here? And is domesticity represented as a compromise, an obstacle to self-reliance, and a façade covering up violence and alienation in the home?

Another recurring image in Emerson's writing is one of "ascent"—rising up, higher, whether toward God or toward self-trust. Does this still apply to "Experience," where "we" find ourselves groggy and bemused and lost? Is Emerson pointedly recalling the opening of Dante's *Inferno*?

> Midway along the journey of our life
>> I woke to find myself in a dark wood,
>> for I had wandered off from the straight path
>
> How hard it is to tell what it was like,
>> this wood of wilderness, savage and stubborn
>> (the thought of it brings back all my old fears),
>
> a bitter place! Death could scarce be bitterer.
>> But if I would show the good that came of it
>> I must talk about things other than the good.
>
> How I entered there I cannot truly say,
>> I had become so sleepy at the moment
>> When I first strayed, leaving the path of truth.

Can the chapter be interpreted on a vertical axis? Can you assess when the narrative descends and when it rises and thereby reveal a design and purpose to what is a disorienting text? Look for instances where Emerson situates the reader on a level, be it high ("Life above life, in infinite degrees"), low ("Power keeps quite another road than the turnpikes of choice and will, namely the subterranean and invisible tunnels and channels of life") or, indeed, in the "mid-world."

Sample Topics:

1. **The death of Waldo:** How does the death of Waldo influence the language and imagery of "Experience"? Discuss images of domesticity and childhood in "Experience."

   This question requires you to note Emerson's imagery and terminology within "Experience." When does he use metaphors or imagery that might suggest—however indirectly—a preoccupation with his dead son? One example is the image of "the boy reading in a book, gazing at a drawing," which redeems the negative view of the Scholar in the preceding lines. The play of children and children's stories are recalled. What might be the purpose of Emerson's own babyish performance ("I clap my hands in infantine joy and amazement") and language ("I make! O no!")? Why does Emerson recall so many images of childhood? Does his grief, or self-reproach, impact (or impose) on his philosophy here? Is this essay a tribute, or shrine, to Waldo? Another reading might be that Emerson is groping toward his own rebirth ("ready to die out of nature, and be born again"). Images of embryos suggest the formation of a new identity. But also remember Emerson's previous use of imagery of children and youth, notably in *The American Scholar.* How does "Experience" revisit the earlier text?

   Look also at the images of domesticity in "Experience." Is domestic life a frequent scene for Emerson's discourse? What differing images are we shown? Under one home's roof "we find tragedy and moaning women, and hard-eyed husbands, and deluges of lethe," while in another is the "old world, wife, babes, and mother, Concord and Boston" while Emerson praises the "potluck of the day." How are both views of domesticity compatible? Which is the authentic one?

2. **Ascent (stairs):** What is the significance of the staircase image in Emerson's "Experience"?

   The opening scene to "Experience" takes place on a staircase. The description is dreamy and obscure, yet it frames the entire discourse to follow. What does it signify? One Emerson scholar has noted that many of Emerson's essays follow one or two ordering principles: polarity and ascension. How does the opening of "Experience" differ from typical images of Emersonian ascent? Can you think of examples from other essays that either support or challenge this assertion? Think, for instance, of the "mysterious ladder" mentioned in "Circles."

Where else does Emerson refer to ascent—or descent, or stasis? Look at the "mid-world" (or "surface") section of the chapter, for example. Does Emerson's favoring of the mid-world confound ascendance? "The middle region of our being is the temperate zone," Emerson writes. "We may climb into the thin and cold realm of pure geometry and lifeless science, or sink into that of sensation." What might this signify, for his larger argument? Critics have suggested precedents for the staircase in literature as well, including Jacob's ladder leading up to heaven, from the Bible. Another comparison has been made with the opening of the epic poem *The Divine Comedy* by the early Italian poet Dante Alighieri, which begins with a descent into hell and closes with an ascent into paradise. Do you think that Emerson is making a deliberate allusion to either text?

Compare and Contrast

The structure and tenor of "Experience" shift and switch to reflect Emerson's argument that temperament and moods color and divert us from reality. Identity itself is in flux in "Experience." There is no anchor or easy index. When is Emerson "honest"? Are Emerson's true feelings over Waldo's death best expressed in the poem "Threnody" or in "Experience"? Some scholars, recoiling from the remoteness of Emerson in "Experience," favor "Threnody" as a more personal, intense document of grief. But does this intimacy make it any more genuine? Do we choose the Emerson we prefer, or the one we believe? In comparing "Threnody" and "Experience" we ask questions about form and content, but also about Emerson as cold philosopher or warm poet.

"Experience" can alternatively be viewed alongside the fiction of its time. Herman Melville wrote that "all men who say yes, lie." Emerson, according to one critical tradition, is included, thinly veiled, among the passengers on the steamboat *Fidèle* in Melville's 1857 novel *The Confidence-Man,* as the optimistic but cold philosopher "Mark Winsome." Melville and Emerson are seen by many literary historians as defining polar opposites of American literature in the period before the Civil War. Emerson, somewhat generalized and in reference only to his early work, is seen as an affirmer, while Melville is seen as the great naysayer, one who said "NO! in thunder." Do the two writers share commonalities, though?

Sample Topics:

1. **"Threnody"**: Compare and contrast "Experience" with the poem "Threnody." How do you explain differences in tone, imagery, and view?

Emerson's poem "Threnody," begun in the weeks after Waldo's death and published in 1847, recalls and mourns the "darling who shall not return." Its subject is at least in part the same as that of "Experience." To what degree are they comparable? Of course, one is an essay (or "chapter") while the other is a poem. Do you consider one form more fitted for describing grief than the other? For instance, does the use of a classic elegy form entail compromise in "Threnody"? Is Emerson bound more to conventions of grief in the poetic form, or does the form allow more emotional articulation? Is conventional expression better suited to the subject than experimentation?

Form aside, you are required to discern less obvious differences. What tonally differentiates the one from the other? Is Emerson cold and remote in one, warm and effusive in the other? Why would he change his tone according to the form of the text? How can you measure this tone? The obvious way is by isolating those instances in "Experience" when Emerson refers to Waldo—or indeed when he seems to refer obliquely to Waldo—and comparing them closely. In "Experience," for example, he remarks that he feels as though he lost a "beautiful estate,—no more." In "Threnody" he laments the loss of "the most beautiful and sweet / Of human youth." You might conclude with a broader question: What does it mean for Emerson to express himself differently in respective forms? Are we to read his poetry as more sincere (or less so) than his essays, for instance?

2. **Herman Melville:** Compare Emerson's thought and expression in "Experience" with those of Herman Melville, particularly in his novel *The Confidence-Man* (1857).

Herman Melville's *The Confidence-Man* (1857) is a novel describing a journey made on a steamboat on the Mississippi, as a mysterious protagonist goes among a number of the passengers, engaging them in philosophical discussions resolving around "confidence." What does this scenario recall about "Experience"? (And what might it mean, if Emerson's essay resembles a work of fiction?) Look at common settings, shared thematic and narrative traits. What is the setting, for instance, for "Experience"? Is it easily defined? There is the unsettling and vague staircase, and then the setting dissolves—"All things swim and glitter." What other water imagery does Emerson invoke, and why? The historical setting for each work is worth studying; both writers were writing in the era of P. T. Barnum, when hoax and illusion were popular preoccupations and fascinations. How is this reflected thematically in the respective texts?

Look also to the form of each work. What narrative or structural aspects do they share? For instance, how might Emerson's "lords of life" be reflected in the multiple voices of Melville's novel, and the shifting identity of Melville's protagonist? You may like to look into the historical background of these two writers. While Emerson never—as far as scholars know—read or commented on Herman Melville, the novelist had some lively opinions on Emerson and they shared a friend in Nathaniel Hawthorne. What were Melville's thoughts on Emerson and transcendentalism? Is *The Confidence-Man* a deliberate and satiric response to Emerson? Do the similarities between the two texts evidence an appreciation of Emerson's views or a rejection of them? And what do any shared aspects of the two suggest about the prevailing critical polarization of the two writers?

Bibliography and Online Resources

Adams, Bluford. *E Pluribus Barnum: The Great Showman and the Making of U.S. Popular Culture.* Minneapolis: U of Minnesota P, 1997.

Cameron, Sharon. "Representing Grief: Emerson's 'Experience.'" *Representations* 15 (Summer 1986): 15–41.

Cook, James W. *The Arts of Deception: Playing with Fraud in the Age of Barnum.* Cambridge, MA: Harvard UP, 2001.

Ellison, Julie. "Tears for Emerson: *Essays, Second Series.*" *The Cambridge Companion to Ralph Waldo Emerson.* Ed. Joel Porte and Saundra Morris. Cambridge: Cambridge UP, 1999. 140–161.

Greenberg, Robert M. "Shooting the Gulf: Emerson's Sense of Experience." *ESQ* 31 (1985): 211.

Hill, David W. "Emerson's Eumenides: Textual Evidence and the Interpretation of 'Experience.'" *Emerson Centenary Essays.* Ed. Joel Myerson. Carbondale: Southern Illinois UP, 1982. 107–121.

Hungerford, Edward. "Walt Whitman and His Chart of Bumps." *American Literature* 2.4 (January 1931): 350–384.

Norwood, Kyle. "Somewhat Comes of It All": The Structure of Emerson's 'Experience.'" *American Transcendental Quarterly*, new series 9.1 (March 1995): 21–39.

Packer, B. L. *Emerson's Fall: A New Interpretation of the Major Essays.* New York: Continuum, 1982.

Reilly, John M. "'Threnody' and the Traditional Funeral Elegy." *Emerson Society Quarterly* 47 (1967): 17–19.

Stern, Madeleine B. "Margaret Fuller and the Phrenologist-Publishers." *Studies in the American Renaissance.* Ed. Joel Myerson. Boston: Twayne, 1980. 229–237.

Tebeaux, Elizabeth. "Skepticism and Dialectic in Emerson's 'Experience.'" *ESQ* 32 (1986): 23–35.

Whicher, Stephen. *Freedom and Fate: An Inner Life of Ralph Waldo Emerson.* Philadelphia: U of Pennsylvania P, 1953.

"FATE"

READING TO WRITE

WITH EMERSON reconciled to "the terror of life" and "the odious facts," "Fate" throws the reader into Emerson's darkest hours and his lowest ebb—or so it is commonly understood. A whole tradition of Emerson scholarship, headed by Stephen Whicher's *Freedom and Fate* (1953), views Emerson's work as following a gradual decline in optimism, reaching its nadir in "Fate," after which his discourse—it is argued— becomes less relevant. Bear this reading in mind, but be ready to challenge it. Indeed, "Fate" only appeared in print as the first chapter of *The Conduct of Life* in 1860, although Emerson had been delivering lectures under this title from December 1851. Between the publication of "Experience" and that of "Fate," two essays glibly thrown together in critical shorthand, 16 years had passed. In between were the books *Representative Men* (1850—which contains the chapter "Montaigne," read by scholars as the prominent connection in the narrative from "Experience" to "Fate")—and *English Traits* (1856), with Emerson's reflections following almost a year in England and France. In between, also, occurred 16 tempestuous years for Emerson and for the country as it moved closer to division and Civil War. Keep in mind the national political scene as you read "Fate"—how does Emerson reflect the larger horizon? Is his still an intensely private, inward-looking meditation, or is it colored by events outside Concord and Emerson's study?

Be sensitive to unheralded changes in the argument—you will remember, from "Experience," Emerson's propensity to change tack and challenge his own claims without any expository announcements. This about-face is almost a signature of Emerson's, and integral to his debt to

Plato's dialectic form. The following excerpt is from the 28th paragraph, one of Emerson's characteristic turning points in his discourse:

> Thus we trace Fate in matter, mind and morals—in race, in retardations of strata, and in thought and character as well. It is everywhere bound or limitation. But Fate has its lord; limitation its limits:—is different seen from above and from below: from within and from without. For, though Fate is immense, so is power, which is the other fact in the dual world, immense. If Fate follows and limits power, power attends and antagonizes Fate. We must respect Fate as natural history, but there is more than natural history. For who and what is this criticism that pries into the matter? Man is not order of nature, sack and sack, belly and members, link in a chain, nor any ignominious baggage, but a stupendous antagonism, a dragging together of the poles of the Universe. He betrays his relation to what is below him,—thick-skulled, small-brained, fishy, quadrumanous—quadruped ill-disguised, hardly escaped into biped,—and has paid for the new powers by loss of some of the old ones. But the lightning which explodes and fashions planets, maker of planets and suns, is in him. On one side, elemental order, sandstone and granite, rock-ledges, peat-bog, forest, sea and shore; and on the other part, thought, the spirit which composes and decomposes nature,—here they are, side by side, god and devil, mind and matter, king and conspirator, belt and spasm, riding peacefully together in the eye and brain of every man.

Now comes the rallying of the counterargument. The same model exists in other essays—several times over in "Experience," for instance, when Emerson emerges from one mood—temperament, lord of life—into another; or in "Circles," when spontaneity and a new circle outdo the previous thought and position. Even in the earliest studies, such as *Nature,* Emerson passes from a gloomy apocalyptic low to a messianic high. Such a pattern is worth noting and anticipating (even if it does not always occur). Emerson's use of polarities—dualities and dialectic—necessitates such moments of about-face and redemption. (Later, having defined Fate's counter, Power, Emerson will ask in paragraph 40 whether "we are permitted to believe in unity?")

Having terrorized the reader with the absoluteness and inescapability of Fate up to this point, Emerson now introduces a paradoxical solution: Fate has its "lord" (recalling, of course, the lords of life of "Experience") in Power. "There is more than natural history." Emerson asks who is the critic who pries into matter? Who is the self speaking now, ready to challenge Fate? In a defiant burst reminiscent of Shakespeare, Emerson now argues, "Man is not order of nature, sack and sack, belly and members, link in a chain . . . but a stupendous antagonism, a dragging together of the poles of the Universe." This choice of words is important—dragging together of poles, or reconciliation of opposites. The synthesis of power and fate will be his eventual purpose as the essay progresses.

Such language is not new to Emerson; such dualities to describe man recall most memorably "Circles"—"I am God in nature; I am a weed by the wall." The low reality of man and his high potential are present in *The American Scholar* in characterizations of men as "bugs . . . spawn" on the one hand and the Scholar's model, Man Thinking, on the other. It is there in the opening of "The Over-Soul," between our "habitual" "vice" and our momentary "faith." That "lightning which explodes and fashions planets" is the same revelation detailed in "The Transcendentalist" as a "flash-of-lightning-faith": when "I should never be fool more." Later, Emerson asks incredulously, "Do you suppose, he can be estimated by his weight in pounds, or that he is contained in his skin,—this reaching, radiating, jaculating fellow?" Wending between the poles, punctuated by pulses of revelation and reversal, is not only Emerson's style; it is his conception of living. By repeating this pattern, however, is Emerson truly pessimistic—discouraged—or immortalized in an uncharacteristic moment? Or does this pulse of faith in turn pass (as a lord of life) to be succeeded by a pessimistic conclusion?

TOPICS AND STRATEGIES

The following section suggests several possible topics for essays on "Fate." They can and should be used as starting points for your own, independent exploration of the essay.

Themes

Given the span of time in which Emerson developed his lecture and then essay of "Fate" (1851–60), time spent meditating on this subject, and given especially the volatility of that particular period, it is unsurprising that Emerson's definition of Fate might be ambiguous and his feeling ambivalent. You may get muddled trying to keep track of whether Emerson sees submission as, finally, unavoidable, or whether Fate can always be dodged; then, whether Emerson sees such a submission as a necessarily bad thing, or whether he sees it as a good, albeit compromised. Emerson pitches Fate against several opposites, trying one duality and then another. Can an overall picture of Emersonian Fate be extracted?

Sample Topics:

1. **Fate:** What is "Fate," as described by Emerson? Is it a power for good or evil?

It should ostensibly be easy to answer this question—Emerson's essay is not short on definitions of Fate. This is, perhaps, its difficulty. There are many, some seemingly contradictory, definitions of Fate (notice, for instance, how many paragraphs begin with the word *But*). You might first line up different definitions and examples and compare them. For instance, what are the various images Emerson uses? At one stage, he describes Fate as like soft, limp bands. Why? Is such imagery consistent with Emerson's other images of Fate? Other examples are drawn from "matter, mind and morals"—from history (the Turks and the Persians: "They conspire with it"), from science ("vesicles"), and from mythology (the limp bands and the "Fenris Wolf" are from Norse mythology; Vishnu and Maya are from Hindu legend). By working toward a concrete definition of Fate using these examples, a larger picture can be formed—even if it only serves to emphasize inconsistencies. Do we expect consistency from Emerson, after reading "Self-Reliance" or "Circles" or "Experience"?

Find those adages and maxims that Emerson scatters throughout the essay, often as starting points for new inquiries. For instance: "Fate is nothing but the deeds committed in a prior state of existence"; "Fate is unpenetrated causes"; "The soul of Fate is the soul of us." What do you think Emerson means by "to use and command" these "facts"? What is "the right use of Fate"? (And what, equally, is its wrong use?) Look also at the synonyms Emerson uses for Fate, and for their opposite terms. Is *Providence* the same as *Fate*? What about *Limitation*; ("*Beautiful*") *Necessity*; *Circumstance*? Look at the different instances when Emerson uses these terms. Are they all the same? Finally, from these examples and illustrations you can infer a tone. Emerson's view shifts fluidly—his opinion itself seems to change—so you must judge, finally, whether the workings of Fate are deemed to be in unavoidable accord with evil, or an affirmation of order. This ascertained, ask further, Do you agree?

2. **Free will:** Is Fate unavoidable? Does Emerson believe in free will?

This question asks you to identify statements that Emerson makes particularly about the extent—if there is any—of man's free will: his ability to determine the direction of his own life. Is Fate compatible with ideas of freedom? Or are Emerson's earlier ideas of self-reliance compromised by a new sense of unswervable inevitability? "We can only obey our own polarity," Emerson writes. Does such an obedience—self-originating—suggest freedom or a state of submission? Are we doomed from "generation"? Emerson's son, Edward, denied that Emerson assigned any ultimate authority to Fate in his notes to his father's essay (see bibliography), but confusion remains even among seasoned critics. How do you think Emerson finally decides? (This polarity is the defining one in an important study of Emerson, Stephen Whicher's *Freedom and Fate: An Inner Life of Ralph Waldo Emerson* [1953]. What is Whicher's thesis?) Isolate Emerson's statements on Freedom and Fate. "Freedom of the will, is one of [Fate's] obedient members," Emerson writes; but then, "Nor can he blink the freewill." Elsewhere he avers that "a part of Fate is the freedom of man." Marshal these and other related remarks and set them against each other. Are all these claims consistent? Test them by reasoning them out. If not, why might Emerson deliberately contradict himself?

Look for those other terms Emerson sets against Fate. "Even thought itself is not above Fate," he writes. How has thought—the life of the mind—previously been represented in Emerson's hierarchy of concepts? "Fate" answers Emerson's earlier essays, such as *Nature.* It would be useful to compare those texts, then. Elsewhere Emerson claims, "Fate, then, is a name for facts not yet passed under the fire of thought," and "Intellect annuls Fate." What about spontaneity and surprise? How were these elements defined in other essays, particularly "Experience" and "Circles"? When Emerson writes about "the power to flux," the "jet of chaos," or the "whim of will," what does he mean? How might chaos, flux, or whim—Emerson's watchword in "Self-Reliance"—survive in a worldview dominated by Fate? How might Emerson's representations of order and chaos have changed over the years, and why?

3. **Power:** What is Power, as defined in "Fate"? What is its relation to Fate?

In the first 27 paragraphs of "Fate," Emerson establishes his view of Fate and portrays it as seemingly inescapable. After paragraph 28 there is a shift when, following Emerson's by-now customary use of polarities, Power is held up as the challenger and baffle, the designated "other," to Fate. This paragraph marks Emerson's about-face: his "and yet . . ." moment in this essay. What happens? The definition of Power is central to the understanding of Fate. What is the nature of their opposition? Emerson says that there is "more than natural history." What does he mean? How might this recall, for example, Emerson's previous dialectic of materialism versus idealism, established in *Nature*? Do Fate and Power supersede this antagonism, or reaffirm it? What exactly is Power? How is it described? Look for those words associated with it: what are *will, freedom, insight, intellect,* and *thought*? Clarity can be lost when dealing purely in abstract terms, so how does Emerson describe and imagine Power? What are its symbols and its exemplars?

An important question to consider is whether Power overcomes Fate, or whether it is vanquished by its opposite. How do the two coexist? Does one win out? Pay special attention to the resolution of the essay. Emerson offers a "key, one solution"—what is it? What does "double consciousness" recall to you from "The Transcendentalist"? What is the "Beautiful Necessity," and why should we build altars to it? Is this an admission of limitation or a final affirmation of Power?

History and Context

Emerson first delivered his lecture "Fate" on December 22, 1851, at the Masonic Hall in Boston. It was the first in a six-lecture series entitled "The Conduct of Life." Almost a year later he would give the lecture in Cincinnati and then a few weeks after that he would read it again in St. Louis in January 1853, reflecting the increasing compass of the lecture circuit and also a marked rise in Emerson's renown and popularity. After this, however, Emerson "retired" that particular lecture. He only decided to turn the "Conduct of Life" lecture series into a book in 1859. It is perhaps significant that he signed the contract for the book only five days after the radical abolitionist John Brown was captured at Harpers Ferry. Spurred and angered by this event, Emerson now put the relatively neglected text "Fate" at the fore of his new book.

In the time since "Experience" much had happened, both personally for Emerson and nationally. *Essays,* second series was published in October 1844. Thoreau had made his experiment in solitary living on Emerson's land at Walden Pond (1845–47). Emerson began writing and lecturing on *Representative Men,* published as a book in 1850. His *Poems* were also published (1846) and from 1847 through 1848 Emerson traveled in England, also visiting France. In national politics, "Fate" came out of an extremely volatile period; 1845 saw the administration of the Democrat James K. Polk (through 1849) and the introduction—and frequent use of—the term *manifest destiny.* It was coined by the newspaper editor John O'Sullivan, who supported the American annexation of Texas with these words:

> The American claim is by right of our manifest destiny to overspread and to possess the whole of the continent which Providence has given

us for the development of the great experiment of liberty and federative government entrusted to us.

How are such themes and ideas seconded or challenged by Emerson in "Fate"? Destiny, or its synonym, Fate, was in the public consciousness set in pronounced opposition to freedom—or at least freedom for some. Expansionism quickly and inevitably impacted the politics of slavery.

American expansionism continued in the Mexican War (1846–48). "The United States will conquer Mexico," Emerson wrote in his journal, "but it will be as the man swallows arsenic, which brings him down in turn." With victory came the acquisition of the "Mexican Cession" (1848)—529,189 square miles of territory formerly belonging to Mexico, including all of present-day California, Nevada, and Utah plus tracts of Arizona, New Mexico, Colorado, and Wyoming. Emerson was right about the arsenic: When California was to be admitted to the Union it was understood that it would be as a "free state"—one where slavery was not allowed. This would duly tip the balance of free states against slavery states, favoring the antislavery movement and antagonizing the Southern states.

This tension (or "polarity" as Emerson might have called it) that wracked the entire nation precipitated the Compromise of 1850, brokered by the "Great Compromiser" Henry Clay and the "Little Giant" Stephen A. Douglas. From this compromise resulted the Fugitive Slave Act, passed in December 1850 and supported by Emerson's erstwhile political hero, Daniel Webster. Now, in his journal, Emerson recorded of Webster: "Fate has been too strong for him." Boston, following Webster, applauded the compromise; not so Emerson. In this failure—this lackluster "reconciliation" of poles—was the germ of Emerson's political involvement. He gave a furious lecture several times against the Fugitive Slave Law in May 1850 (seven months before his first lecture on "Fate"). While he stopped lecturing on "Fate" after January 1853, he gave a second lecture against the Fugitive Slave Law in New York in March 1854.

America was simmering over slavery throughout the 1850s. The country was increasingly polarized between the North and the South, abolitionist and proslavery. (Did such a polarized national state exert an influence—albeit subtly—on Emerson's way of thinking in oppositions, and his search for reconciliation of these opposites?) Stephen Douglas introduced the Kansas-Nebraska Act, which was passed in

May 1854, by which bill the two new territories were deemed open to "popular sovereignty" in the question of slavery. In other words, the territories would be free states or slave states according to the politics of their settlers. This precipitated a mad rush by partisans on both sides to the territories. Come the vote, fraudulent voters from Missouri assured the establishment of Kansas as a slave state, and bloodshed and division ensued in the four-year conflict dubbed "Bleeding Kansas" by Horace Greeley.

The Kansas-Nebraska Act led also to the abandonment of the old Whig Party and the establishment of the Republican Party in opposition to a now predominantly Southern, proslavery Democratic Party. Emerson was lifted well out of the purely abstract speculation of his earlier writings by the violence around him. He was roused by the betrayal he felt by Webster and by Boston in supporting the Fugitive Slave Act; he was roused again when the Massachusetts abolitionist senator Charles Sumner was struck until unconscious on the floor of the Senate by a Southern congressman in 1856 (again, over the matter of Kansas), and yet again when the radical abolitionist John Brown was hanged after his capture at Harpers Ferry in 1859. Even if they are not referred to explicitly in the essay, all these events—these many currents and narratives—inform "Fate." A bitter Emerson reflects now: "Our America has a bad name for superficialness. Great men, great nations, have not been boasters and buffoons."

Sample Topics:

1. **The Fugitive Slave Act:** How is the Fugitive Slave Act reflected in Emerson's essay "Fate"?

   What was the Fugitive Slave Act? When was it passed? You should acquire a good knowledge of this bill and its background. Be aware of the dates of the significant events related to the act, and correspondingly the dates of composition and revision of the text, along with those dates when Emerson was reading the lecture "Fate." How closely does Emerson's composition of the essay tally with national developments? While Emerson's subjects may seem to exist on a plane above time and space, "incompetent to solve the times," note how his use of abstractions mirrors events in history. What is the connection between fate and slavery? How does slavery lead us to ideas of fate? Southern slaveholders and their defenders claimed a biblical precedent for slavery, as though the practice was foreordained by God and so right (such rationales can be traced in studies of American slavery). Emerson, meanwhile, opposes fate with freedom, the latter of which is—more obviously—a central consideration in any discussion of slavery.

Note the overt remarks Emerson makes about politics. Look for any suggestion of a political position. For example, early in his discussion of power—when he begins a counterargument against Fate's totality—Emerson writes that "nothing is more disgusting than the crowing about liberty by slaves, as most men are" and that the Declaration of Independence is "some paper preamble." Where does Emerson locate himself, in the American tradition, with such comments? How are the ideals of the "founding fathers" challenged by Emerson? Elsewhere, Emerson remarks on politics and fate: how any person's political bent is already destined in the womb, "this a Whig, and that a Free-Soiler." What kind of a view of political discrimination does this suggest? Do you agree? Does Emerson suggest, then, that slave holders are already destined in the womb, as are slaves? Is this a positive conclusion, or a negative one? How might the events of his time have influenced such a conclusion? Look also at Emerson's two lectures on "The Fugitive Slave Law," which were developed and delivered alongside "Fate" (1851, 1854)—what themes do the texts share, and what other resemblances? Do you believe that the act precipitated Emerson's thinking on Fate? If so, why does he not mention it by name in "Fate"?

2. **Bleeding Kansas and John Brown:** To what extent do the events of "Bleeding Kansas" and the career of John Brown inform the writing of "Fate"? What does Emerson's identification with Brown signify?

As with the previous question, this question requires a good knowledge of the national history behind the text, as well as a good command of the text. What was "Bleeding Kansas"? The term was coined by Horace Greeley, editor of the *New York Tribune* and associate (if not friend) of Emerson. The early history of Kansas, its place in the center of a national debate about expansion and slavery, is integral to the story of John Brown. Is an understanding of the life of John Brown, in turn, integral to an understanding of "Fate"? If you research the complicated history of the composition of "Fate," you will find that Emerson delivered the lecture form of "Fate" between 1851 and 1853, six years before the events at Harpers Ferry. How, then, is "Fate" about John Brown?

Certain themes are associated with John Brown and his story—violence and martyrdom among them. What does Emerson say about these? How does John Brown measure with the Emersonian hero, and accord with the "right use of Fate"? Look at Emerson's other statements on Brown, from his journal and from his speech given in Salem in January 1860. Does Emerson's identification with Brown mark a departure from the Emerson of earlier works? Brown has been defined as a terrorist—a word loaded with special meaning in our own times. Was Emerson condoning terrorism? Northern abolitionists raised money to buy guns and ammunition for Brown's "army." Is such a figure—mired in violence and controversy—an emblem of a new philosophy? If so, how? You might also look at Henry David Thoreau's various speeches and writings on the subject of Brown, which Emerson admired. Is Brown a useful index to the direction these thinkers took beyond transcendentalism?

3. **Manifest destiny:** Is Emersonian "Fate" the same as "manifest destiny"? Compare the two concepts.

Fate and *destiny* are synonyms. Is it coincidental that Emerson wrote "Fate" in the wake of the coining of the term *manifest destiny*? When was the term used, and how was it applied? You should look at the various presidents who used "manifest destiny" and its trappings as part of their campaign and administration. A policy of westward expansion was prosecuted with special vigor under the Democratic Presidents Polk (1845–49), Pierce (1853–57), and Buchanan (1857–61). Manifest destiny suggests a national destiny for America, a mythology that inspired a good part of the country. How does Emerson's Fate resemble this national myth? Is it a positive support of the cause (as *The American Scholar* promoted the nationalist ideal of Young America)? Or is it a critical and negative imagining of the ends of fate and destiny?

Can Emerson's polar opposites fate and power be compared to the Democratic Party (on one side) and the Republican Party on the other? What were Emerson's views on Kansas, manifest destiny, and expansionism? Check biographical sources, journals, and correspondence.

Philosophy and Ideas

While Emerson drew some of his impressions on Fate from political developments around him, other speculations also fed his developing philosophy. Emerson's interest in natural history meant that he was aware of theories of evolution well before the publication of Charles Darwin's *Origin of Species* (published in 1859; Emerson still sought a copy in early 1860). Evolution had grim implications for a predominantly Christian nation, disorienting, unsettling implications that Emerson seems to meet head on in "Fate." "All we know of the egg, from each successive discovery, is, *another vesicle*," he writes, starkly reducing the planet to its basic protoplasm, "and all that the primary power or spasm operates, is, still, vesicles, vesicles." Is this simply another flourish, like the "weed by the wall" of "Circles," bound to be followed by a countering upswing, where he declares the might of man, or is this all Emerson now sees— vesicles, vesicles?

Emerson's scientific (bordering pseudoscientific) ruminations lead him also into questions of heredity and race. Theories of race raged throughout the country in these fraught, anxious times, arguments on both sides being drawn from religion and science and pseudoscience alike. The latest scientific discoveries and theories could be exploited by partisans on both sides of the slavery question, for instance. Emerson plunges into such speculations, thinking of African Americans but also other immigrants to America—Jews and Irish. What are his conclusions? What are his views, equally, of his own race—and his family?

For Emerson, ideas of evolution were no threat to ideas of religion. Thus alongside his scientific meditations, this essay sees Emerson, as one critic has it, finally conceding "the dignity of those American Calvinists" (Richardson, 501). Whether this is "final" or there has been a Calvinist streak in Emerson throughout his writing is arguable. Of particular note here is Emerson's reference to an American tradition of looking and bowing to Fate much older than 1845, in the Puritan emphasis on predestination and election. How do Puritan notions of Fate infiltrate Emerson's discourse?

Sample Topics:

1. **Evolution:** Is Emersonian Fate biological evolution? Are we solely products of our biological makeup according to Emerson?

"The Book of Nature is the book of Fate," Emerson writes, anticipating the great book of nature, Darwin's *Origin of Species* (published in England in 1859 and in America, 1860—the same year as "Fate"). Emerson had been interested in evolutionary science as far back as 1833, when he visited the Jardin des Plantes in Paris and remarked upon the "occult relation between the very worm the crawling scorpions & man" (recounted in his journal). How does Emerson use evolutionary science in his argument for the dominance of Fate? Look, for instance, at the third paragraph of the essay. Emerson, dismayed at the failure of reform movements even in schools, concludes, "We must begin our reform earlier still,—at generation: that is to say, there is Fate, or laws of the world." What does he mean? Generation is, here, the act of human procreation. What does Emerson then imply? Are we the product of our "vesicles"—our flesh? Does Emerson abandon idealism for materialism? (Remember in *Nature*, when even our bodies were defined as "NOT-ME"?) Where else does Emerson focus on generation and the formation of the embryo?

Look also at Emerson's other use of biological terminology. "A vesicle lodged in darkness . . . became animal; in light, a plant." All is vesicles, he writes. Does Emerson believe this, or is he (as he has before) stating one case the better to challenge that case subsequently? For instance, Emerson revisits the pseudoscience phrenology in paragraph eight. How did Emerson view phrenology in "Experience"? Has his opinion changed since? Look further back, to *Nature*. How does Emerson use evolutionary examples differently? Look, for instance, in the "Discipline" section, where he detects "the type of the human hand in the flipper of the fossil saurus." In the second half of "Fate," when Emerson begins to consider opposites to fate, does he stand by this evolutionary model? Or does he abandon it— "Man is not order of nature, sack and sack, belly and members, link in a chain"?

2. **Race and heredity:** To what extent is Emersonian Fate dictated by either race or heredity?

To answer this question, you might select those passages of the essay where Emerson concentrates on questions of genetic inheritance from the family, and of racial—or national—traits and identity. Does one's race define one's destiny, according to Emerson? Do all Neapolitans mature into "scoundrels"? Such a supposition would be viewed as unfair discrimination in our own times, but what about in Emerson's time? Is Emerson a racist? National attitudes to African Americans, while mixed, were clear enough in this period preceding the Civil War, but does Emerson challenge those prevailing ideas or endorse them? And what does he say about other races—Jews, Irish, French, Italians, German, English, Arabs? Each race is discussed in "Fate." For instance, Emerson predicts "a great deal of guano in their destiny" for the "German and Irish millions." How does Emerson reimagine immigration, expansion, and "manifest destiny"—or, indeed, the later term *the American dream*? What exactly does Emerson mean by *race*, indeed? Late in the essay he remarks that "the first and worst races are dead. The second and imperfect races are dying out." Who are these races, and what does he suggest by *imperfection*?

Is there any trace of fascism in Emerson's discourse, such as when he writes, "The more of these drones perish, the better for the hive"?

The question also asks you to look at the related theme of family inheritance. If not by our race, are we absolutely determined by our family background? "How shall a man escape from his ancestors?" Emerson asks and remarks later that "men are what their mothers made them." You might research Emerson's own family to examine his speculations on this subject. What was his relationship with his parents? Was he "made" by his mother? (Why did he choose the example of the mother, for instance, and not the father?) Emerson's younger brother Robert Bulkely was developmentally challenged; two more brothers became insane. Does Emerson's thesis on family and fate mask his own anxieties? As with all the suggestions made by Emerson, you should also ask yourself whether he believes this himself or whether he is voicing a position to challenge later on. Does Emerson sustain these ideas or revise them?

3. **Election and providence—Calvinism:** Is Emerson's Fate the same as Calvinist predestination?

Another form of Fate recalled by Emerson is the Puritan tradition of "predestination." This idea was developed in the writings of John Calvin (from whom we get the term *Calvinism*), a French theologian of the 16th century. The belief was that God had decided the fate of men—whether they would go to heaven (these were known as the elect) or hell—before he created the world, and that there was nothing that could be done about this. There was no sure way of knowing whether one was among the elect or not. Thus Puritans lived their lives knowing they were predestined, but agonizingly not knowing how. You can study more about Calvinism and predestination—historical responses to the doctrine, how this concept affected Puritan culture. How might Emerson's concept of fate be indebted to this earlier tradition?

Look at the language Emerson uses to describe "Our Calvinists, in the last generation." Does he praise his Calvinist forebears or condemn them and their beliefs? Look also for Emerson's use of words such as *providence*—again a loaded term in the discussion of Puritan New England. What does *providence* mean and signify? How might this relate to Emersonian *Fate*? When you have studied the extent of Emerson's recourse to Puritan terminology and doctrines, you should further consider the significance of Emerson's making peace with his Calvinist heritage. Is a Calvinistic notion of predestination a gross betrayal of Emerson's earlier philosophy? Is there a dismal defeat in his apparent embracing of such a grim worldview? Or does Emerson truly accept these values?

Language, Symbols, and Imagery

While national historical and political events simmer beneath the surface of "Fate," as discussed earlier, Emerson's personal history is also reflected in the essay in his choices of images and examples. Margaret Fuller, Emerson's close friend and correspondent, died in July 1850, while returning to America from Italy with her Italian husband and son. Her ship sank off the very coast of Fire Island, New York. Emerson spent the next two years gathering material for and editing the *Memoirs of Margaret Fuller Ossoli* (published in February 1852), the same period in which he composed and first gave the lecture "Fate." How does this death haunt the text of Emerson's essay?

Emerson had himself spent the period from October 1847 through July 1848 in Europe—England for the most part. His impressions, which were eventually collected in *English Traits* (published in 1856), were of an empire in decline. He recoiled from industrial England (especially the city of Birmingham) and found disappointment and oppression at every turn. How did Emerson discern Fate in England's corruption (as he saw it)?

Sample Topics:

1. **Margaret Fuller and images of death at sea:** How is the death at sea of Margaret Fuller reflected in "Fate"?

Does the image of Margaret Fuller's dying at sea off Fire Island haunt the text of "Fate," as the death of Emerson's son Waldo's (arguably) haunts the essay "Experience"? What do the contexts of each reference to death at sea suggest, if applied to the death of Margaret Fuller? For instance, when Emerson writes, "learn to swim, trim your bark, and the wave which drowned it, will be cloven by it, and carry it, like its own foam," what is the lesson? Was Margaret Fuller fated to die, or could she have avoided death if she had "learnt to swim" and "trimmed her bark"? What example does Emerson draw from Fuller's death; what lesson does he learn?

Note any appearances of sea imagery. How does Emerson's present use of water or sea imagery differ from earlier usage of similar images? Think, for instance, of "Experience," in which "All things swim and glitter." Does the same remain true for Emerson now? Research also the life and death of Margaret Fuller, and Emerson's relationship with Fuller. What did her death mean to him particularly? How would her death have impacted on Emerson, carrying the "weight of the Universe" with it?

2. **Images of England:** How did Emerson's visit to England (1847–48) influence his concept of fate, and the writing of his essay?

To one critic, at least, Emerson's visit to England inspired his writing of "Fate" as much as the Fugitive Slave Act. Do you agree? A good way to begin such an inquiry is to read Emerson's journals from his stay in England. What were his immediate impressions? You can find those impressions consolidated and expanded in the book *English Traits*. What is Emerson's response to England? Is it predominantly negative or positive? What does he praise, and what are the faults he finds? Is he fair or biased? Do you find the same nationalist resentments that bristled in *The American Scholar*?

Mark the various examples Emerson takes from England in "Fate." For example, the Kings College chapel, the steam engine, the jokes in *Punch* (a London humor magazine), the

Englishmen who mature into conservatism—how are these used in his discourse on Fate? What about England's state at that time—its industry, its people, its arts—illustrates or advances Emerson's personal vision of Fate? For example, how does Emerson utilize the steam engine (paragraph 44)? How does the correct use of steam suggest the correct use of Fate? A knowledge of the English situation of this time—the "spirit of the times," as Emerson has it—will help your inquiry. How is Emerson's description of America different from this? Make a studied contrast. Remember, for instance, Emerson's dramatic rebirth in a "new yet unapproachable America I have found in the West" (from "Experience"). Is America still a solution to or redemption of England—and, so, Fate?

Bibliography and Online Resources

Buell, Lawrence. "Emerson's Fate." *Emersonian Circles: Essays in Honor of Joel Myerson.* Ed. Wesley T. Mott and Robert E. Burkholder. Rochester, NY: U of Rochester P, 1997. 11–28.

Cole, Phyllis. "Emerson, England and Fate." *Emerson: Prophecy, Metamorphosis, and Influence.* Ed. David Levin. New York: Columbia UP, 1975. 83–105.

Conner, Frederick William. *Cosmic Optimism: A Study of the Interpretation of Evolution by American Poets from Emerson to Robinson.* New York: Octagon Books, 1973.

Emerson, Edward. "Notes." *Complete Works of Ralph Waldo Emerson.* Vol. 6. *The Conduct of Life.* Ed. Edward Waldo Emerson. Boston: Houghton Mifflin, 1904. 327–434.

Emerson, Ralph Waldo. "The Fugitive Slave Law." *The Portable Emerson.* Ed. Carl Bode and Malcolm Cowley. New York: Viking Penguin, 1981. 541–557.

———. "John Brown: Speech at Salem, January, 1860." *The Portable Emerson.* Ed. Bode and Cowley. New York: Viking Penguin, 1981. 569–572.

Lopez, Michael. "The Conduct of Life: Emerson's Anatomy of Power." *The Cambridge Companion to Ralph Waldo Emerson.* Ed. Joel Porte and Saundra Morris. Cambridge: Cambridge UP, 1999. 243–266.

Packer, Barbara. "History and Form in Emerson's 'Fate.'" *Emerson: Bicentennial Essays.* Ed. Ronald A. Bosco and Joel Myerson. Boston: Massachusetts Historical Society, 2006. 432–452.

Reaver, J. Russell. "Emerson's Focus in *The Conduct of Life*." *South Atlantic Bulletin* 45.4 (November 1980): 78–89.

Richardson, Robert D. *Emerson: The Mind on Fire*. Berkeley: U of California P, 1995.

Rusk, Ralph L. *The Life of Ralph Waldo Emerson*. New York: Charles Scribner's Sons, 1949.

Thoreau, Henry David. "A Plea for John Brown." Witherell 396–417.

———. "Martyrdom of John Brown." Witherell 418–421.

———. "The Last Days of John Brown." Witherell 422–428.

Whicher, Stephen Emerson. *Freedom and Fate: An Inner Life of Ralph Waldo Emerson*. Philadelphia: U of Pennsylvania P, 1953.

Witherell, Elizabeth Hall, ed. Thoreau: *Collected Essays and Poems*. New York: Library of America, 2001.

SELECTED POEMS

("The Concord Hymn," "The Sphinx," and "Brahma")

READING TO WRITE

EMERSON WROTE in a love letter to Lydia Jackson, before she became his wife: "I am born a poet, of a low class without doubt yet a poet. That is my nature & vocation." He was courting her, and so defining himself in what was—we assume—his most candid and vulnerable voice: Emerson saw himself as a poet. Should we take his poetry more seriously than his essays or addresses, then? Does Emerson articulate better his philosophy through poetry or through prose?

Another question to ask is whether we should read Emerson's poetry as illustrations or confirmations of his essays, or whether they should be read as wholly separate. Does one explain the other, or are they best treated as products of a separate intelligence? One way to find advice as to how to read Emerson's poetry is in his own remarks on poetry and the poet. From *Nature* (particularly the chapter "Beauty") and *The American Scholar* Emerson privileges the poet as a special figure in society. Read "The Poet" from the second series of *Essays* for the most thorough meditation on the poet's duties and art.

The following excerpt is from "The Sphinx," stanzas 14 and 15:

> "Dull Sphinx, Jove keep thy five wits!
>   Thy sight is growing blear;
> Rue, myrrh, and cummin for the Sphinx—
>   Her muddy eyes to clear!"

The old Sphinx bit her thick lip,—
    Said, "Who taught thee me to name?
I am thy spirit, yoke-fellow,
    Of thine eye I am eye-beam.

"Thou art the unanswered question;
    Couldst see thy proper eye,
Alway it asketh, asketh;
    And each answer is a lie.
So take thy quest through nature,
    It through thousand natures ply;
Ask on, thou clothed eternity;
    Time is the false reply."

The form of Emerson's poetry is, surprisingly, relatively safe and conservative. He has a reputation for flubbing meter occasionally, which may rather have been a deliberate disdain for exactness, but as a rule he did not experiment in form as, for instance, Walt Whitman did. Do not become flustered by the poetic form and feel the need to overstate the structure of the poem. Notice how Emerson uses the form to reflect his content. For instance, "The Sphinx" features an alternation between lines ending in "masculine" syllables and lines ending in "feminine" ones. Can you identify which endings are which? How is this fluctuation related to the subject or a theme of the poem? Emerson stresses the substance of the poem over its form. He writes in "The Poet": "it is not meters, but a meter-making argument that makes a poem. . . . The thought and the form are equal in the order of time, but in the order of genesis the thought is prior to the form."

The featured stanzas contain exchanges from both sides of the Sphinx-poet (female-male) dialectic. Which position is the reader expected to take? Whom should we sympathize with? Emerson's writing of "Circles" has been confidently dated as happening only months before he submitted "The Sphinx" for publication in the *Dial*, so both texts might partake of a common viewpoint. In "Circles," Emerson describes a constant cycle of assimilating and superseding, so that one solution never has any permanence but is absorbed and exceeded. Equally, the contest of two ultimately untenable positions might anticipate the "lords of life" that will occur in a few years in "Experience."

The 14th stanza begins with the poet (teasing or consoling?) the Sphinx for her "blear" sight. Perception is called prominently to our attention, with the two positions vying over who sees more clearly. (Eyes, and perception, are also integral to Sophocles' telling of the life of Oedipus. Is there a connection?) Clear perception, though, would be less and less of a possibility to Emerson in this period, leading up again to the writing of "Experience," when he declared that all perception was necessarily "blear." With the application of his various balms, however, the poet effects a change in the Sphinx. The Sphinx trumps the poet's apparently self-satisfied answer to her riddles by a new revelation of identity ("Who taught thee me to name?"), claiming now to be the "spirit" and "yoke-fellow" of the poet, the "eyebeam" of his eye. In addition, the poet is the "unanswered question"—is this the secret that "the ages have kept" (stanza one)?

The pair are transformed from antagonists to partners, from duality to unity. We are reminded of those natural partners that complement each other, featured in the fifth stanza: "Each the other adorning, / Accompany still; / Night veileth the morning, / The vapor the hill." By this exchange (or by the eye salves?), also, the Sphinx is transformed from sluggish, drowsy (the same word used to describe "our" state at the start of "Experience"), dirgeful and dull to "merry" and "crouched no more in stone." The exchange—or rather, the response (solution?) that the Sphinx provides ostensibly for the poet—animates and liberates the Sphinx herself. Their dialogue is not necessarily the legendary duel between Oedipus and the Sphinx, ending in death for one participant, but a conversation ending in completion, animation, transcendence for one. The poet, perhaps unwittingly, provides a dialogue for the Sphinx by which she achieves her own solution, just as, in "all conversation between two persons, tacit reference is made, as to a third party, to a common nature. That third party or common nature is not social; it is impersonal; is God" ("The Over-Soul").

TOPICS AND STRATEGIES

The following section suggests several possible topics for essays on "The Concord Hymn," "Brahma," and "The Sphinx." They can and should be used as starting points for your own, independent exploration of the essay.

"The Concord Hymn"

The "Concord Hymn" (as it only later became known) is an example of "occasional verse"—verse written for a particular occasion. It is also perhaps his best-known work (having been drilled to schoolchildren), if not his most representative. It was composed for a recital at the unveiling of a memorial obelisk commemorating the heroism of the Lexington Minutemen at the battle of Concord, during the War of the Revolution. The stone was erected on land that once belonged to the Emersons, owned in 1837 by Emerson's step-grandfather, Ezra Ripley. The former Emerson home, the Old Manse (later the home of Nathaniel Hawthorne), overlooks the land and the historical North Bridge where the battle raged. The poem was sung by a choir to the tune of "Old Hundred," an established hymn. It was published as a "broadside" (a single printed sheet) and handed out among the audience at the occasion, with the title "Original Hymn." Emerson's first proper collection of poems would not be published for another nine years (*Poems,* December 1846). When this collection was published, the "Concord Hymn" was the final poem in the collection. What does such placement suggest? Does the lengthy period between these dates suggest an admission, on Emerson's own part, that the "Concord Hymn" was not typical of his poetry or satisfactory to him?

Themes

When Emerson composed the "Concord Hymn," his first book, *Nature,* had been published (September 1836). Many of Emerson's enduring themes and ideas are already present in *Nature.* Can the same be said of the "Concord Hymn"?

Sample Topic:

1. **Recurring ideas:** Which characteristic themes of Emerson's later writing are already present in the "Concord Hymn"?

While the "Concord Hymn" is short and, for Emerson, distinctly unambiguous, plenty of his recurring ideas and themes can be glimpsed in miniature in the poem. Think, for instance, of Emerson's interest in "nature." In the "Concord Hymn" nature is named: "Bid Time and Nature gently spare / The shaft we raise to them and thee." Furthermore nature is described in the flood (line one), the breeze (line two), the "green bank" (line nine), the "dark stream" and the "soft stream" (lines eight and nine). How is nature characterized in this instance? Why is the stream both "dark" and "soft"? How does this reflect Emerson's meditations on the subject in *Nature*? Other recurring themes include time and memory, freedom and independence. Despite its brevity, the poem is rich with Emersonian themes. It is not sufficient simply to point these out, however; identification should be accompanied by explanations of where Emerson uses these themes more fully, and how he uses them. Is his use of these themes in the "Concord Hymn" consistent with his use of them elsewhere? What might account for any difference of usage?

History and Context

The "Concord Hymn" describes—although only briefly—the fighting that began the Revolutionary War ("the shot heard round the world"), in the battle of Concord, on April 19, 1775. The battle was fought on land belonging to the Emersons. The poet's grandfather, William Emerson, had been instrumental in mobilizing the Minutemen, and, as their chaplain, had preached the rightness of resistance to the English. He was at the battle (although, as a minister, he could not fight), while his family—including Emerson's beloved aunt, Mary Moody Emerson, then a baby—watched the fighting across the meadow from their home, the Old Manse. The most detailed account of grandfather Emerson's prominent involvement in the battle of Concord and the formation of the Minutemen can be found in the biography of Mary Moody Emerson by Phyllis Cole (see bibliography).

For the greater part, the "Concord Hymn" is less a paean to revolution than it is about time passing, and ways of remembering honorable men—an ongoing interest for Emerson. Concord had celebrated its bicentenary in 1835, for which Emerson contributed an oration on the history of the town, to which he dedicated a considerable amount of research. Emerson spoke to survivors of the battle of Concord about their experiences—or at least what they could remember. How was the Revolutionary War remembered in 1837?

Sample Topics:

1. **Emerson and the Revolutionary War:** How influential were the battle of Concord and the Revolutionary War on the "Concord Hymn" and on Emerson's other works?

> The idea of revolution in the abstract occurs repeatedly in Emerson's writing. In the Divinity School Address, for instance, he writes, "Wherever a man comes, there comes revolution." In "Self-Reliance," he says that "greater self-reliance must work a revolution." Is Emerson's appetite for revolution tied to the Revolutionary War, and is the "Concord Hymn" an indicator of this? To answer such a question, you should familiarize yourself with the part Emerson's family played in the Revolutionary War. What was the role of his grandfather, William Emerson? How was this tradition passed down, and how did Emerson perceive it?

Philosophy and Ideas

In September 1835, less than two years before the performance of the "Concord Hymn," Emerson gave an oration he had written, again for a Concord town celebration. This time, it was the bicentennial of Concord, and Emerson read aloud *A Historical Discourse, Delivered before the Citizens of Concord, 12th September 1835*. On July 29, 1835, he had written in his journal:

> I replied this morn. to the Committee that I would do what I could to prepare a Historical Discourse for the Town Anniversary. Yet why notice it? Centuries pass unnoticed. The Saxon King was told that man's life was like the swallow that flew in at one window, fluttered

around, & flew out at another. So is this population of the spot of God's earth called Concord. For a moment they fish in this river, plow furrows in the banks, build houses on the fields, mow the grass. But hold on to hill or tree never so fast they must disappear in a trice.

How does such a journal entry read, alongside the "Concord Hymn"? One is a private statement, one a very public one. What are the differences in the composition of such texts? Which are we more inclined to believe? Which is the real view of Ralph Waldo Emerson? The "Concord Hymn," unambiguous as it seems, becomes less legible when we read it alongside Emerson's more challenging statements on themes and ideas featured in the poem—ideas of self and society, and ideas of duty to ancestors and history, among others.

Sample Topic:

1. **Votive stone and history:** Are notions of historical veneration and remembrance compatible with Emerson's philosophy as articulated in his essays?

   Emerson's poem "Concord Hymn" and the events it describes are both gestures of historical veneration for an earlier generation. It is a public performance of participation in family and community. Are the formal unveiling of a "votive stone" and an occasional poem to mark that event in any regard a compromise of Emerson's later values? Think, for instance, of Emerson's relations with community, or society. Is such participation—and a text composed expressly to be sung by a chorus—consistent with values emphasizing self-reliance and solitude? Think, also, of Emerson's verdict on history and veneration of the past. Emerson began *Nature,* published a year before "Concord Hymn," with the words "Our age is retrospective. It builds the sepulchres of the fathers. It writes biographies, histories, and criticism." Is such an antipathy consistent with the spirit behind the "Concord Hymn"?

   How does Emerson address the past of Concord here? Is it with civic pride, for instance? With family pride? What does it mean for Emerson to identify with a specific place and time? By comparing attitudes to community (and solitude) or to history in *Nature* (or another essay) and the "Concord Hymn," you might isolate resonances or contrasts that, when examined closely, highlight inconsistencies—or dualities—in Emerson's overall view. Such inconsistencies provide excellent positions for analysis.

Form and Genre

The "Concord Hymn" enjoys an unusual place in Emerson's canon. It is familiar to schoolchildren, while being scarcely discussed by higher-level scholarship (one critic, Leslie Fiedler, calls the poem "popular sub-poetry"). Why do you think this is? The poem lacks many of the qualities that mark Emerson's more typical work—complexity, obscurity, ambiguity. Does this make it a less interesting or more interesting work? And how does it stand relative to those other works? Did Emerson intend it as a serious work, or was it written only as a social obligation to his hometown?

Sample Topics:

1. **Apprentice work:** Is the "Concord Hymn" a characteristic Emerson poem? Is it equal in complexity, form, and language to his later, work, or is it juvenilia?

   Does the "Concord Hymn" prepare a reader for Emerson's later writing (either his poetry or his prose)? Is it representative of Emerson's thought, or is it an early anomaly, completely unlike what was to follow? To answer this question, you will need to identify those tenets that are classically "Emersonian." Think, for instance, of self-reliance. Does the "Concord Hymn" address questions of selfhood and solitude? It was sung by a chorus at a public event—hardly the model of solitude. (Perhaps Emily Dickinson provides the ideal model of the solitary poet.) Consider other recurring images and philosophies in Emerson's work (nature, idealism, dualism). Are they present here? Are they contradicted here?

Another way to consider the poem is through its form and language. Emerson, it has been argued repeatedly, is difficult, obscure, fragmentary, whimsical. Is this true of the "Concord Hymn"? Are there ambiguities, as we find in "Experience"— or in "Brahma," or "The Sphinx"? Is it a "difficult" poem, or straightforward? Are short poems necessarily unambiguous? Ask yourself, Who was Emerson's audience for the poem? Was it phrased especially for his audience, and if so, is this a compromise of Emerson's usual standards? Look furthermore at the form. The "Concord Hymn" was sung to the tune of an old hymn (a common practice). Is such a dogged observance of a standard form typical of Emerson? Look at the forms of other poems. Should it be read solely as an apprenticeship to what followed?

Compare and Contrast

The recital of Emerson's hymn at Concord (Emerson was not in attendance) occurred less than two months before his reading of the commencement address *The American Scholar* at Harvard for the Phi Beta Kappa society. Since both were composed and performed in the same period, what similarities do they share?

Sample Topic:

1. *The American Scholar:* Compare the "Concord Hymn" with *The American Scholar.*

A question like this asks you to compare two texts that are, apparently, very different. One is poetry; the other is prose. One is short, composed of only 16 lines, while the other is much longer, composed of 50 paragraphs. However, you can assemble similarities also. Both texts were written for public performance at specific occasions. Both texts were composed in the summer of 1837, and while the "Concord Hymn" was performed on July 4, *The American Scholar* was read out on August 31. These and other similarities and differences in the composition of the texts should be assembled and examined.

Next, you should examine the texts. Since the "Concord Hymn" is so relatively short it can be dissected minutely. Question and turn over every word or phrase for inferences. Do you recognize any repetitions of ideas from *The American Scholar*?

Bibliography and Online Resources

Cole, Phyllis. *Mary Moody Emerson and the Origins of Transcendentalism: A Family History.* New York: Oxford UP, 1998.

———. *The Cambridge Companion to Ralph Waldo Emerson.* Ed. Joel Porte and Saundra Morris. Cambridge: Cambridge UP, 1999. 30–48.

Emerson, Ralph Waldo. "A Historical Discourse, Delivered before the Citizens of Concord, 12th September 1835." *Complete Works of Ralph Waldo Emerson.* Vol. XI. *Miscellany.* Ed. Edward Waldo Emerson. Boston: Houghton Mifflin, 1904. 27–86.

Fiedler, Leslie. *Waiting for the End.* New York: Stein and Day, 1964.

"The Sphinx"

"The Sphinx" was submitted for publication in the *Dial* on November 24, 1840, and printed in the edition for January 1841. When Emerson's *Poems* were published in 1846, the first poem in the collection was "The Sphinx." Emerson personally decided on the order of the poems, and "The Sphinx" was his favorite. However, when the posthumous *Complete Works* was collated under the editorial eye of his son, Edward Emerson decided to change the configuration of *Poems,* relegating "The Sphinx" to eighth place because he did not want the poem at the entrance (or "portal"—that is, the door) of the collection:

> In the mythology the Sphinx let no man pass who could not solve her riddle; and Emerson's Sphinx has no doubt put off, in the very portal, readers who would have found good and joyful words for themselves, had not her riddle been beyond their powers.

Instead, as editor, Edward chose to begin the collection with "Good-Bye," a poem his father wrote in his youth (1823) and disliked. The poem's reputation for difficulty, then, preceded it.

One critic has called "The Sphinx" Emerson's "most typical poem." It has been called obscure, unintelligible, and "Emersonian"—as though the last is a synonym of the first two. Other critics see it as a "condensation" of Emerson's ideas. What might be meant by this? Can you see which Emersonian concepts are "condensed" in this 17-stanza poem?

Themes

Emerson provided a "solution" to his mysterious poem in a notebook entry of 1859, which was eventually printed in the edition of his *Poems* collected by his son Edward. "I have often been asked the meaning of the 'Sphinx,'" Emerson writes;

> It is this,—The perception of identity unites all things and explains one by another, and the most rare and strange is equally facile as the most common. But if the mind live only in particulars, and see only differences (wanting the power to see the whole—all in each), then the world addresses to this mind a question it cannot answer, and each new fact tears it in pieces, and it is vanquished by the distracting variety.

Can such a "key" be trusted, however? Why did Emerson write such a solution, particularly in a private notebook, not intended (ostensibly) for publication? Then, is his explanation any clearer than the poem itself? Some critics have called this "explanation" offhand and too simple. Does it match the poem at all? Furthermore, other critics would argue that Emerson has no more authority than any other reader to interpret his poem. Even if we do believe he is the paramount authority, Emerson has shown more than once a propensity to lie or to misrepresent his views, if only to excite new questions. As he remarks in the poem, "Each answer is a lie." Alternative readings of this confusing poem exist ("So take thy quest through nature, / It through thousand natures ply"), one of which sees the subject's theme as that Emersonian perennial, the Fall of Man.

Sample Topics:

1. **Perception of identity:** Is "The Sphinx" about the uniting power of the perception of identity? Do you find Emerson's "explanation" of his poem convincing?

Emerson claimed that "perception of identity" was the main theme in his poem "The Sphinx." To prove—or disprove—his solution, you should gather any references in the poem to perception and identity. Such language will be familiar to readers of his essays, in which eyes and perception recur. So, for instance, Emerson writes of "the babe by its mother" who "Shines the peace of all being, / Without cloud, in his eyes." The Sphinx, conversely, has "muddy" eyes and tells the poet, "Of thine eye I am the eyebeam." Where do you recall such language elsewhere? Find examples from Emerson's other works. For instance, in "Fate" Emerson also speaks of "eyebeams" ("Well, they had a right to their eye-beams, and all the rest was Fate"). The transparent eyeball of *Nature* towers over his works as perhaps Emerson's defining image. Yet "The Sphinx" also reflects later writing, when Emerson has become less sure of his perceptions. Among the Sphinx's list of man's sins is that he "creepeth and peepeth," recalling Emerson's remark in "Experience" "Nature hates peeping."

When you collect and examine these uses of language related to perception, remain critical. Look also for chinks in Emerson's explanation. Can—or should—a poem be readily explainable by its poet? Is not the essence of poetry to say that which pedestrian prose cannot, in a way that prose cannot? Be ready to challenge Emerson's explanation then. Or, if you believe that Emerson's explanation is the right one, support your testimony thoroughly, and if possible examine alternative readings and show (using the text) why they are wrong. Henry David Thoreau, the writer and friend to Emerson, wrote a lengthy stanza-by-stanza analysis of "The Sphinx" in his *Journal* (1:229–237).

2. **The Fall of Man:** "It is clear, of course, that the Sphinx demands an explanation for the Fall of Man" (Whitaker). Is the Fall of Man the central theme of Emerson's poem—and his larger philosophy?

"It is very unhappy, but too late to be helped, the discovery we have made, that we exist," Emerson writes in "Experience."

"That discovery is called the Fall of Man." What is the Fall of Man, and what does Emerson interpret it to signify? The term has a biblical origin and describes the degeneracy of humanity, following Adam's disobeying God in the Garden of Eden and his consequent banishment. How is this interpreted by Emerson, in "Experience" and other works, but particularly in "The Sphinx"? Having defined the Fall of Man satisfactorily, your next task is to ascertain that it is an underlying theme—if not the central theme—of "The Sphinx."

In stanza six, for instance, the Sphinx describes "the babe by its mother" with the sun as its toy; while in stanza seven she turns to man and finds only "an oaf, an accomplice." How does such a transformation or decline occur, according to Emerson? Is this Emerson's interpretation of the Fall? What solution to this question does the poet provide? What, for instance, is recalled by the "alternation" and "strong pulses" of the 13th stanza? "Man lives by pulses; our organic movements are such," Emerson writes in "Experience"; "the mind goes antagonizing on, and never prospers but by fits." Is this the same as the "double consciousness" of "The Transcendentalist" and the faith that occurs "in moments" of "The Over-Soul"? Is the poem, indeed, a "condensation" of Emerson's whole philosophy—and is Emerson's philosophy itself "an explanation for the Fall of Man"?

Philosophy and Ideas

"The Sphinx" has three speakers—the narrator (Emerson?), the Sphinx, and the Poet. For the most part it is a verbal exchange—almost a duel—between the Sphinx and the Poet. Why are these two grouped together? Do they represent polar opposites to each other? Another question worth asking is, Who emerges triumphant from this dialogue? And, once the victor is identified, what are the implications of that victory?

Sample Topic:

1. **Who is the victor?:** Who, in this dialogue, triumphs, the Sphinx or the Poet? What is the significance of this exchange and its resolution?

This question focuses on the dialectical nature of the poem. In a pattern familiar to readers of Emerson's essays, the narrative is structured around setting up two opposed arguments and running them against each other to—potentially—arrive at a solution. One Emersonian solution is to accept both arguments (the "double consciousness" of "The Transcendentalist" and "Fate"). Does "The Sphinx" fit this pattern? First, you should clarify the participants in the dialectic and what they represent. Who is the Sphinx? There are Sphinxes in Greek and Egyptian mythology; where does Emerson draw his from? What does the Sphinx represent? To Thoreau, it was "man's insatiable and questioning spirit." Who is the poet? Is it Oedipus (the classic foil to the Sphinx)? Or is this poet comparable to the heroic figure of Emerson's essays, from *Nature* through *The American Scholar* to "The Poet"? Is he foil to the Sphinx or vanquisher? There is a third present—the narrator. Is it Emerson? Why does Emerson not class himself as the Poet? And does he—Emerson, the third party—benefit? Which side does this narrator favor—and which side does the reader take?

Identify also the substance of their dialogue. What is the issue? Identity, says Emerson. The Fall of Man, says a critic. Is the dialogue resolved, the riddle solved? Depending on the identities of the participants and their subject, the outcome can have radically different meanings. Is it optimistic or skeptical? Is the Sphinx's final dissolution ("She melted into purple cloud") a defeat or an apotheosis? And which outcome would be an Emersonian affirmation, and which a statement of Emersonian skepticism?

Form and Genre

The best-known literary appearance of the Sphinx is in the play *Oedipus the King,* by the ancient Greek poet Sophocles. In this play, the Sphinx is portrayed as a monster that waits by the side of the road for passersby, whom it quizzes with a riddle. If they fail to answer the riddle, the Sphinx kills them. If the lucky participant correctly answers the riddle, the Sphinx shall die. Oedipus correctly solves the riddle and the Sphinx is defeated (the answer to the riddle is, Man). Does Emerson's poem follow the same form—that of a riddle?

Sample Topic:

1. **Riddle:** Is "The Sphinx" a riddle? What does it ask? What is its solution?

An awareness of the mythology behind the Sphinx, particularly the Sphinx's riddle to Oedipus, might help you with this question. By framing the story as a dialogue between the Sphinx and the poet, is Emerson suggesting to his readers that this is a riddle with a definite solution? Or is it, equally, a riddle without a solution? "All is riddle, and the key to a riddle is another riddle," Emerson writes in the essay "Illusions" (first published in the *Atlantic Monthly,* November 1857).

This question asks you first to identify what constitutes a riddle. Find a definition, and preferably some examples from literature. The original riddle of the Sphinx would be a useful start, particularly because of its specific solution. Having established a definition of the riddle, dissect Emerson's poem with this form in mind. What questions are asked by Emerson's Sphinx? The first one, for instance, is "Who'll tell me my secret, / The ages have kept?" Why does the Sphinx not have the solution to her own secret? Interrogate such ambiguities. The entirety of the second stanza seems to be a question—at least, it ends with a question mark. Three further questions are voiced through "the great mother," ending: "Who, with sadness and madness, / Has turned my child's head?" What solution is offered by the poet? Further clues might be found in Emerson's other writings on the Sphinx. Emerson refers to the myth in *Nature* (chapter 4, Language), "History," and the second essay titled "Nature" in the second series of *Essays.*

Bibliography and Online Resources

Child. "Emerson's 'The Sphinx.'" *Explicator* 31.3 (November 1972): item 20.

Emerson, Edward Waldo, ed. *Complete Works of Ralph Waldo Emerson.* Vol. 9. *Poems.* Boston: Houghton Mifflin, 1904.

Morris, Saundra. "The Threshold Poem, Emerson, and 'The Sphinx.'" *American Literature*. 69.3 (September 1997): 547–570.

Smith, Gary L. "The Language of Identity in Emerson's 'The Sphinx.'" *ESQ: A Journal of the American Renaissance* 29.3 (3rd Quarter, 1983): 138–143.

Sophocles. *The Three Theban Plays: Antigone, Oedipus the King, Oedipus at Colonus*. Trans. Robert Fagles. New York: Viking, 1982.

Thoreau, Henry David. *The Journal of Henry D. Thoreau*. Ed. Bradford Torrey and Francis H. Allen. 14 vols. New York: Dover, 1962. Walcutt, Charles.

Whitaker, Thomas R. "The Riddle of Emerson's 'sphinx.'" *American Literature* 27.2 (May 1955): 179–195.

"Brahma"

As "The Sphinx" did, the later poem "Brahma" acquired notoriety for its obscurity. And as with the earlier poem, "how to read" "Brahma" has been a much-contested subject. "Brahma" was published in November 1857, in the first number of the *Atlantic Monthly* (alongside three other poems and the essay "Illusions"). By this time, Emerson was at the height of his popularity; he was a "public intellectual." After the poem was published and duly syndicated across the American press, it mystified the nation. Literary criticism became a national pastime, as parodies of the poem sprang up throughout the many magazines and newspapers:

> If the grey tom-cat thinks he sings,
> Or if the song thinks it be sung,
> He little knows who boot-jack flings
> How many bricks at him I've flung.

Editors clamored to deride the poem or explain it. "A poem in which no one can find a meaning must be acknowledged a very great success," said the *New York Times*; "none but a man of genius could have produced such an exquisite piece of no-nothingness" [*sic*]. A torrent of letters followed, defending and lampooning and endeavoring to explain "Brahma." "It is fashionable to call [Emerson] incomprehensible," wrote one correspondent to the *Boston Courier*; "this is partly due to the subjects he chooses." Explanations ensued, showing that at least some of Emerson's public knew enough about Hindu theology and myth to recognize the allusions behind the poem and possessed the sophistication to suggest that Emerson might be adopting a persona for the poem. "It is not an expression of Emersonian sentiments," the *Courier* correspondent continues, "but merely a poetical presentation of Brahma speaking as Brahmins believe he would speak."

During 1844–45, Emerson had been reading Indian scripture, including the *Vishnu Parana*, from which he found inspiration for "Brahma":

> What living creature slays or is slain? What living creature preserves or is preserved? Each is his own destroyer, as he follows evil or good.
> (Carpenter 1930, 114)

An important text, the Bhagavad Gita (which is extracted from the epic *Mahabharata*), had arrived in Concord in 1843, and in 1856 Emerson read from the collection of writings called the Upanishads the following:

> If the slayer thinks that I slay, or if the slain thinks I am slain, then both of them do not know well. It (the soul) does not slay, nor is it slain.
> (Carpenter 1930, 116)

Knowledge of the substance of these sacred books can arguably explain Emerson's poem in a way that a knowledge of Sophocles' *Oedipus the King* does not explain "The Sphinx." Still, "The Sphinx" and the later "Brahma" tend to be associated with each other, both popularly (as conundrums and subjects of burlesque) and in scholarship (as poems with a similar form and subject).

Philosophy and Ideas

The meaning of "Brahma" can be made clearer than that of "The Sphinx," perhaps, because it is easier to identify credible sources to the poem, although this might equally lead any reader into an overly simplified understanding of the poem. Nevertheless, a familiarity with the Bhagavad Gita and certain passages of the Upanishads will undoubtedly inform you well with regard to Emerson's ideas.

Sample Topic:

1. **"Brahma" and its meaning:** What is "Brahma" about?

First, this question requires you to research the meanings of foreign terms. Most obviously, you should clarify the meaning of the word *Brahma*. Be careful and precise in acquiring definitions, because very similar words (such as *Brahma, Brahman,* and *Brahmin*) each have different—if only subtly distinct—meanings. Emerson himself mixes terms up, indeed (see McLean, 116). A canny reading of the Bhagavad Gita—which is composed of only 18 "lessons"—will help you find precedents for many of Emerson's ideas and images. An overview of the Upanishads will explain further. Studies of Hindu mythology and thought will also explain these terms and ideas. It is not enough, however, to robotically identify the meanings and their sources. Studies exist that already do so. What are their specific meanings for Emerson and his audience? For instance, how does "Brahma" sit in relation to Emerson's existing philosophy? Does it update, challenge, or reconfirm it? Is it, as with "The Sphinx," an encapsulation of Emerson's many different ideas?

When you have adequately explained the poem's immediate allusions, next start the process of deeper interpretation of the work. What are its universal themes? Questions of unity, immortality, and identity are all addressed in "Brahma," among others. Look also at the narrative. Why is Emerson using a persona ("Brahma") as the speaker? Is this narrative view comparable to other narrative masques used by Emerson (for instance, in "Circles" or "Experience")? Does Emerson himself espouse these values? Check with statements made in the journals, or in essays like "Plato" (*Representative Men,* 1850) and "Illusions" (*The Conduct of Life,* 1860). The poem has been charged with espousing nihilism, for instance, and elsewhere for exhibiting a studied indifference, for wholly failing to discriminate between killer and victim. Is such a philosophy an affirmation or a negation? What does it mean to "turn thy back on heaven"? How might this be read by Emerson's Christian readership? Take the poem from abstraction and timelessness back to its scene of writing and its market. How does such a stance challenge New England tradition and values? And what has Brahma or Vishnu to do with an America on the brink of Civil War?

Form and Genre

While it has been argued that "The Sphinx" and "Brahma" fundamentally present the same idea, the latter poem has a far greater popularity among scholars, perhaps because it seems to have a key and a solution. Quite promptly after its publication, even as halloos of protest and burlesque went up in the presses, studious and pedantic explanations of the poem were also printed in the more sensible newspapers. Does this apparent resolution to the poem satisfy us as readers, however? And is such a ready answer consistent with Emerson's prevailing philosophy?

Sample Topics:

1. **Paraphrase:** To what extent is "Brahma" a paraphrase of ancient Indian literature and how far is the poem an independent exposition of Emerson's own ideas?

Is "Brahma" solely a paraphrase (that is, a rewording of a preexisting text) from the Bhagavad Gita, the Upanishads, and Emerson's other reading among the Indian sacred scriptures? This question asks you to identify the extent of Emerson's use of Indian scripture, but also to be aware of how much of the work was his own, based on ideas of his own. A look at studies of the poem will show you the process by which the poem was written. For instance, from Emerson's journals we find that the poem was originally entitled "Song of the Soul," with the name *Brahma* (in parentheses) appended later. What does this suggest? When did Emerson first read the various Indian texts; what are the dates of influence? Familiarity with the entire creative process of a work helps you identify any sources of influence.

Against his reading of Indian texts, think of Emerson's earlier works and thought. What echoes can you find in "Brahma"? What, for instance, of "The Over-Soul"? What similarities can you find between Emerson's representation of Brahma and his concept of the Over-Soul as laid out in his (earlier) essay? What, also, of the use of paradox and contradiction throughout the poem? Where does Emerson use such traits, and—again—are they instances prior to his reading of the Indian texts? For example, in "Self-Reliance" (written in 1840) Emerson declares that "a foolish consistency is the hobgoblin of little minds." He celebrates whim and self-contradiction—values propounded again in "Circles" and "Experience." Furthermore, why should it matter whether "Brahma" is solely a paraphrase? Does this make the poem slighter, or of less importance? Is Emerson's use of ideas from books consistent with his own philosophy? (Think, for instance, of *The American Scholar*, with its claim "Each age . . . must write its own books" and "the guide is a tyrant.")

Bibliography and Online Resources

Allen, Gay Wilson. *American Prosody.* New York: American Book Company, 1935.

Anderson, John Q. *The Liberating Gods: Emerson on Poets and Poetry.* Coral Gables, FL: U of Miami P, 1971.

Cameron, Kenneth Walter. "The Reception of Emerson's 'Brahma': Parodies and Paraphrases." *American Renaissance Literary Report: An Annual* 2 (1988): 165–223.

———. *The Voice from Nirvana: Emerson's "Brahma."* Hartford, CT: Transcendental Books, 1997.

Carpenter, Frederic Ives. *Emerson and Asia.* Cambridge, MA: Harvard UP, 1930.

———. "Immortality from India." *American Literature* 1.3 (November 1929): 233–242.

Chandrasekharan, K. R. "Emerson's Brahma: An Indian Interpretation." *New England Quarterly* 33.4 (December 1960): 506–512.

Francis, Richard Lee. "Archangel in the Pleached Garden: Emerson's Poetry." *ELH* 33.4 (December 1966): 461–472.

Leidecker, Kurt F. "Emerson and East-West Synthesis." *Philosophy East and West* 1.2 (July 1951): 40–50.

McLean, Andrew M. "Emerson's *Brahma* as an Expression of Brahman." *New England Quarterly* 42.1 (March 1969): 115–122.

Morris, Saundra. "'Meter-Making' Arguments: Emerson's Poems." Ed. Joel Porte and Saundra Morris. *The Cambridge Companion to Ralph Waldo Emerson.* Cambridge: Cambridge UP, 1999. 218–242.

Yoder, R. A. *Emerson and the Orphic Poet in America.* Berkeley: U of California P, 1978.

INDEX